One O'clock Jump

One O'clock Jump

The Unforgettable History of the
Oklahoma City Blue Devils

Douglas Henry Daniels

Beacon Press

Boston

Beacon Press
25 Beacon Street
Boston, Massachusetts 02108-2892
www.beacon.org

Beacon Press books
are published under the auspices of
the Unitarian Universalist Association of Congregations.

09 08 07 06   8 7 6 5 4 3 2 1

This book is printed on acid-free paper that meets the uncoated paper
ANSI/NISO specifications for permanence as revised in 1992.

Composition by Wilsted & Taylor Publishing Services

Library of Congress Cataloging-in-Publication Data

Daniels, Douglas Henry.
  One o'clock jump : the unforgettable history of the Oklahoma City Blue Devils /
Douglas H. Daniels.
     p. cm.
  Includes bibliographical references and index.
  ISBN 0-8070-7136-6 (cloth : alk. paper)
  1. Blue Devils (Musical group) 2. Jazz musicians—Oklahoma—
Oklahoma City—Biography. I. Title.

  ML421.B64D35 2004
  782.421643'092'2—dc22   2004015080

For Naima, Anissa, and Kyrah

"*The evenings began with the more formal steps, to popular and semi-classical music, and proceeded to become more expressive as the spirit of jazz and the blues became dominant. It was then Jimmy's voice began to soar with the spirit of the blues that the dancers—and the musicians—achieved that feeling of communion which was the true meaning of the public jazz dance. The blues, the singer, the band, and the dancers formed the vital whole of jazz as an institutional form, and even today neither part is quite complete without the rest.*"

—RALPH ELLISON, "Remembering Jimmy," *Shadow and Act*

CONTENTS

Prologue

Deep Deuce and Oklahoma City's Musical Heritage

Late in the afternoon, the blind musician and his three sons left their home in a row of frame buildings on South Geary Street on Oklahoma City's east side in the 1920s. The Christian family lived just north of the railroad tracks. Their neighbors were strictly working class except for the café proprietor, who lived on the corner, and a shoemaker; most neighbors in their block were laborers, porters, maids, servants, and laundresses. All were renters. Clarence and his wife, Willie Mae, headed the Christian family, and they roomed with her parents, Ella and John George, in a house they rented for twenty dollars monthly. All of Willie Mae's family were Texans who migrated to Oklahoma City from Bonham in North Texas around World War I,[1] except for John George, who was from Kentucky. Clarence, the father, was possibly from Bonham, too. He was born around 1872, was literate, and worked as a hotel waiter in 1910. He and Willie Mae married in 1904, and Edward, their first child, was born in 1907, Clarence around 1911, and Charles in 1916. It is not clear why the family migrated to Oklahoma with their three boys. The opportunities available in Oklahoma City may have been deemed greater than those in nearby Dallas, or perhaps it was because they had relatives in the new state's capital. Tragedy befell the family at some point, because the father went blind. Later, after her husband died around 1929, Willie Mae worked as a hotel maid, trying to support her parents and boys. Fortunately, music saved them.[2]

Perhaps the youngest boys came out of the house first, while Edward led his father. They carried a battery of musical instruments, many of them stringed. The father played bass guitar and sang, and the youngsters sang, too, and performed. "The musical brothers inherited their talent from their father, an early day bass guitarist-singer with a versatile group of string and woodwind players who used a wide variety of wood flutes, the now obsolete 'C' clarinet, and plectrum instruments now seldom seen." Though Charles Henry attained considerable fame as an electric guitarist, both his brothers were musical. Edward, for example, "had the rare gift of 'absolute pitch,' a remarkable memory and almost singly taught himself to be an excellent dance orchestra pianist and arranger." He also wrote a column for the city's *Black Dispatch* in 1935. They were one of many musical families in the capital—there were also the Rushings and the Whitbys, for example.[3]

Troubadours during the jazz age, the blind guitarist and his three sons entertained every night at the city's Concord Airdrome. They also strolled through the white neighborhoods singing—and the boys probably dancing, too, when they were young. They played popular songs, folk songs, whatever the public requested, and they managed to collect enough every evening to support the family.

On their way west, they passed Douglass High, where the legendary Zelia Breaux, who was in charge of the music program in the five Black schools, taught music. She was a major force on the music scene in Oklahoma City for three decades. She started a band at Douglass in 1923, and Lawrence Williams, one of the original Blue Devils, was a member along with Edward Christian. Breaux also organized pageants and musicals at the school, at the Aldridge Theatre that she co-owned on Second Street, at the state fair and civic affairs, and at the 1939 World's Fair in Chicago.[4] The Christian boys would have heard one of her rehearsals as they made their way westward.

At the corner of Stiles and Second sat Slaughter's Hall, built by the local physician, and bands such as the Blue Devils and Gene Coy's Black Aces played for dances atop this three-story structure. Schoolboy Ralph Ellison, a youngster in the 1920s and later author of the acclaimed novel *Invisible Man*—as well as cultural critic and chronicler of these golden years in Oklahoma City's music history—sat in on rehearsals with the Blue Devils, where he picked up pointers and gave his opinion on musical issues.[5]

As the quartet made their way up Deep Deuce, heading west, they passed the shops, restaurants, boarding houses, and businesses lining both sides of the street. Porters, cooks, waiters, and maids lived alongside Second Street professionals. The Blue Devils occasionally stayed in the boarding houses, or rented rooms, as in the case of Blue Devil bassist Walter Page, who lived with his sister, wife, and two children in the building of the local undertaker, Willis Tucker, at 311 East Second.[6]

Just west at 307½, set on the back of the property, was the Rushing home, where real estate agent Andrew Rushing lived with Cora, his wife, and their son Evoid, who was a shipping clerk and formerly a student at Wilberforce, a Black college in Ohio. In front and on the street sat a confectionery store–diner, where their oldest son, Jimmy, worked after returning from Los Angeles in 1925. He fed down-and-out musicians who were stranded in town, sang popular songs and some blues, played a little bit of piano, and sought a career in show business. In 1927 he joined the Blue Devils, but prior to that he played and sang at private house parties and semiprivate Elks smokers.

Clarence Christian and his sons continued westward, passing the *Oklahoma City Black Dispatch* building on the corner of Central and Second, and the Central Hotel, just around the corner, where the original Blue Devil, Willie Lewis, lived. The musical "brains" of the band, Lewis was a composer of sonatas as well as a music and language teacher. Just north up Central Street was the home of local businessman Sidney D. Lyons, who played guitar for his family's amusement and, in the 1920s, purchased a mechanical piano worth more than three thousand dollars for his home. The 200 block of Second Street contained more barbershops and stores, but at the crest of the hill on the northeast corner was Avery Chapel A.M.E. church, where the choir rehearsed for Sunday services.

Music was everywhere on the east side, and the blind man and his three sons drew upon this tradition and took it with them into the heart of Oklahoma City. Thanks to the writing of Ralph Ellison, the journalistic efforts of Roscoe Dunjee, editor and publisher of the *Oklahoma City Black Dispatch,* and the reminiscences of old-timers, Second Street—also known as Deep Second and Deep Deuce—became as legendary as Eighteenth and Vine in Kansas

City, Bourbon Street in New Orleans, and Central Avenue in Los Angeles. In addition to at least one of the Christian brothers, Edward, Walter Page, Jimmy Rushing, Henry "Buster" Smith, William "Count" Basie, Eddie Durham, Oran "Hot Lips" Page, Lester "Pres" Young, and a host of lesser-known musicians performed with the Blue Devils, one of the first jazz bands in the city—and a band recalled as one of the very best in the Southwest.

Today this rich heritage is celebrated annually. Originally the festival took place on historic Deep Second, where celebrants closed off the street and hung a banner from one side to the other, proclaiming "Charlie Christian Festival." Every year musicians play and sing, dancers do their thing, vendors sell barbecue, sodas, ice cream, and T-shirts, and the district's unique heritage is preserved. In 1996, pianist Juanita Bolar, wife of the former Blue Devil Abe Bolar, performed; the two had played on some of the early rock and roll records of the 1950s. If this book succeeds in acquainting readers with the history of a singular jazz band that came out of Oklahoma City, then they, too, can appreciate and enjoy the heritage that Oklahomans have known about for nearly a century.

CHAPTER TWO

Oklahoma City Pioneers

Readers of histories of jazz would not expect Oklahoma City to have a thriving jazz scene from the music's beginnings. In the Sooner State's capital, as in other urban areas, the music known as jazz can be traced to the 1920s, and in that city, the Oklahoma City Blue Devils were clearly the dominant band. They were, in fact, a match for Bennie Moten's band, from Kansas City, and countless others in Texas, Oklahoma, and Missouri—not to mention other bands in the prairies and plains of the nation's heartland.[1]

Nestled in the valley of the North Canadian River in the midst of the rolling prairies that had been Indian Territory, Oklahoma City was founded after the run of April 22, 1889, when settlers converged around the Santa Fe Railway station site and made ten thousand homestead claims in one day. It became the state capital in 1910.[2]

Some African-Americans came to the Indian Territory, as it was known in the late nineteenth century, with the Native Americans— the Creeks, Choctaws, Chickasaws, Cherokees, and Seminoles— who were relocated from the eastern U.S. to west of the Mississippi, safe from harm—or so some said. Some of these Blacks were slaves, others were freedmen. Some African-Americans came with the rush of 1889, when a number of them settled in Black towns, forming their own communities at Boley and Langston in the late nineteenth and early twentieth centuries.[3]

By 1900 more than 55,000 African-Americans resided in Oklahoma and the Indian territories. Black farmers owned land valued at about $11 million and totaling more than 1.5 million acres, but their farmland acreage decreased as the number of white migrants increased.[4] In Oklahoma City in 1910, Blacks numbered 6,546, barely 10 percent of a population of 64,205, and in the next decade they increased to 8,241 (out of a total of 91,295 residents). By the end of the 1920s, this Black population grew to 14,662 (out of 185,389 total).[5] This growth indicated the existence of a vibrant and dynamic population of urban residents.

◆ ◆ ◆

Oklahoma City's area in 1920 was 18 square miles, with 138 miles of paved streets. It had nine fire departments, fourteen banks, including a Federal Reserve Bank, eleven hospitals, two vaudeville houses, and nine picture shows. Its waterworks included a $1,500,000 reservoir with a capacity of 7,000,000,000 gallons. It was the distribution center of the motion picture industry and possessed five daily newspapers and twenty-five other publications in 1926.[6] Within the separate school system for Blacks, Inman E. Page, the father of Zelia Breaux, supervised five institutions: Douglass, with a principal and twenty-seven teachers; Bryant and Dunbar, each with its own principal and fifteen teachers; Orchard Park, with a staff of five; and Choctaw, having a staff of three.[7]

Even before statehood, Jim Crow restrictions were established, though they were not as oppressive as in the Deep South. The Oklahoma Territory set up a separate system of public schools for Blacks in the 1890s, and Oklahoma City started a school for African-American children in 1891. Langston University, commonly called the Colored Agricultural and Normal University, was set up near Guthrie in 1897; this was the only institution of higher education for Blacks in Oklahoma. For a few years, local option prevailed, whereby voters in each county decided whether to have segregated schools. Then in 1897, one year after the famous *Plessy vs. Ferguson* case, in which the Supreme Court declared that racially segregated facilities were legal, the Oklahoma Territory adopted segregation by law.[8]

Despite considerable opposition to their voting, Oklahoma Blacks fought for this right in court and won in 1915, a time when their fellow African-Americans were disenfranchised in the Deep South. Despite this success in the courts, they failed to overturn laws forbidding intermarriage and supporting restrictive housing ordinances, Jim Crow schools, and segregation in railway cars and other public facilities.[9]

Though hemmed in socially and physically, and excluded from Oklahoma churches, clubs, and societies, Black Oklahomans created their own social life, one that was particularly rich with schools, businesses, churches, clubs, fraternities, sororities, and other institutions. Besides farmers, Oklahoma attracted a professional class of Black clergymen, doctors, dentists, lawyers, and affluent businessmen who operated cafés, grocery stores, hotels and rooming houses, barbershops, and pool halls. These people included the Reverend John W. Dunjee, who migrated with his family from Minnesota in 1892, the father of Roscoe Dunjee, editor of the *Oklahoma City Black Dispatch,* and Drusilla Dunjee Houston, feature editor of the *Dispatch* and author of such works as *Wonderful Ethiopians of the Ancient Cushite Empire.* The Reverend was among the elite, bringing not only his savings of several hundred dollars but an extensive library, the result of forty years of collecting.[10]

When the Reverend's spouse, Lydia Ann Dunjee, died in 1928, the full role of the couple in the Oklahoma City community was summarized and praised during the service at Howard Metropolitan C.M.E. (Colored Methodist Episcopal) Church. Born free in Virginia in 1846, she was one of ten children. She met and married her husband after the Civil War, and they had five children who grew to adulthood. "She was [the Reverend's] faithful assistant in the building of ten representative churches in large cities of the North and East." She played a similar role in Oklahoma, where her husband was appointed by the American Baptist Home Mission Society of New York, and she was eulogized as "an unusual home-maker, a devoted mother, a woman far ahead of her time . . . quiet, modest, cultured, progressive in things worth while."[11] She was eighty-two at the time of her death.

A number of elderly pioneer women played prominent roles in the Black community of Oklahoma City and throughout the state. Mrs. Thomas Foster, who came with the eighty-niners, exemplified the frontier spirit of the late nineteenth century, a heritage she sustained until her death in 1930 at the age of eighty-seven. She was born a slave in Kentucky in 1843 and was described by the *Dispatch* as "a woman of extreme force and power." Her daughter, Uretta, married Professor J. D. Randolph, and when he came to Oklahoma in 1889, she accompanied her daughter's family. The professor was the first Black person to instruct in the Oklahoma schools.[12] Mrs. Foster was separated from her own mother at the age of three, and when her mother died years later, she "raised and brought to honorable marriage" her eight siblings. "From these stern trials...[she] developed not the soft, easy gentle nature of many of us who fail to render great life service to our families; but was full of fire and bluntness." This Oklahoman "was made of that stuff that makes great pioneers and which made this the great state it is."[13]

Self-educated, she was also a Baptist church member for over sixty years, and lived by the dictum that "He that provideth not for his own, is worse than an infidel." After joining the Randolph household, she worked night and day washing clothes and sewing, and managed to send three grandsons and a nephew to Meharry University, the African-American medical school in Nashville. She worked even after her family told her to take it easy, and when her grandchildren married, "out of her own earnings, [she] was able to offer each substantial help in buying the first home." Indeed, the Randolph family, "our largest and perhaps most devoted family group, owes much of their solidarity to the labor and sacrifices of this grandmother who worked beside their devoted parents." They included the dentist Thomas J. Randolph; James L. Randolph, pharmacist; Iphagenia, a Dunbar School teacher; and Madeline, who instructed at Choctaw School.[14]

Another pioneer, Mrs. Edith M. Rushing, was also praised at her funeral when she died in 1928. The resident of 923 East Seventh Street and mother of twelve children was nearly eighty-seven years old at the time of her death. She came to Oklahoma with her husband, P. R. Rushing, in 1896. She was a member of Avery Chapel and, from the cards and floral offerings present at the funeral, active in or at least respected by the Missionary Society, the Deaconess Board of Avery Chapel, and Lily White Rose Court. Her surviving relations included her son, Andrew Rushing, of Rushing Confectionery at 307½ East Second Street; his son, James Rushing, the famous singer with the Blue Devils, Benny Moten, and Count Basie; and Wesley Manning, a blues pianist and major influence on his cousin James. As Andrew Rushing prospered, he built a home on the lot behind his store and eventually went into real estate.[15]

The *Dispatch* recognized another pioneer mother, Elizabeth Whitby, who died at the age of 80 in Wewoka, Oklahoma, in 1930. She was the mother of Dr. A. Baxter Whitby, an Oklahoma City dentist, Grand Master of a local lodge, and father of the saxophonist Francis "Doc" Whitby. Mrs. Whitby was born a slave in Texas, and she "fought down the obstacles of environment, educating all of her children and living to see all of those who reached adult age, recognized as prominent and useful citizens of the nation." Her daughter, Mrs. S. L. Brown, was an instructor in the Wewoka Schools. With Mrs. Whitby, as with the other pioneer mothers, what is remarkable is how successful her children and grandchildren were, and the degree to which she was active in the social and economic life of Black Oklahoma City.[16]

Dr. W. H. Slaughter was just such a community-oriented Oklahoman. Born in Alabama around 1873, he came West and married a grandchild of Mrs. Foster, and he and his wife Edna raised two children, Wyatt Jr. and Saretta, both of whom were active in community affairs in the capital city. The doctor built the three-story brick Slaughter building, known not only for its dances that sponsored local bands, but also for its offices, the Dunbar Library, and a roof garden—particularly valued in an era before air conditioning.[17] It was located at the corner of East Second and North Stiles, and in 1923 the *Dispatch* described it as "the finest building owned and controlled by Negroes in the Capital."[18] Dr. Slaughter was elected Convention Manager of the Oklahoma City Negro Business League in 1927; he also served as treasurer of the Stonewall Finance Company and, in addition, of the Avery Chapel A.M.E. church and the local medical society. The doctor was chairman of the Board of Great Western Hospital, which served the Black community. Moreover, he was praised as "owning valuable rural property in addition to his urban properties."[19]

Other Black businessmen, such as Alphonso Hall, were also quite successful. Mr. Hall was described by the *Dispatch* as "one of the substantial property holders of the race" in the capital. He erected a building named after him and owned Hall's Hardware Store on North Central. Hall's Hall was located on the northwest corner of Second and Central. Stores and apartments occupied the first floor, while the Elks had their offices on the second; Victory Lodge No. 248, I.B.P.O.E.M., was on the third floor.[20]

Sidney D. Lyons became rich with a business that catered to the needs of African-Americans for distinctive hair products. "Mr. Lyons is one of the wealthiest men of the state and have property interests amounting to several thousands of dollars."[21] His East Indian Toilet Goods Mfg. Co. prospered in the 1920s to the extent that Lyons and his wife took a vacation trip in the summer of 1926, visiting Chicago, Detroit, New York, and other Eastern cities. His interest in music was evidenced by *Dispatch* reports that he bought a mechanical piano for $3,500 and was "seen picking the guitar on the lawn of his home for the entertainment of his family."[22] One of his relations was another of those who benefited from the prosperity of the roaring 1920s: Ruby Lyons, proprietor of the Men's Rest Billiard parlor, who distinguished himself by purchasing a new car, "a Lincoln Sport Roadster," in 1927 as a present for his wife. "She got tired of riding in a Pierce Arrow... so I decided to give her a Lincoln thrill."[23]

When a representative of the Black insurance company North Carolina Mutual visited Oklahoma City, he reported that "the Negroes were doing more here in the commercial world than anywhere he had been in the state." Among the establishments "doing a real business here" and supported by the Negro Business League was The American Iron and Metal Company, managed by J. E. and W. J. Edwards. They also owned the Enterprise Filling Station and the Blue Bird Taxi Line.[24]

The levels of organization of Black Oklahoma City were quite remarkable, as was the degree to which different institutions were interconnected—not only the schools with the churches, but the fraternal orders with both of them, and with the *Dispatch*, the local bands, and Oklahoma Blacks in general. The interpenetration of church and press is clearly evident in the life of Roscoe Dunjee, son of the Reverend, who grew up in Oklahoma City, attended his father's church regularly, and had at his disposal his father's vast library. He was a steadfast advocate of civil rights for Black Oklahomans, and he was editor of the *Dispatch* from 1915 until the mid-twentieth century. This staunch Republican was also a supporter of the teaching of Black history, as was his sister, Drusilla. He also served as president of the National Negro Business League, was an investor in the Security Life Insurance Company, and was recruited by the Knights of Pythias as a speaker and organizer. This fraternal order adopted the *Dispatch* as its official organ.[25]

Fraternal orders were interlinked, and it was in the spirit of promoting their goals that members often belonged to more than one order. In 1921, Oklahoma's Odd Fellows had a roster made up largely of Pythians. So it was with pride that Roscoe Dunjee announced in the *Dispatch*'s columns in 1923 that he had been awarded the commission of "Colonel Aid-de-Camp Major General" in a letter from a Major General of the Uniform Rank in the American Woodmen. The Uniform Rank, Dunjee continued, was "the fastest growing fraternal military unit" in the U.S., having in three years' time added 305 drill companies and 51 musical organizations to its ranks. Somewhat playfully, Dunjee concluded, "Just keep it in mind, its [*sic*] no longer 'Editor,' its 'Col. Aid-de-Camp Major General Roscoe Dunjee.'"[26]

The close relationship among fraternal orders, the churches, and local bands was evident one Sunday in late winter 1926, when the cornerstone of the New Quayle M. E. Church was laid at the corner of Second and Lindsay Streets and under the direction of the Knights of Pythias Lodges of Oklahoma City. W. T. Tucker, the local undertaker and Chancellor Commander of St. Charles Lodge No. 28, acted in the capacity of Grand Chancellor. At 2:00 p.m. in the afternoon, the Pythians lined up in front of their temple, at 206 East Second, behind the Oklahoma City High School Band; other lodge members—men and women in their own respective orders—also lined up: Christopher Columbus Company No. 1, the Mary L. Barnes Company C.D.C., and the Sisters of the Court of Calanthe. Paraders passed through the east side streets, and then at the church and before services they sang the Pythian ode. The pastor turned the services over to Acting Grand Chancellor Tucker, and after the fraternal order's rites were concluded, made his own remarks. Members of the order made a "liberal" donation to the church.[27]

The fraternal orders also had their own musical organizations. In the spring of 1923, "over 200 Elks and their friends" left the capital city for a "gala occasion" in Guthrie, fifty miles to the north. After the parade, "a monster reception was held...all Wednesday night," while the Ideal Jazz Band of Oklahoma City performed. Dr. T. J. Randolph, Exalted Ruler of Victory Lodge No. 248, was in charge of what the *Dispatch* referred to as "a pilgrimage." Around the same time, both the "Famous Ideal Jazz Band" and the "Blue Devil's orchestras" were scheduled to play at Guthrie's city hall. The Blue Devils performed regularly at Pythian affairs, as its musical director, Willie C. Lewis, was an active fraternity member.[28]

Black pioneer residents of Oklahoma City combined the versatility and resourcefulness of the Southwestern frontier with a measure of urbanity and sophistication that allowed them to enjoy the unique opportunities of an expanding urban area. The tremendous increase in population in the 1920s indicated the promise of this emerging metropolis. Some Back residents were prosperous as a result of their professions and businesses, some benefited from their pluck and frugality, and many depended upon the hard work and savings of their slave forebears who had the foresight to move to Oklahoma. This community provided fertile grounds for the development of a rich Southwestern music tradition that is often overshadowed by the emphasis on Kansas City.

CHAPTER THREE

Blue Devil Phoenix

Swing era musicians accorded a rare place to the Oklahoma City Blue Devils, the jazz band that started in the Sooner State's capital in 1923 and broke up in West Virginia in 1933. For bandleader Count Basie, it was the model for his swing combo at the Reno Club in Kansas City in 1935; within a few years, Basie's orchestra acquired an international reputation as a leading exponent of what was called Kansas City swing. In fact, he believed the Blue Devils to be the best band he ever heard, surpassing even Bennie Moten's Kansas City outfit. In his autobiography, Basie recalled how much the Blue Devils impressed him when he first heard them in Tulsa, Oklahoma, one summer day in 1927: "Hearing them...was probably the most important turning point in my musical career so far as my notions about what kind of music I really wanted to try to play was concerned." Basie reminisced, "There was such a team spirit among those guys, and it came out in the music."[1]

Blue Devil tuba player and bassist Abe Bolar, from Guthrie, Oklahoma, contended, "That's the first bunch that came here that could do both well [play and solo with feeling—that is, 'get off']. There was a couple of conservatory musicians in there, especially the piano player...Little Willie Lewis." He explained, "They *all* were good. In other words, they set a piece of music up there, and no rehearsals or nothing, they went on *down*. They were good musicians."[2] This was the first band of its kind local Oklahomans had ever seen, and the first that they could copy from.

The Original Blue Devils, circa 1925: Walter Page, Ermal Coleman,
Edward McNeil, Lawrence Williams, and William C. Lewis

Despite their name's suggestion that they were a blues band, this
was not the case for the founders. "They weren't so much on blues,
cause they were from somewhere else. They weren't what you called
good blues players." The blues tradition was very strong regionally,
however, in Oklahoma and Texas. "The people *here* were the ones
that played the blues. People around in *this* part of the country
played the blues [Oklahoma and Texas]."[3] The Devils embraced
blues traditions gradually through the 1920s until the blues influence was evident in, for example, their recording, "Blue Devil
Blues."

Bennie Moten liked them so much that, starting in 1929, he
succeeded in getting several of them—first Eddie Durham, the
guitarist-trombonist/arranger/composer, and Basie, then singer
Jimmy Rushing, and next trumpeter-singer Oran "Hot Lips" Page,
then eventually bassist Walter Page—to join his band. Even before
Moten died in 1935, Basie recruited former Blue Devils—Henry
"Buster" Smith and Lester "Pres" Young, Leonard Chadwick, Rushing, and Walter Page—for his bands and for the Reno Club job. In a
few years of touring, the Blue Devils became one of the premier ex-

amples of Kansas City swing. Significantly, the orchestra's roots were as much in Oklahoma City as they were in the Missouri city.[4]

With their almost reverential focus on New Orleans, Chicago, New York, and Kansas City, jazz historians have neglected a number of cities besides Oklahoma City—including Tulsa, Dallas, Houston, San Antonio, Sioux City, Iowa, and Minneapolis—the heartland of the nation. This vast region was covered by the Blue Devils, and by focusing upon their singular esprit de corps, social origins, early music education, and various activities as musicians, we grasp their significance as a remarkable band that stayed alive more in the memories of old timers than in published histories of the music.[5]

Unlike Bennie Moten, whose success was attributed as much to his links with Kansas City's political machine as it was to his recordings, the Blue Devils were rooted in Oklahoma City's Black community. The band's ties to the existing Oklahoma political structure are unknown at this point. (Before the Depression and Franklin Roosevelt's first term, Black Oklahomans were Republicans in a region dominated by the Democratic Party.) We do know, however, that the Blue Devils were a democratic entity, a "commonwealth band," as they termed it, with no leader who received more money than the others. (In his band, as leader/manager/pianist, Moten received twice a musician's share.)[6]

The Blue Devils did have managers, but they were always members of the band, and everyone shared equally in the proceeds. Pianist Willie Lewis was said to be the "brains" behind the band during its initial years, 1923–1928.[7] Then Walter Page took over these responsibilities until he left for Moten, temporarily in 1929, and then permanently in 1931. When Page left, James Simpson took over management; then around 1932, Buster Smith and Ernie Williams began running the band's affairs. However, these members did not make decisions for the band; in other words, they were not managers whose word was final. The Blue Devils' motto was "All for one and one for all"—like their heroes of the movie based on Alexandre Dumas' *The Three Musketeers.* Members had some say in their choices, and they all voted on major decisions. This was typical of many bands in the Southwest until they abandoned this form of organization for the more familiar one during the Depression.[8]

The Blue Devils' connections and activities within the capital city's Black community were one of the most remarkable aspects of the band.[9] Its various sources of support—the local theater owner, different businessmen, fraternal organizations and social clubs, Charleston champions and blues dancers, and city dwellers on the east side—are what made the band such a "phoenix": it repeatedly reformed after disbanding, following changes in leadership and personnel, and started over again with a slightly different name—but always as the Blue Devils, either Walter Page's Blue Devils or, later, the Thirteen Original Blue Devils. They recorded two selections, "Blue Devil Blues" and "Squabblin'," in 1929 but ultimately failed to make it to the big time. The orchestra floundered and broke up in 1933 partly because of the hard times of the Depression, but also because they were in Virginia and West Virginia, more than a thousand miles from their base of community support.[10]

The founding Blue Devils, in particular, were not roving musicians with few meaningful social connections or none at all, like the legendary blues ramblers and "rolling stones" of African-American folklore. Nor were the founders musical illiterates—Lewis, Rushing, and Walter Page attended college. In fact, one of the features of the Blue Devils was the role that the more skilled musicians assumed in instructing self-taught band members like Buster Smith to the point he not only learned to read and notate music, but became the band's arranger within a few years' time.[11]

The typical jazz history traditionally focuses upon different styles corresponding to specific cities or regions—"New Orleans," "Chicago," "Kansas City," and "Western swing," during the music's early history. However, with the exception of Walter Page, who went to school in Kansas City, none of the Blue Devils came from any of these jazz meccas, suggesting that this interpretation is overly simplistic. Texas musicians (Oran Page, Eddie Durham, and Buster Smith) and band members from states like Iowa (Le Roy "Snake" Whyte), Illinois (Willie Lewis) and Indiana (Ermal Coleman), and states as distant as West Virginia (Reuben Lynch) and North Carolina (Ernie Williams) came to the Oklahoma capital, home of singer James Rushing and the Christian brothers—Clarence, Edward, and Charlie. These different geographic origins of the Blue Devils suggests that the music they played was at least as much national as it was regional.[12]

The unique spirit of brotherhood among band members kept them in the band, many staying on through thick and thin. One must wonder how they functioned for so long and why they continued to revive the band, despite the constant loss of personnel and the unfavorable developments in the music industry. There is also the issue of how the band developed institutional ties to the local African-American community.

The original band was perhaps a temporary affair, in that the "internationally famous Blue Devil Orchestra" accompanied the blackface comedian and vaudevillian Billy King in the road show "Moonshine," with its "dashing Creole Beauty Chorus," at the Aldridge Theatre on Second Street, in the heart of Oklahoma City's African-American community, in the winter of 1923. The blackface figure in the *Oklahoma City Black Dispatch* advertisement reminded readers of the minstrel tradition that set the tone for the musical, as it did for most Black entertainment during the jazz decade and for years prior to that—a tradition so powerful that even Black performers wore blackface, imitating whites. "Moonshine" was probably on the Theater Owners' Booking Association (TOBA) tour, the Black circuit started after World War I, and probably combined song, dance, and comedy, like the traveling road shows that vaudevillians Bert Williams and George Walker popularized earlier in the century.[13]

In its summary of the musical, the *Dispatch* made it clear that jazz was featured, noting "Jazz music of the livelies [*sic*] sore [*sic*] played by an orchestra superior to anything ever heard in Oklahoma City." The musical was "one of the brightest and fastest moving entertainments." Billy King "ranks with the best," and as for the rest of the troupe, "Every member of the company can dance well and with much grace, most of them can sing." The star of the show, Miss Margaret Scott, "the Creole Nightingale," is "the possessor of a fine soprano voice."[14]

The Blue Devil Orchestra, however, "alone is worth the price of the show." Moreover, "it is to the jazz music and the dancing girls that the production undoubtedly owes most of the success which it has met with this season." As for the music accompanying the show, "all of it is of the jazz type, [and] will satisfy the audience from the start." The *Dispatch* concluded, "This is a production worthy of your patronage and there will be nothing said or done to mar the minds of the most refined audiences."[15]

But that specific band, Walter Page claimed, "broke up the next year in Texas," so he formed a second version, recruiting Buster Smith and, a few years later, Rushing, Williams, Oran Page, and other stalwarts.[16] This lineup was the band that captivated Moten. Smith and Ernie Williams were the leaders of the third version, The Thirteen Original Blue Devils. Significant for its legendary reputation as a band that would not die, it was said to have broken up in Bluefield, West Virginia, about the time "Ernest Williams and his Thirteen Original Blue Devils" performed at the annual Musicians' Ball at Paseo Hall in Kansas City in the spring of 1933.[17] There was still another reincarnation when Eddie Christian, brother of the famous guitarist Charlie, revived the Oklahoma City band around 1935—at least we have a photograph with "Blue Devils" etched into the surface of the print.[18]

In the spring of 1923, after the Oklahoma City Elks entrained for the state's former capital in Guthrie, the Blue Devils were featured at a dance held at the town's city hall. On Christmas Eve of 1923, the Devils played for the chauffeurs' organization at Slaughter's Hall. Their performance was so outstanding "the crowd was unwilling to leave the Hall when the lights went out." A few days later they performed again at the Hall, offering "an entire change of musical numbers" to "a larger crowd" than on the evening before. The next night they played at a Midnight Ramble at Hall's Hall following the Aldridge's first show.[19]

They were versatile, too—a band for the entire African-American community and for white audiences as well (in separate presentations, of course, as Jim Crow ruled in Oklahoma). In January 1924 they entertained dancers at the Bell Hops' Ball, and the event was so successful that dancers requested a second performance. The Coleridge Taylor Choral Club treated the public to an event highlighting the band's thorough knowledge of music: "The Blue Devil Orchestra will render classical and sacred music during the program," which included Mayor Cargill as the principal speaker. This Christmas presentation was held at the Aldridge Theatre, and the *Dispatch* praised the band's relationship to the community and noted its popularity: "This musical organization has been serving the community need for high class music for the past few weeks and their programs are always a drawing card."[20]

The Aldridge, the local vaudeville and movie house, also needed their services. As Walter Page, one of the Blue Devils' founders, recalled, "we were playing in the silent picture houses a lot for movies like *The Ten Commandments* with *appassionatas, andantes, pianissimos* and all those things."[21] That summer of 1925, the Blue Devil Orchestra provided music at the reception in honor of the Supreme Chancellor of the Sons of Damon and Pythias at the Winter Garden, "one of the coolest and largest social centers of Oklahoma."[22] Later in the year, they held forth at "perhaps the most elaborately arranged and enjoyable affair" of the season, the "Alegria Heurreux's" annual social event, held at the Hall auditorium and described as a "formal soiree" on the club's invitations.[23] On Christmas Eve 1925 the orchestra was featured at the first annual charity ball at Slaughter's Hall, where a Charleston contest was held that evening at 11:00 p.m. and prizes were given away.[24]

Of course their popularity was not limited to the capital, because they played the surrounding towns like Enid and El Reno, as well as Guthrie. In late winter 1926, the *Dispatch* maintained that the orchestra would be performing in El Reno "ten strong," and the following week, the newspaper reported that "the dance given by the Blue Devil Orchestra in El Reno Tuesday night was a success in every way." It added, "the people of El Reno proved that they appreciate good music and know when the Devils are billed to play that is all they may expect." That night patrons included people from El Reno, Chickasha, Enid, and Kingfisher, "and a host of the dance-loving public from Oklahoma City were loyal to their favorite orchestra."[25]

While there is ample information on the band's activities, biographical data on Billy King and the founding Blue Devils are limited. There is a rare *Dispatch* report on a birthday party for the head of the road show with which the Blue Devils started their career. (No Blue Devils mentioned any history of the outfit taking place before the beginning of 1923.) The veteran showman Billy King made a speech in winter 1923 at the East Side Cafe, right across from the Aldridge Theatre on East Second Street, and the *Dispatch* summarized it in early February. His statement allows us to consider the specific social values that he supported—values that sustained the Blue Devils, and were in turn put into practice by band members during their stint with the band and throughout their entire lives. In some ways the speech embodied the self-help philosophy of the late Booker T. Washington, founder of Tuskegee Institute, but it also reflected an abiding religious faith typical of millions of devout African-Americans in the nineteenth and early twentieth centuries. The event was his surprise fifty-fourth birthday celebration, and the Blue Devils performed.

King expressed his appreciation for their expressions of gratitude and, also, a bit of paternalism characteristic of older vaudevillians: "Children ... I do not know how to tell you how glad I feel to have you prepare this treat for me." After more than thirty years on the road, "this is one of the happiest moments of my life ... your bright faces and your youth reminds me that I ought again tell you what I am always saying to you. Try to lift yourself in your profession, try to live clean." He maintained that just as some said *he* had successfully risen to the top, so could *they*. "Save your money and try to put it to good uses and purposes as you see me doing day by day."

He then asked how many hoped to be with him the next year, and after all hands were raised, he asked how many intended to attend services at C.M.E. Church. The response was identical, reflecting their unanimity on these core African-American religious values. After the speech, he kissed each and every one of the nine chorus girls, "blondes and brunettes," and Marshal Rogers, King's partner, "came in for second honors during the affair."[26]

Billy King was "one of the greatest and funniest blackface comedians of minstrel reputation seen on the boards" in the early decades of the twentieth century. Introduced to Chicago audiences in the musical comedy *A Night at the Masquerade,* King "woke the people up to his own peculiar and original style of drollery" in the Grand Theater in the summer of 1915. A second presentation, *My Old Kentucky Home,* on that occasion featured the comedian "in a burlesque show dog character [that] was extremely funny and redeemed his power to draw as a minstrel flavored comedy star."[27]

Born in 1869, the aspiring young vaudevillian went off to New York City in the 1890s and was told by an *Indianapolis Freeman* journalist to be sure to look up the living legend of the stage, Sam Lucas.[28] He was eventually very successful catering to Black audiences; in one season "a single musical production of Billy King grossed $200,000." In the late 1920s King retired from show business and went into real estate in Chicago. During his days of glory, he "was a State Street citizen's idea of a millionaire ... [and] was the first of the theatrical luminaries to sport a high-powered, flashy, block-long automobile with a chauffeur." His driver, Marshal Rogers, became his protégé, and he, too, became famous as a comedian.[29]

The *Dispatch* article is significant for other reasons than the solidarity and core values that were praised and endorsed by members of the company. In addition to the few biographical details on King, the article also lists the vaudevillians and musicians. The newspaper named the members of the Blue Devils, musicians subsequently mentioned as among the band's original founders—Ermal Coleman, Ed McNeil, Lawrence Williams, Walter Page, William Blue, and William Lewis.[30]

Aside from mention in local newspapers during the band's heyday, Lester Young, Buster Smith, and Walter Page were the first Blue Devils to shed light on the history of the band. Allan Morrison, who wrote an article on Lester Young in *Jazz Record* in 1946, described it as "one of the most exciting combinations in jazz history." Young recalled how "We got around everywhere, but we starved to death.... We had no capital, no bookings, no nothing." He concluded, however, that "it was one great band that played some fine music."[31]

Buster Smith also stressed the hardships they faced when he was interviewed ten years later. The Blue Devils recruited him in Dallas in 1925, but he said little of the band other than to describe its breakup around Easter time in 1933. "Nobody had any money so we talked two cab drivers into taking us [to a gig three hundred miles away]. When we got there, we found out it was a commission job and the fellow who hired us didn't have any money either." On top of this, their instruments were attached because of their debts, they were thrown out of their hotel, and finally the survivors decided to hobo their way back home on freight trains. After that, several remaining members joined Bennie Moten.[32]

The biographical information available on some of these Blue

Oklahoma City Blue Devils, 1932

Devils reveals their social origins and values and the musical training that permitted them to play for a variety of occasions, for every
stratum—from the social elite to the chauffeurs and bellhops, and
for the dancers on Second Street and from outlying areas. Though
Walter Page did not stress pianist Willie Lewis's role in the band, he
praised him as one who "had come out of Polytechnic school in Peoria and had a fast, powerful left hand that really jumped." Furthermore, "he'd learned to write music like I had."[33]

Lewis, the band's first music director, was the son of William
Henry Lewis, a paper hanger–painter born in Pekin, Illinois, in
1861, who married Emma Belle Turner, from Hannibal, Missouri,
in 1890. Evidently the Lewises prospered sufficiently to send their
sole son, William Cecil, born in 1895 in Peoria, to the local college
on the eve of World War I. Either the family's financial condition or
Lewis's earnings from music allowed him to attend a music conservatory and an African-American university in Ohio.

We know only a little about Lewis's musical background. He
studied at the local Polytechnic Institute (later Bradley) from 1915 to

1917, and while the curriculum may have included music, Lewis followed a Liberal Arts program with courses in English, French, German, history, math, and woodworking, while singing in the school's choir. He also attended the Boston Conservatory of Music, and was said to be a graduate of Wilberforce, the African-American institution in Ohio. In 1923 and 1924 Lewis roomed at 214 North Central, in Oklahoma City, and in 1926 he was listed as a music teacher in the *Oklahoma City City Directory*. A businessman as well as a member of the Knights of Pythias and Elk lodges, he was said to have "organized several classes in languages" in addition to teaching pianoforte and music theory.[34]

Lewis was one of the first Blue Devils to be praised in the *Black Dispatch*. Early in 1926, in anticipation of his appearance with the band at a dance at Hall's Hall, the newspaper columnist wrote: "If you haven't got your dancing habits on you had better put 'em on 'cause Lewis is sure goin' tu whip 'Ida I Do' over those piano keys until you can't rest."[35] In the summer of 1928, Lewis joined Alvin "Fats" Walls's orchestra, which had recently been organized in Oklahoma's capital; saxophonist Theodore "Doc" Ross and Harry Youngblood, on trumpet—future Blue Devils—were members of Walls's orchestra at this time.[36] In the late 1920s the pianist disappeared from the *Oklahoma City City Directory*. Evidently the hardships of a traveling musician took their final toll in 1934 in the midst of the Great Depression: Lewis died in Bismarck, North Dakota, while with Wee Willie's Memphis Blue Devils, in the autumn of that year.[37]

Lewis's versatility was evident in that he offered music instruction in Oklahoma City. "Pupils of William C. Lewis" gave classical music performances at the Pythian Temple on a Sunday afternoon in Oklahoma City, in January 1926. Bernice Burnett, daughter of the local businessman Abner Burnett, and later wife of the Blue Devil drummer, Ed McNeil, was featured in this piano recital; she accompanied singer Lonzetta Townsend on "The Brown Bird Singing," performed four selections from the First *Peer Gynt* Suite, op. 45, and closed the recital with a Beethoven sonata, op. 10, no. 3. Compositions by Brahms, Mozart, Chopin, and Scriabin were among the selections featured, so it is clear that Lewis, like Page, was well trained in Western classical music.[38]

Indeed, Lewis also composed music in the European classical vein. During the jazz age, this pianist was cited as "perhaps one of the outstanding musical composers of the Southwest." Lewis's love for the classics reminds us of Scott Joplin, the ragtime composer who wrote *Treemonisha*, a ragtime opera, and of James P. Johnson and Thomas "Fats" Waller, contemporaries of Lewis who also had an abiding respect for European classical music.[39]

The Blue Devil music director was a member of the Pythians, and for one of their sessions in the summer of 1925, he performed one of his compositions, a Sonata in F minor, as well as *Kol Nidrei*, a paraphrase on an ancient Hebrew melody.[40] This particular piece was sung and played by Jews in their synagogues on the evening of Yom Kippur—and solely on this occasion.[41] During the 1920s, he spent three years writing a sonata. By the summer of 1928 he had "completed work on a sonata in E flat Minor, that he will play for the first time during the sessions of the Pythian Grand Lodge" in July. Indeed, he had "favored the Pythian Grand Lodge three years ago with one of his wonderful compositions," probably a reference to the Sonata in F minor. Lewis was widely respected by not only the Pythians but by others in the Oklahoma Black community, and "his new number," the *Dispatch* forecast, "is destined to be extremely popular."[42]

Walter Page was the third Blue Devil who was interviewed, by Frank Driggs, shortly before the bassist died in 1957. Following World War I he played with Bennie Moten, then he joined the first Oklahoma City Blue Devils, and he mentioned how the band started with Billy King's road show on New Year's Day 1923. Page recalled that trombonist Ermal Coleman was the leader, William Blue was the clarinetist, Lawrence Williams was the cornetist, Eric [Edward] McNeil was on drums, and Willie Lewis was on piano—six in all—typical of jazz combos of the day. He related how they drank a lot, "had a ball, lots of fun," but broke up "the next year in Texas."[43]

Significantly, Walter Page was another early Blue Devil with a thorough grounding in music theory. Born in the small town of Gallatin, Missouri, in 1900, he was a member of a very large family and the grandchild of Clara Page, a Missouri native born before the Civil War. Walter Page's father, Edward W., was one of Clara's children, fifteen of whom lived with their mother in Union Township in 1900. Illiterate—but a homeowner—she saw to it that all her children attended school. In 1904, Walter and his mother, Blanche Marshall Page, also from Gallatin, moved to Kansas City, where he grew up with music all around him. Moreover, his mother was quite an active worker in Ebenezer A.M.E. church, and also in civic affairs. She was evidently deeply involved in community building and uplift, and this appears to have influenced her only son.[44]

Page heard the singing of spirituals and religious songs in the A.M.E. church in Kansas City, but there was also a music teacher in the family—Aunt Lillie, his father's oldest sister.

In Kansas City, Page recalled, "there were three brothers next door to me who played...bass horn...baritone horn bass clef... [and] baritone treble clef." On the other side of the street lived two other brothers—Joe, who played cornet, and Frank, who played bass horn. Page's friends taught him to play bass horn, and by high school he was on bass drum in their band.[45]

At Lincoln High he studied under Major N. Clark Smith, one of the famous music teachers who trained generations of musicians in Kansas City, St. Louis, and Chicago. Major Smith was a composer of some renown, and his posts included Tuskegee Institute.[46] The former army bandmaster played all instruments and started Page on bass; he was also given credit for having his students "sing the cantatas like *Elijah* and...play arrangements for the brass band." The teenage Page found it all "very inspiring." After graduation, he studied music at Kansas University (University of Kansas) and later recalled that he completed a three-year course in one semester, studying sax, violin, piano, voice, composition, and arranging.[47]

Page represented the generation whose grandparents were enslaved, and whose parents taught the importance of education and community uplift. For the source of his ideas about community involvement, we only have to look to his mother; several local ministers praised her leadership when they spoke at her funeral services, which nearly nine hundred mourners attended in Kansas City in spring 1934.[48] As an educated African-American, he appreciated the principles of self-reliance preached by Booker T. Washington, so Page also enrolled in and completed "a three-year course on gas engines." In the midst of World War I, he enlisted in ROTC and received a commission as second lieutenant as well as chief musician. Through his various courses of study, Page "qualified [as] an A-1 cook, cabinet maker, carpenter, musician, and mechanic." The war ended, however, and Page left college to work as a Pullman porter on the Union Pacific, traveling to Denver and Cheyenne. But he never left music: from 1918 to 1923 he performed with Bennie Moten, but after joining the Blue Devils, Page was a stalwart until circumstances forced him to quit and join Moten in 1931.[49]

Edward "Crack" McNeil, the band's first drummer, was one of the original members—a founder, so to speak. We know less of him than of Page or Lewis. He, too, died in his prime, in spring 1935. He came from Kansas City and was listed as a musician in the *City Directory* in 1926, but he left the Blue Devils two years later. He also played in Andy Kirk's Clouds of Joy, but in 1928 he was an assembler in the Alligator Manufacturing Company.[50] He may have taken the job to better support his wife, Bernice Burnett, daughter of a local grocer. In fact, McNeil worked as a clerk in his father-in-law's grocery store in 1931. He lived with the Burnetts, as well, in a large frame house at 838 Northeast Seventh Street.[51]

In April 1935, returning home around 3:30 a.m. after playing at Slaughter's Hall, McNeil retired as usual. A few hours later, his wife "was awakened by an apparent struggle on the part of McNeil to breathe." He was "half sitting up in the bed, but slumped over just as she awoke." She was unable to awaken him, so she told her father, and they called the doctor, who insisted he go to the hospital. He died at St. Anthony Hospital "following futile efforts of pullmotors and other modern methods" to arouse him from unconsciousness. The "expert drummer," who "had a reputation in his line all over the United States," died of "acute myocarditis" at the age of thirty-five, just as swing was about to become a national rage.[52]

At the time of McNeil's death, Edward Christian praised the drummer in his weekly *Dispatch* column, *Musical Low-Down*. Rarely did he write as highly of any musician as he did of McNeil. He noted that former Blue Devils Coleman and Simpson "say that every musician must pay their respect" to him. Christian added, "There are not going to be any excuses, for the first reason that Mr. McNeil

Edward McNeil, Blue Devil Drummer, circa 1925

was one of the best friends the musicians had. As for myself, I would dislike having to personate any musician that doesn't pay his respects to Mr. McNeil.... Every Cat that can blow a horn is expected to be on hand to do anything that may be asked of him." He concluded, "Musician friends, we have lost one of the best friend[s] we had."[53] McNeil personified the ideals that Blue Devils identified with and practiced for much of their lives.

Another founding Blue Devil, the trombonist Ermal "Bucket" Coleman, was also the band's business manager. He hailed from Indianapolis, Indiana, according to Buster Smith. The Manuscript Census and *Indianapolis City Directory* confirmed his recollections.[54] In 1920 Coleman and his wife, Lillie, resided at 912 Muskingham near downtown. Coleman was one of the oldest Blue Devils, born in Indiana in 1896. He earned a living as a dance musician in 1920 and was an army veteran. Even when he was holding nonmusical jobs, he was involved with the music world in one way or another. For example, the *Oklahoma City City Directory* listed him with Hallie Richardson in 1930; Richardson kept a shoeshine stand on Deep Deuce and, most significantly, was known as the musician's friend. The next year Coleman opened Bucket's Restaurant at 311½ East Second Street, and then for the next three or four years he led a band known as his Pails of Rhythm.[55]

He, in fact, employed former Blue Devils after the band's demise. For example, after Walter Page left Bennie Moten, he performed with Coleman, and so did James Simpson, in spring 1935.[56] The trombonist was the third founding Blue Devil to pass—just a few years after Lewis and McNeil. His good friend, the drummer known as "Bozo" (James Bowler), took him back to Indianapolis when he became ill in 1936. Perhaps his illnesses were too serious for any doctor, as the death certificate listed uremia as the main cause of death along with heart disease ("myocardial degeneration") and kidney problems ("nephritis with edema"), as well as afflictions from which Black men suffered more than the general population—arteriosclerosis and hypertension, in that order. He died in early winter 1937 in an Indiana veterans' center, at the age of forty.[57] His widow, Lillie, probably provided the details of his short life for the death certificate.

Thornton Blue, another member of the first band, was one of the more elusive Devils in terms of biographical details. One reason he was difficult to trace was his name—it was not Thornton Blue, but William Thornton Blue, and he was born in 1902 or 1903, in St. Louis. He evidently was not a Devil for very long. We know he was a schooled musician, not only because he was a bandleader, but because his father was also a musician. The *Argus*, the St. Louis African-American weekly, reported that Blue was "well known as a clarinet and saxophone player, having played here for several years with one of the leading bands"; he stayed with this band for only a few years and went to New York City. In late spring 1928 he took his own band to Paris, where he had a six-month contract at the Ambassador Club. Then he joined Noble Sissle's band in Paris before returning to the states to perform in the outfits of Cab Calloway and Dave Nelson, King Oliver's nephew.[58]

Around 1925, when the Blue Devils floundered, Page launched the second version of the band; he enlisted Buster Smith after hearing him play in a speakeasy in Dallas, Texas. Unlike Willie Lewis and Walter Page, Smith came much closer to the ideal of the untutored jazzman; he was also known as a peerless bluesman and an inspiration for saxophonists Lester Young and Charlie Parker. Until Smith came on the scene, it does not appear that hot soloists were among the original Blue Devil band members. Unfortunately, the one time the *Dallas Express* mentioned them performing at Chester Park in Dallas, no band members were named.[59]

While not a founder, Jimmy Rushing, said by some to be an early Blue Devil, was mentioned in 1926 in the pages of the *Dispatch,* but it is not clear that he was a band member at this time. He was, however, a winner at the Mardi Gras Ball where the band played that winter—Rushing and his partner, a Mrs. Jones, tied another couple for first place in the waltzing contest.[60] Basie corroborated the fact that Rushing was a superb dancer and quite fleet of foot as well, often racing Bennie Moten in the 1930s.[61]

The singer, drummer, and M.C., Ernie Williams, was a Blue Devil during the band's last years, but in 1926 he was a champion dance contestant; his specialty was the Charleston, and he was known as "the best Charleston King in the Southwest." While his status as a Blue Devil at this time is uncertain, his dance talent once again reveals the versatility of band members. The music and the dancing were integrally related, and someone who excelled in one often excelled in the other, as well.[62]

Despite the myth that early jazz musicians were untrained, it is fairly clear that the original Devils were not musical illiterates. By the same token, neither were they rootless individuals, devoid of social ties to the community in which they lived. They embraced the values that King endorsed the night of his birthday celebration. Their band was also a veritable school for untutored musicians, and they performed for different social classes and occasions—not only in the Black community, but for white audiences as well, such as the dancers at Oklahoma City's Ritz Ballroom.[63]

Besides maintaining a jazz band, the musicians' efforts took institutional form in still another way. Three were instructors at the

Coleridge Taylor School of Music in Oklahoma's capital. Late one autumn afternoon in 1923, the Coleridge Taylor Choral Club gave its first recital, and William C. Lewis and W. S. Page were its directors. A local community member gave a speech, "Community Needs," no doubt stressing self-help as well as the need for philanthropy. The evening's affair featured piano and vocal solos by members of the community. Interestingly, the *Dispatch* reported that Walter Page "will also render a cello solo on his new $700 cello, which has just been purchased," evidence of the bassist's prosperity.[64]

From the Pythian Temple, at 206 East Second Street, the three professors of the Coleridge Taylor School offered classes to prosperous members of Oklahoma City's Black community. Walter Page's specialties were violin, cello, reed instruments, and harmony, while Lawrence Williams instructed in cornet and other wind instruments, and William C. Lewis taught German and French, indicating the importance of the European tradition in the school that was named after the famous Black composer of classical music.[65]

Through the music school and choral group, these three Blue Devils tapped the resources of the prosperous African-Americans in the capital city who wanted their children to perform the "art music" taught in the universities and conservatories of the U.S. and Europe. Band members also utilized other venues. Lawrence "Inky" Williams, the cornetist and Blue Devil who was at Billy King's birthday celebration, was director of the band at Douglass High School, which had a particularly strong music emphasis.[66]

Significantly, the Blue Devils developed ties with different segments of the Black community, not only through the Coleridge Taylor School, but at public dances, by means of membership in fraternal organizations, at the Aldridge Theatre on East Second Street, in the local high school, and in other ways. Page told of the famous Oklahoma music instructor Zelia N. Breaux, who taught at Langston, the Black university (over which her father, Inman Page, presided), and who became head of the Black schools' music programs in 1923. In 1919 with her business partner, Fred Whitlow, she opened up the Aldridge Theatre, named after the famous nineteenth-century African-American actor Ira Aldridge, and she was one of the community people who encouraged and supported the Blue Devils despite the fact that jazz was not her forte.[67]

As Page explained, the band had "gone on to a little theater in Oklahoma City and one of the co-owners fell in love with me." She wanted him to accompany her on the road as her assistant, and, he recalled, she "had big ideas and wanted to form a band in the cadet corps in the school in town with me as the director." Given Zelia Breaux's activities in the schools, Page's account suggests that he was referring to her and her support of the band. In any case, the Blue Devils often played at the Aldridge Theatre when they were in town, especially in the 1920s. With only five pieces and Page playing cued cello parts, they "sometimes . . . sounded like ten."[68]

Community support also came from a group of businessmen. Page reminisced about one time around 1927, when the band either rested or failed after Ermal Coleman left: "I had to scuffle around for a while trying to keep my family together, and I decided to get together with some of the influential men I knew around Oklahoma City." They all gathered in a hotel room while the bassist "told them I wanted to organize a big band, and that I needed money to get them together all in one place." Because of the group's roots in the capital city and the services they had provided to Blacks over the years, "one of the men put them up in a large room and fed them all" until they were self-supporting again.[69]

It is noteworthy that Page wanted to enlarge the band, suggesting that he was sensitive to the most recent developments in jazz bands. Around this time small jazz combos of five to six were adding musicians until they became a group of nine or ten, or still larger. Duke Ellington was among the bandleaders who, following in the footsteps of Fletcher Henderson, enlarged their units to become what were later known as full-fledged swing bands. This then became the second version of the band—Walter Page's Blue Devils (James Simpson, Jimmy LuGrand and Lips Page, trumpets; Eddie Durham and Dan Minor on trombone; Buster Smith, Reuben Roddy, and Ted Manning on reeds; Turk Thomas on piano; Reuben Lynch on guitar; Alvin Burroughs on drums; and Page on baritone sax, bass violin, and bass horn).[70]

Band members' testimony suggests that their sense of shared identity was as important as the techniques of arrangement, the inventions of soloists, the propulsive swing, or the blues harmonies. Numerous individual sacrifices and displays of solidarity ensured the band's persistence and, also, its legendary stature in the folklore of territorial musicians. When circumstances reduced the band to four or five musicians, its ever-loyal stalwarts always revived it. Buster Smith resurrected the band after Eddie Durham, Walter Page, Oran Page, Jimmy Rushing, Bill Basie, and Dan Minor left for Moten: "Ernie [Williams] and I kept that band...sometimes there wasn't but five pieces in it." This happened again when Leonard Chadwick and Le Roy "Snake" Whyte left in winter 1932–33. But Williams and Smith refused to give up, and "always kept adding one and bringing the band back to where it was supposed to be—twelve or thirteen."[71]

Many Blue Devils had close social ties with the Oklahoma City Black community, marrying and starting families and belonging to organizations such as the fraternal orders. Trumpet player James Simpson came to the Blue Devils in the mid- or late 1920s; he was one of the more versatile and community-oriented musicians. A native Oklahoman, born around 1908 or 1909, he was an electrician as well as a musician, and he suddenly emerged on the scene and became a leader of the band in 1929.[72]

Simpson's various activities were typical of some band members. He and his wife, Ada, were listed in the *City Directory* in 1930 and 1931 as residing on "Deep Deuce" at 323 East Second Street. Around 1932, he opened the S and H Smoke Shop across the street at 316, and also the Rhythm Club, a nightspot just two doors down at 312. In 1934 he was head of the American Federation of Musicians local and resided at 311½ East Second. The next year, Edward Christian, in his weekly column for the *Dispatch,* named Simpson as one of the outstanding area musicians along with former Blue Devils Leonard Chadwick, Harry Youngblood, Ermal Coleman, Edward McNeil, T. B. Thomas, Walter Page, and Abe Bolar. Simpson was, furthermore, active in the African-American community as a member of the Elks.[73]

This trumpet player first appeared in the *Dispatch* as a bandleader in his own right in 1926. He and his KVOO Broadcasting Syncopators gave Oklahoma City a surprise dance shortly before Christmas that year. Around New Year's that winter, Simpson, "with his broadcasting artists," was slated to entertain the Elks and the

Daughter Elks for their smoker at Slaughter's Hall. The very next month, he was praised as former head of the Black Aces and current head of KVOO's radio staff orchestra. He was also said to be "making good." Moreover, "as of old whenever his orchestra gives a dance the hall is packed." Such was his popularity that he was scheduled to play at Slaughter's Hall for the Pink Bow Club's masquerade ball six months prior to the occasion.[74]

He was thus a prime candidate to serve the Blue Devils, which he did for at least four years. In the early 1930s, Simpson appears to have alternated with Walter Page as manager of the Blue Devils, each using his name to headline the band—"James Simpson and His Famous Blue Devils" and "Walter Page and His Original Blue Devils." In 1931, a *Dispatch* article, "Elks Charity Ball Nets Nearly $200," referred to "Page's Blue Devils"; a year later, in the *Chicago Defender*, the band is referred to as "the original '13 Blue Devils'" and Simpson is listed, but not Walter Page, who had been replaced by Abe Bolar. By 1935 Simpson had reunited with Walter Page, Ermal Coleman, and Edward McNeil in Coleman's Pails of Rhythm.[75]

Blue Devils were community-oriented, whether in their relationships with musicians or—through other institutions—with churchgoers, fraternity brothers, family, and friends. Ermal Coleman, another original Blue Devil, opened up a headquarters for performers, with an office, reception area, and rehearsal rooms at 325 East Second, in late 1933; at the time, he was with the Harlem Devils.[76]

Unlike Bennie Moten's band or the big-time East Coast bands, the Blue Devils were strictly a grass roots organization, part of the loose social network of African-American urbanites in the Southwest. The business community came to their rescue at least once, and perhaps in gratitude, the Blue Devils played for the Oklahoma City Negro Business League in 1925. They also performed for the Pythian Grand Lodge that same year and, in 1931, at an Elks charity ball, where they successfully raised nearly two hundred dollars to assist homeless and impoverished Black Oklahomans during the Depression. Their community service helped to spread their name: "The whole [Elks] affair would have been impossible but for the unselfish service of Mr. Walter Page and his famous Blue Devils." The next month they performed for the Elks again, at Slaughter's Hall, part of a series of entertainments that culminated in the Elks convention in Denver in mid-1931.[77]

Differing from more prestigious bands in another respect, the Blue Devils provided opportunities for younger musicians to trade expertise with them. Author Ralph Ellison explained that when he was a band student at Douglass High School in Oklahoma City, he lent his mellophone to Oran Page, and other Blue Devils borrowed mellophones from high-school bandsmen "in order to play special choruses." Ellison pointed out that "in exchange I'd insist upon being allowed to sit in on trumpet during a Blue Devils rehearsal." Also, "I'd be asked to arbitrate when they got into arguments over interpretation." Occasionally he played solos with them at weddings.[78]

Other Blue Devils met community needs more informally, through their own practices, sometimes to the dismay of family members. Years after he left the band, Oran Page's dedication to helping young musicians exemplified their creed. In an article announcing his death late in 1954, the Kansas City *Call* pointed out that the trumpet player's "family and friends complained frequently that he was too generous with his talents [but, nonetheless, he] remained anxious to help young musicians. He listened to their problems and gave them advice." His apartment—in New York's Harlem —"became a haven for musical tyros." Page explained, "Somebody's got to look after the future generation of musicians." He was forty-six when he died.[79]

The "all for one and one for all" attitude of the bandsmen mirrored the community spirit of the Oklahoma frontier. Their appeal to different segments of the community, across class and racial lines, took place because the capital city was newly settled, and hard and fast class lines were not yet drawn in the early and mid-1920s; by the end of the decade, many Black Oklahomans had soirees and social affairs in their homes, with music by Zelia Breaux and by pupils of Professors Lewis and Page. Hardening of class lines occurred near the end of the decade as some residents became rich from oil, and others from commerce, and then the Depression set in. These hard times, with the long lines of unemployed, created greater distances between Oklahomans.

About this time, in 1931, band members began to travel even farther, into Iowa and Minnesota, for example, before heading East, late in 1932, in pursuit of the success that Moten's band garnered when it went East. For African-Americans, the Blue Devils became meaningful symbols of the persistence of the archetypal Black musician—unknown, struggling, but overcoming formidable odds to successfully earn a living, raise a family, and satisfy his aesthetic needs through swing music. Hot soloists could swing with contagious enthusiasm and solo at great length, creating triumphant moments in the lives of a people subjugated by racism, discrimination, and low wages in the prairie and plains states west of the Mississippi. By staying with the band as long as they did, band members proved their stamina, conviction, and willingness to take a chance on swing music by casting their lot with a group whose existence was a symbol of the vitality of a people.

CHAPTER FOUR

Texas Bluesman

Henry "Buster" Smith, the Professor of Swing

Henry Franklin "Buster" Smith performed "with virtually every important band that played the free-wheeling 'Kansas City' style," and was designated an important mentor by no less than Lester "Pres" Young and Charlie "Yardbird" Parker.[1]

Born in Alsdorf, just south of Dallas, Texas, on August 26, 1904, Buster was named Henry after his mother's father. He was the eldest of five brothers, and the youngsters grew up in cotton country in north Texas in the World War I era. After harvest time in late summer and fall, various family members played musical instruments, some of which they had constructed during the winters. The father played guitar, while the mother played piano. They also attended church all year round, and the grandfather was particularly pious and strict.[2]

Smith's birth in 1904 coincided with the boll weevils' invasion of the cotton crop, and during his childhood the pest created havoc in the South's cotton economy, launching the migration of Blacks and whites to nearby cities. This was probably one reason the family moved to Dallas about the time that Buster became a musician. The Smiths were also ambitious. "Our family picked cotton. We ran back and forth between the farm and Dallas trying to raise enough money to pay for the home in Dallas we were buying."[3]

They were also family-oriented and depended upon everyone's contributions to better their condition: three generations lived together in rural Texas and in Dallas in the 1920's—the grandfather, three of his children, including the saxophonist's mother, and Henry's four brothers. Their family—and their mother, in particular—provided a focus for their activities and concerns during much of their lives.[4] Like some other Blue Devils, Henry grew up in an extended family, and information about his father is practically nonexistent. Significantly, all members of the family, including his grandfather, were literate. The neighbors were mostly white, farmers and farm laborers, except for three Mexican families that came into the U.S. at the time of the Mexican Revolution. His mother's father, Henry H. Johnson, a fifty-four-year-old widower and farm laborer in Delta County, Texas, headed a household of eleven members in 1920. They included his son, Tracy, a farm laborer at twenty-five; his daughter, Ileana (or Arleana), who was thirty-five; her five boys—Henry (sixteen), John (fourteen), Boston (twelve), James (nine), and Floyd (seven); and a family of three boarders. Neither Johnson's grandsons nor the boarder's child attended school that year, though they were listed as literate—indicating the low priority the state of Texas placed on the education of Black children at the time.

All we know of their father is that he was presumably alive in 1920, because Mrs. Smith was listed as married instead of widowed, and he was from Texas; he also made and played his own guitars and banjos. In 1920, the Johnsons and Smiths lived as share-croppers or farm laborers and had a street address, which suggests that the area where they lived in Delta County was not as rural as it might have been.[5] Ten years later Arleana Evans was widowed, but it is impossible to determine whether the deceased (Evans) is the boys' father or stepfather. The Dallas household that she headed was still an extended family, and now all their neighbors were Black. Her oldest son, Henry, was a Blue Devil rooming in Oklahoma City, but the other four sons remained in the household she headed, and so did her father, her brother Robert, and a grandson. Now Dallasites, they had been swept up in the industrialization of this urban area. While the Smiths were laborers, and still renters, too, they worked in a variety of enterprises, including a construction company and a hotel, while the uncle was a driver for a wholesale house. They apparently took care of the grandfather, Henry Johnson, who was no longer working. It is likely that Henry Smith's uncles, Robert and Tracy Johnson, were the guitar players on his mother's side that he mentions in the interview quoted below.[6] Smith explained that his introduction to music came when he was four or five years of age: "The blues was all around, growin' up, picking. . . . I heard them work songs, church hymns."[7] The family kept an organ, and "I'd come in from the fields and play an old organ." With his brother Boston assisting, Henry worked the keys while Boston pressed the pedals. "I tried that blues on my uncle's pump organ in Ennis." He explained that his mother disapproved,[8] and that his grandfather "used to come in and whip me for playing organ while they were out in the field working." The old man claimed that playing music would lead to no good, so the family had to get rid of the organ. "After that I didn't get near another instrument till I was about eighteen."[9]

Nonetheless, his family's musical influences were considerable. Smith reminisced, "during the winter time when they can't do nothing [field work], it was cold, and there wasn't no radio or TV then, so they. . . learned [to play music], and some of them was playing in the *church*."[10] His family "learned how to play them organs, and them things, back in them days. That's all the musical instruments they had, and an old guitar." In a rare statement about his father, he explained, "My old dad, I've seen him sit down, several times, and just sit up and get him a stick and a bucket, and saw it off, and a pan or something, make a guitar, an old banjo or something, and sit around and pick on it" during the winter. "That's all the amusement we ever had. On my mother's side, it was just a musical family." Smith had "two or three uncles, they all could play guitar." He summed up his career in one sentence: "I just loved music, and I just played any instrument, first start off playing an old guitar, and I put it down, start playing an old clarinet, and put that down, and learn how to play the saxophone in three days, cause the saxophone and the clarinet have practically the same fingering."[11]

One day around harvest time in 1922, Smith saw a used clarinet in a shop window in Celina, and promised his mother he would pick enough cotton—four hundred pounds a day for a week—to pay the sum of $3.50 for the clarinet. In fact, he "picked *over* four hundred for five days" and taught himself to play by watching others in Dallas's "Deep Ellum," the African-American district on the edge of downtown, where musicians performed and crowds of sightseers ambled about on weekends. The bands that made the circuits—Alphonso Trent, T. Holder, and George E. Lee—also influenced him. Dallas itself boasted such bands as Trent, Fred Cooper, and Carl Murphy's Satisfied Five. Dallas' Deep Ellum was famous for its sights, its hawkers, musical entertainment, milling crowds, and weekend visitors from the country and other towns. Smith maintained, "Man, Deep Ellum was wide open... Friday, Saturday, and Sunday was the most crowded. There'd be medicine show men, right out in the broad open, sellin' that medicine." The bluesman T-Bone Walker "got started... dancin' for them medicine shows in Deep Ellum." City-dwellers and visitors congregated along the railroad tracks that ran down the street: "You could see everybody you knew in Deep Ellum, they'd hang out by the railroad tracks and listen at the medicine shows and then go to the Tip Top." This nightclub was popular because "they used bigger bands." It was "about two doors down from the Ella B. Moore Theatre," which opened in 1925.[12]

Church music and the guitar playing of his father and uncles were Smith's first influences. As he explained his training: "I just picked it up little by little by watching people who played that same instrument." His method was "just watch them and listen and pick up more and more." On the new record players of the 1920s, Smith listened to recordings of reedmen Sidney Bechet and Woodie Walder, as well as "Tommy Dorsey quite a bit."[13]

Despite his longtime association with the alto saxophone, from early in his career, Smith was a multi-instrumentalist who could play the clarinet, saxophone, guitar, and banjo. Of the famous New Orleans virtuoso and soprano saxophonist, Sidney Bechet, Smith said: "I tried to copy behind him. I'd buy all his records and listen to him."[14] He rarely failed to mention the singular influence of Jesse Hooker, "an awful good clarinet player who used to play down on the Central track at the Tip-Top Club." Significantly, his mentor "couldn't read [music] either." At the dawn of the jazz age, Hooker was one of the few clarinet players in Texas, Smith claimed. "A little short fellow. He was a whole lot of player. He was one of the best ones around here." Indeed, Smith "used to follow him around. I'd go up and listen to his band before we went up there and play behind them." Listening to Hooker "gave me ideas."[15]

Before he was a professional musician, Smith earned money as a dishwasher, and also by working with a group of electricians wiring ice houses in Dallas.[16] Within one year after the family moved to Dallas in 1923, he was playing in public, having left school after the seventh grade. Smith helped his mother, as she was "alone with us five boys so I had to help bring in a little money." In his first years as a musician, he performed in a trio with Voddie White, pianist, and a drummer, in lowdown spots. "Nothin' but blues. Chock houses."[17]

Smith grew up around the blues and played it from the beginning of his career, in the joints that served the homemade liquor—"chock"—that gave these places their name. "We didn't play nothing but chock houses [sometimes referred to as "chalk" houses, where a very powerful local brew was served]. Slow blues was what you heard in the chock houses," where "they'd be sellin' pig ankles, pig feet, pig ears, and they have a big tub full of chock with a dipper in it sittin' up on top of the piano." It was all-you-could-drink in these "good time houses." Smith recalled, "You'd hear that slow blues and there'd be fightin'."[18]

It is likely that Smith forgot some of the venues where he performed in the first year or so of playing. He may have been the Henry Smith performing at the Dreamland Theatre in Tulsa's new Greenwood District in 1923, but he never mentioned this in interviews.[19] He also played with Albert Dominique, the New Orleans bandleader, who "changed his name to Don Albert because later on he organized a big band around [Dallas]." Smith maintained their models were Duke Ellington's and Fletcher Henderson's bands. In fact, "A lot of these ideas were from records that he had then. I learned how to arrange, and how to voice the instruments and what not."[20] At first, however, Smith maintained, "I wasn't reading music." Like Eddie Barefield and other excellent young jazzmen, in Albert's band, "they just played by ear . . . we had about five pieces together [alto sax, clarinet, trumpet, trombone, banjo]. We played in a place called the Tip-Top . . . down on the Central [track]." Smith was the only Texan in the band; the others were from New Orleans. They played, he recalled, "rhythm and blues." Albert liked the local scene so much that he ran a club for a local resident "for years and years" in Dallas.[21]

In 1925, Smith took up the alto saxophone. He was in a three-piece band with Jesse Dee, "a drummer, and he had an alto and drums, too. So he didn't like the alto, so he let me have his old alto." The only other alto player in Texas, Smith recalled, was M. J. Collins, known as "Sauerkraut." "All of them cats, played all that technique on the instrument. And I had all of their records. So I'd follow behind them, and add a little something to it." At that time he never used instruction books, and he never practiced scales.[22]

When he joined the Blue Devils and left Dallas, Smith liberated himself from the injustices of race relations in Texas. He explained how one day he went to visit "one of our old friends, a lady... [from] down there where I was born and raised... raised on the farm with us," who was ill. He went to see Mrs. Whittaker at her home in North Dallas and stayed with her at his mother's request until around 10:00 p.m., when he left to bicycle home. Two plain-clothes detectives stopped him and accused him of stealing:

" 'Hey, boy, where you been?' And I tells them where I been. 'Where you work?' During that day we have to tell all that. So I told him where I work. 'No, you been somewhere stealing.' I said, 'No, man, I can't steal nothing.' He said, 'You lie!' and hauled off and slapped me and knocked me off the bicycle. Then when I come to myself I could hear him say, 'Bout the time I get my gun out you better be around that corner.' And I got on my bicycle and went around that corner so fast that I ran up against the building. And that's what... [changed] my mind, gentlemen. I said I'm gonna leave Texas. So when the Blue Devils came through and when they came back here... I said I'm gone."[23] The Blue Devils were the first larger combo that he joined. He encountered them one summer when they came to Dallas. In fact, "they got here and got stranded here... came here with about eight pieces and they... couldn't get out of town." Smith reminisced, "they stayed around here about a year-and-a-half or two years, and they geared the band back up." More than thirty years later he recounted, "It all looked pretty good to me so I joined up with them."[24]

The band, at the time, was led by Ermal Coleman, from Indianapolis, "a fine trombone player," who "came down with a boy that played a whole lot of drums, in fact, I never heard anybody that played any more drums than him—a boy called 'Crack' [Edward

McNeil]...a great drummer." Bassist Walter Page also "played tuba and a good baritone sax," and "everybody thought it was great the way he'd run from one instrument to another."[25] Smith must have been somewhat reluctant to join them because he told them he could not read music, but they answered, "That's all right. Read the... books, and you can start right on the course." Until then, they said, "we'll just play the intro and you come in, and the way you play, you'll make it!" In another instance, because he was new to the band and did not know the arrangements, Page cued him with a whistle when it was time for him to come in.[26] The actual story of his becoming a Blue Devil is complicated, insofar as he left the band and went back to Dallas over a pay dispute. He recalled that they left Texas in the fall of 1925 and played some Halloween dates. Yet Smith complained for the first time about this stint during an interview deposited at the Institute of Jazz Studies: "They gave us [Smith and his friend] about ten or fifteen dollars less than they did the other fellows." He didn't understand the reasoning for the disparity, and left with his friend, but the band "come back next spring...they come back to Dallas and picked us up again....We stayed with them then."[27]

At first, Smith's approach was entirely that of a self-taught musician. He never consulted instruction books or practiced scales, he simply listened to the records of Bechet, Walder, Dorsey, Fletcher Henderson's band, and others, and he played along with his heroes in the way that so many young players did, beginning in the 1920s.[28]

Like other self-taught musicians, he made some very basic mistakes. James Clay observed, "When he first started playing the clarinet, he played it backwards. People freaked. I couldn't believe it myself. And he was pulling it off. They said, 'Hey, Buster, you're playing it backwards, my man. Turn it this way.' He did and just kept on playing."[29]

In his early twenties he had "earned a reputation as a kid wonder, a player of unlimited ability." He also claimed that he taught Sammy Price piano in 1924. Allegedly, Price approached him: "Buster, I want to learn how to play piano. Can I come over?" Smith was accommodating, teaching Price just as others had taught him: "Well, come on out . . . I'll show you a few chords." What he demonstrated was "nothin' but the blues."[30] As for his soloing and learning to read and write music, Smith explained, "I used to bang around on the piano a little bit. I'd study those chords. I'd try to put as many notes as I could within the chord for a change—for the chord to change. I'd turn back with something or other, and I'd study those chords, and I'd notice that 7 means one thing, 6 means another thing, diminished means another thing, augmented means another thing."[31]

While maintaining he learned all this more or less intuitively, he also recounted how different musicians introduced him to reading music, and how he taught music to others. Blue Devil Willie Lewis, a "great piano player, sight reader . . . take a liking to me, and he say, 'Now, I'm going to show you something.'" Lewis "got that little old book of instructions, and he showed me the right hand notes and all of that." Johnny Clark, a banjo player, also befriended him, and "showed me the value of note[s], when I first tried to learn how to read" in Dallas, when he was getting started as a musician. Clark played with Jesse Hooker in the 1920s, and "he'd get off work at night, and we go out there [to his home] and sit up around 2 or 3 o'clock in the morning." As Smith explained, "I was just crazy about music. And I just didn't want to give the music up. And I wanted to see what I could do, just running around and hearing all that different music, and guys playing and going on."[32]

◆ ◆ ◆

By the time he joined the Blue Devils he had been introduced to reading and notating music.[33] Smith was a member during the Blue Devil's barnstorming days. They traveled far and wide, "all over the South," and into southern Texas, and "even got up into New Mexico and Colorado a few times."[34] "We played around Dallas, Houston, Oklahoma City, Kansas City, and those places." In 1927 "we saw Basie in Kansas City playing the piano in a show with the Whitman sisters." Because "there wasn't much happening there," they convinced him to join them. Smith claimed they returned to his hometown of Dallas "and stayed around here till the last of 1928, went back to Kansas City for about three months, and then we moved back to Oklahoma City and started working at the Ritz Ballroom." They alternated this winter job at the Ritz with summers at the Cinderella Garden in Little Rock. They did this "three or four years—steady work the whole time" and had only eight days off a year.[35]

The reedman took credit for recruiting his fellow Texan, Oran "Hot Lips" Page. In Tyler, a north Texas town and site of some Black colleges, Page performed with Sugar Lou and Eddie and their seven-piece band in 1928. Smith confessed, "I'm the one who stole him." Page was singing and playing trumpet at this time. A year after Page joined, the other Blue Devils started their exit for the Moten band. Durham went first, then Basie, followed by Rushing, and early in 1931, Oran Page. Finally, Walter Page left the Oklahoma City outfit the next year. Smith persevered, however, recruiting new members with the help of Ernie Williams—Charlie Washington, Le Roy "Snake" Whyte, Abe Bolar, Lester Young, Jasper "Jap" Jones, and others.[36]

◆ ◆ ◆

The band endured, despite these defections, because "Ernest Williams and myself, being the oldest men in the band, took over and carried it all over into Virginia and around, and kept it together." Williams became the drummer, and sang as well. Smith recounted how "Ernest and I got to be real good friends." They saw the Blue Devils "dwindle down several times to five or six pieces and we'd have to build it back up again." They "kept that up about three years," until the band's demise in West Virginia in 1933.[37]

Smith learned about arranging while with the Blue Devils and was their main arranger after around 1928. He began this new dimension to his career, he recalled, in Little Rock: "I was the only arranger in the band. I had to do all of it." He worked from the piano, like many arrangers.

> The first thing I had to write . . . was for the saxophone. I found out that the saxophone, the alto player, was in the same line and the same key that the trombone player is, but the trombone is in bass clef and alto is in treble clef. But they're

on the same line. So I found out that the tenor and the trumpet was on the same line—the B-flat instruments. And the clarinet was a B-flat instrument; it's the same key and it's on the same line. So I had to write saxophone parts first. Then I found out what the trombone was and the bass fiddle and all that, and the trumpets and all that, and then I got to write for the brass section.

His work was extremely tedious; he listened to records, and "I'd take the whole thing down...every note, every one of them. The only thing I didn't write down was the drummer." Smith explained that "sometimes I'd write the drums, though, but mostly the drummers, they wouldn't read it anyhow, so I wouldn't write it." For a show, drummers might show off, but otherwise, "back in them days they just kept time. They didn't play no fancy stuff." If the drummer took a solo, then "he'd play what he wanted to play."[38] Still the band depended on "head arrangements" (memorized, unwritten arrangements) as well, and once they had memorized Smith's arrangements, they no longer needed the sheet music.

Touring in the Deep South and on the Southwest frontier, they ran into the problems that plagued traveling Black bands and shows for so much of jazz and U.S. history. Smith recalled how in Odlow, Oklahoma, "playing the second floor for a man who had a dance hall up there...in a white place and everything," the boss man paid them at 11:00 p.m. and left, and they had to play until midnight. Everyone in the audience left "except one great big guy who looked like a big prize fighter.... He pulled off his shirt" after getting drunk, and had nothing but his pants on. He even removed his shoes and stood at the door. "I'm gonna whup every one of you when you come out, one by one," he told them "You all think you're smart. I'm gonna whup every one of you." They were worried, because no police were around. "We looked out the window out there, wasn't nothin' out on the street. No cars, nothin'. [They were] all home."[39] Not wanting any trouble, they were perplexed about what to do, and then the banjoist, Reuben Lynch, a rather large man, came to their rescue. "You all want to get out?" he said. And they responded, "Yeah, sure. We got to get back to Dallas. We got to go home." He told them, "Just follow me." He folded up one of their metal music stands. "He rolled that thing and batted that guy right in the back of the neck, draw that thing and batted him clean down the steps with that thing, right down into the street." The bully exclaimed, "Whoever did that, I'll kill you. I'll bust your brains out." Smith chortled with some delight, as he remembered their triumph, "but see, we all got in the car and flew! Ha-ha!"[40]

In a similar incident in Palestine, Texas, the town sheriff, another bully, "comes down with two big pistols on, and he wouldn't let nobody dance but himself! In other words, he didn't want nothing but 'Turkey in the Straw' all the time." As a result, "wasn't nobody dancing but him, by himself, standing out there with some big boots on, right in the middle of the floor." Everybody just stood around. Smith recalled he was a "bad man, so wasn't nobody said nothin' to him; all the people were standing around and listening to it!" This went on the entire night! The boss man came up and said, "He's the baddest man in this part of the country.... Go ahead, I'm paying you. Go ahead and play. Don't make no difference. There's nobody gonna dance."[41]

One time in Texas when some white men came up to the bandstand at intermission and asked band members where they were from, they all replied, "Dallas," especially those who were from up north. One of the whites remarked, "See that big nigger laying out there, sitting there?" He was referring to Jimmy Rushing. The stranger said, "My daddy sure could use him down on his plantation ... He got three full niggers down there like him. I sure could use him down there, because he could kill a whole lot of hogs and things." The Blue Devils "just sat there and looked at him," and started playing again after intermission. They understood the whites were trying to start something, and by saying nothing—a form of passive resistance—they avoided disaster.[42]

Smith was one of the first Blue Devils singled out for praise by the *Black Dispatch* shortly before Christmas in 1926. The weekly wrote of "The Famous Blue Devil Orchestra with Buster, the Star Sax specialist," and their return to Oklahoma City from a tour of the South.[43] In the autumn of 1928, Smith was featured in a Kansas City *Call* photograph of the band along with four other members—

Walter and Oran Page, Jimmy Rushing, and William Basie. By this time the band numbered eleven and also included the composer and arranger Eddie Durham.

The Blue Devils were an integral part of the Oklahoma City community and the Southwest in the 1920s, staying in a local boarding house and residents' homes, performing at dances for various local social clubs and organizations, and attending college games. In autumn 1929, the band—eleven strong—piled into their cars and, along with other Oklahomans, drove down to Dallas for the famous football classic: the Panthers and Wildcats at the Texas State Fair. Local African-American college football teams battled before hundreds, including Roscoe Dunjee, the *Dispatch* editor who reported the affair.[44]

The makeup of the band on this occasion is telling. Both Walter Page and the subsequent leader, James Simpson, were in attendance. Alvin Burroughs (or Burrows), drummer; Reuben Lynch on banjo; and Charlie Washington, pianist, made up the remainder of the rhythm section. The reeds were Reuben Roddy, Buster Smith, and Bell [Bill] Owens. The brass included Simpson, Oran Page, and Druie Bess. James Rushing completed the band. Basie and Durham appear to have left by this time.[45]

As leader of the Blue Devils in the early 1930s, Smith had progressed considerably from a self-tutored amateur to star soloist in one of the top territorial bands in the Southwest. His newfound skill in writing arrangements would serve him well during the swing era with Basie's orchestra and with other outfits in subsequent years. His persistence personified the spirit of the band and the values they upheld. But he could not foresee what a calamity the Depression would work on jazz bands and popular entertainment. However, while the movie industry with its "talkies" meant the end of vaudeville, and of productions like Billy King's that launched the Blue Devils, jazz bands adapted by performing in movie houses before and after the main feature. Moreover, they still accompanied the musicals and floorshows in movie houses and the nightclubs modeled after New York's famous Cotton Club. After the Blue Devils became stranded in West Virginia and disbanded, their spirit and bonhomie persisted in the Moten and other bands they joined, as well as in other aspects of their careers, for much of their lives. This was the case with Smith and his career, first in New York and then, from the middle of World War II, in Dallas, where he lived, led bands, and wrote music for nearly half a century.

CHAPTER FIVE

The Voice of Deep Deuce

James A. Rushing and East Second Street

Jimmy Rushing usually gave his date of birth as August 26, 1903; he was the first child in the family living at 307½ East Second.[1] Actually the correct year of his birth was 1899 according to the 1900 Manuscript Census for Oklahoma City.[2] It was not uncommon for show business people to shave a few years from their age. He added only a few biographical details in interviews, such as in *Down Beat* when he discussed the blues: "My father played trumpet" for the Knights of Pythias. "There were a lot of lodge bands in the Middle West. [His father's band] would play some jazz sometimes. They'd catch one of those good tunes." Indeed, "every now and then they would step out of bounds and play the St. Louis Blues, Memphis Blues, and numbers like that." He could easily recognize his father's trumpet playing from a distance: "When the band passed my house...I could hear them on the next street...[and] could tell when my father wasn't playing. He played very high and very strong.... I'd say to my mother, 'Pop's blowing now, mom.' And she'd say, 'Yes, I know.'" He asked how she knew, and she responded, "Because he's so brilliant, so strong."[3]

His mother's singing influenced him, as well. She played piano and sang in church choirs. In fact, she "was the best church singer I ever heard. Anywhere!"[4] In 1957 he attributed his singing to a relative: "I always could sing because I got it from my uncle," Wesley Manning, a sporting-house pianist from Mississippi.[5] The youngster listened to him practice, "and he taught me how to play piano."[6] As a matter of fact, "I got a lot of my blues from him." He also mentioned Mamie and Bessie Smith as influences, "among others," but he claimed that he did not take his own singing seriously: "it was only a hobby of mine."[7]

In a 1966 interview he explained, "I started singing in school, for the Easter pageants, and for Christmas programs and church affairs." He did so well, "I was holding down the first tenor chair in the choir. This all came about because both my parents were musical [and my mother] . . . got me in there [the choir] when I was real young."[8] At some point his parents "first tried to get me to take up violin, but I wouldn't, couldn't," and he turned to Wesley Manning, "who was responsible for me singing the blues . . . and used to practice at our house all the time." As a result of Manning's instruction, "I got so I could play anything I could hum, even though I could only play in three keys: B flat, E flat, and C."[9] Rushing also "used to play piano at house-rent parties . . . I was a big-time piano player . . . but I was singing louder than I was playing. . . ."[10]

Clearly the marching band of the fraternal lodge, the church choir, and jazz and blues were powerful but not contradictory sources of his music education. As Rushing explained, "In the old days we used to call out, 'Give us some of that old church harmony,' but we meant the blues, for spiritual [sic] and the blues with us always ran neck and neck."[11] Then too, there were the street singers on the sidewalks outside the church, lodge, and sporting house. When he heard Big Bill Broonzy on a record, Rushing reminisced, "That was one of the greatest country blues men. . . . His songs and the way he performed them took you back to the old times, when they used to sing on street corners." Rushing recalled that "when I was a kid, fellers used to gather together with a guitar, a jaws-harp and just sing the blues." He remembered them vividly during his days in the Southwest. "These street blues singers were all over the country, but they were going strong around Kansas—and no one seems to realize that." They "used to jam all night in Kansas City."[12]

Rushing's father did not like blues or the sporting life and feared their allure for his firstborn son. He was like many respectable urban dwellers who held in disdain the entertainment milieu of the sporting houses and sundry "resorts" where gambling, alcohol, and prostitution flourished. He must have been aware that Manning's singular influence went beyond the blues. As Jimmy Rushing recalled: "Each morning when [Wesley Manning] came home he would bring in his hat full of money, which he collected in tips for entertaining the patrons. He would say to me—'dig your hands into that, boy!' and I would grab as much as my little fist could hold and take it all to school with me next day."[13] Rushing reminisced, "That used to be a big influence on me, too."[14]

When his mother died at the age of eighty-one in 1961, the veteran singer revealed a detail of his life that he had not revealed in earlier interviews. His mother actually conspired with him against his father's wishes. "She used to unlock the door to the piano room to allow me to practice when dad wasn't looking." As noted, Mr. Rushing "objected to my being an entertainer because musicians played in 'sporting houses' at that time." The young pianist explained his motivation: "I was determined to make it." His mother's encouragement was significant in this respect, because she was his "great inspiration," and used to tell him, "Whatever you're going to be, be a good one."[15]

He also mentioned another institution that was influential in his music training—his school. Oklahoma law required segregated schooling for African-Americans, and in Oklahoma City, the Black youngsters attending Douglass High School studied music under the tutelage of Zelia Breaux after 1918, but there probably was music instruction before her arrival.[16]

Rushing was the grandson of Oklahoma pioneers who settled in the territory in 1896.[17] His family imparted to him a highly developed music tradition, as "I heard music in my home all my life," but they also gave him a sense of history—not so much personal family history as the history of his people. He never talked about his grandparents in interviews, but he explained once that "the blues . . . come from way back in slavery days, from the time when those people weren't treated right. A man would have a plantation with as many as 200 working for him—150 of them would be singing spirituals, and the other 50 would be singing he or she songs, or songs about other private affairs." Blues, work songs, and spirituals came out of the same historical experience.[18]

His family's roots were in the Deep South. His father, Andrew Rushing, was born in Alabama at the end of Reconstruction in 1876, and Andrew's parents were also from that state. Jimmy Rushing's mother, Cora, came from Tennessee and was born in 1880. Wesley Manning—who appears to have been the son of Cora's sister, and thus was Jimmy Rushing's cousin, not his uncle—was born in Mississippi, a state noted for its blues traditions, around 1890.[19] Andrew and Cora's second son, Evoid, was born in 1903 in Oklahoma.[20] The young couple resided with Cora's mother in 1900; Andrew worked as a meat salesman that year, and in 1920, as a porter at the Oakland Motor Company, while Cora was a maid in an undertaking establishment.[21]

The Rushings were not only pioneers in the Oklahoma territory, but quite enterprising, as well. Around 1926 or 1927 they opened a confectionery store and small restaurant, where Jimmy worked before joining the Blue Devils. In 1947 the *Black Dispatch* columnist Jimmy Stewart reminisced, "Some of us still recall Jimmy Rushing making hamburgers and dispensing root beer out of that large wooden keg at his dad's café . . . in the gay twenties." With violinist Tennie Dixon, he "was the chief musical entertainment for high school parties during the early 1920s." Then his father built another dwelling on the rear of his property and went into real estate, in which he evidently prospered.[22]

Both sons benefited from the family's prosperity. Andrew had married well. His wife's mother, Bettie Mason, an illiterate laundress, owned her own home at 414 East First Street where the Rushings and their infant son, James, lived with her in 1900. Both Jimmy and Evoid attended Wilberforce College, the African-American institution in Ohio. Jimmy enrolled for only a year, in 1918–1919, and studied music, but left, he claimed, for a career in show business. From Ohio he made trips to Chicago's South Side to hear the new music. Then he worked as a hotel bellboy in Oklahoma City in 1920, and when he earned good tips, he could finance trips to Texas and California with his savings.[23]

Jimmy was different from his younger brother, who appeared to be a model son, if the *Dispatch* columnist's report of his "high marks" in college and his return to Wilberforce in 1920 was any indication.[24]

As a youngster Jimmy Rushing chafed under his father's strict regime, and, just like the Blue Devils' Leroy "Snake" Whyte and Lester Young, he used to run away from home. Rushing went to Texas, to Chicago, and in 1923 as far as Southern California. At first, he was content to sneak out his bedroom window and into the nightlife his father found so abhorrent. "After they'd go to sleep, I'd slip out my bedroom window... I was still pretty young, still wearing short pants, but I'd join my friends at a party where they'd have me playing the piano and singing all night long."[25] Of course his parents were angrily waiting for him when he returned.

Clearly the music as well as the love of travel were powerful attractions for him. "I ran away from home to go to Chicago to hear all those bands I'd heard so much about... Erskine Tate, Dave Peyton, Tiny Parham, Carroll Dickerson, and boy, did they have some bands." He also liked Coon-Sanders, who were at the Blackhawk Café, and Isham Jones, "because he could play the 'Wang Wang Blues' better than anyone I ever heard." A rover if not a rebel ("I used to like to travel and roam around a lot in those days. You couldn't keep me in one place very long."), on still other occasions, "I'd sneak off and run down to Texas all the time, and I heard some marvelous bands there."[26]

After his forays into the Midwest and Texas, he went to Los Angeles in 1923.[27] In one interview, he claimed that he married, or that he came West to get married ("I came out here [Los Angeles] incidentally to marry"), but little is known of this part of his life.[28] He claimed that his professional debut was in the Quality Night Club, where Hollywood movie stars liked to meet and "drink cases of gin."[29]

In Los Angeles, Rushing often played in rough-and-tumble after-hours spots rivaling those in Oklahoma City and Chicago. "One of the places I worked was the 'Jump Steady' Club. Boy, was this a rough place. You had to check your weapons at the door before you could get in." For one night every week, the free food was divine: "They used to barbeque a whole hog and slice it up and pass it out free: the only thing you paid for was the beer. Every Friday night was hog and beer night."[30]

In California he met New Orleans pianist and composer Jelly

Roll Morton: "I'll never forget him.... He'd walk in, listen to somebody play the piano for a while, and then he'd say, 'Whenever you see me walk in, get up off that piano.' "[31] This was when Morton lived in Los Angeles, during one of his sojourns on the West Coast before he went to Chicago late in 1923 and on to international fame.[32]

Rushing recalled that Morton played downtown, "and when he'd come up to the 'Jump Steady' they locked up the house and things really were swinging." Whenever the pianist came into the club where Rushing played, the two invariably "split the take half and half, which was alright by me 'cause Jelly really brought in the money." After about three years on the West Coast, Rushing returned to Oklahoma. [33]

These sojourns in the Southwest, the Midwest, and on the Pacific Slope were crucial to his music education and to his understanding of the nightlife and entertainment worlds in general. When he listened to the street-corner singers of the Southwest, he was immersed in the blues that he had been taught by his cousin, Wesley Manning. Hearing Morton as well as other New Orleans musicians in California, he learned about collective improvisation, and with the Midwest musicians, Dave Peyton and Earl Dickerson, he was introduced to Chicago's big-time entertainment world. While New Orleans's and Chicago's influences on the history of jazz are well known and widely accepted, aside from the work of Tom Stoddard, Larry Gushee, and Phil Pastras, the West Coast's early contribution is rarely examined.[34]

As Rushing and others have noted, the Los Angeles scene was particularly rich, especially with Crescent City musicians: "That's where I met all the New Orleans boys like Jelly Roll, Dink Johnson, Mutt Carey, Buddy Petit and all of them."[35] After he returned to Oklahoma City to work in his father's diner on Deep Deuce, he no doubt regaled his friends with tales of faraway places and the music he heard, while continuing to sing. From these days he was remembered as a friend of the hungry musician. Budd Johnson, who was stranded with fellow band members several times in his youth, recalled: "the only thing saved us is Jimmy Rushing's people always owned a restaurant in Oklahoma City, and he made it possible for us to eat over there, in his parents' restaurant."[36]

Interestingly, Rushing gave a version of the Blue Devils' origins that stressed its Texas roots: "In 1925, the Billy King group toured Texas with a show. Some of the boys from this show formed a band called the Blue Devils and I joined them and toured the South and Southwest in 1927 and 1928."[37] Then the pianist Bill Basie came to the Southwest with a show and joined the Blue Devils until winter of 1928–1929. In 1929 they made their first and only record, of "Blue Devil Blues," featuring Rushing, and "Squabblin'," an instrumental.[38] Rushing recounted that in 1929 Bennie Moten became leader, and Rushing stayed with him until his death. After Moten's nephew, Buster, "kept the band going for about a year after, then it broke up." Basie then formed his band "and we went up to Chicago through 1935/36." The singer added, almost as an afterthought, "We played the Reno Night Club and also broadcast over radio station WHB." Then he related the familiar story of how Benny Goodman and John Hammond heard them on the radio in Chicago, came to hear them, and the rest was history.[39]

Before considering more closely his stint with the Blue Devils, it is worthwhile to examine further the sources of Rushing's inspiration as a singer and musician, as well as the nature of his social life in Oklahoma City in the early 1920s.[40] Of course, among singers of Rushing's generation, Louis Armstrong's influence was paramount: "At one time I used to sing really like Pops; so like him in fact that people used to ask me why I sang that way. My only answer was because I liked to sing that way." Eventually, "I finally got away from Pops' way of singing and formed my own style." Still, Armstrong's pervasive influence was still acknowledged, as "even now if I ever get stuck when I'm singing I drop right back on Pops style—it's the basic way of jazz singing and you can't get away from it." Rushing concluded, "He's the boss and it's inescapable."[41]

Rushing heard Armstrong in Chicago during one of his collegiate sojourns, or from his Hot Five records of the mid-1920s. While he often followed the scripted jazz history, emphasizing Kansas City's influence, he nonetheless observed that Chicago was "the greatest city for jazz in the whole of the United States. . . . and it was the place which set the pace as far as jazz is concerned for a long time."[42] Besides Armstrong and the blues queens, among the singers he mentioned were Bertha "Chippie" Hill and Caroline Williams, who "Was great at the blues. . . . this was way back in 1923, before my time. Used to idolize those singers." There was also Jessie Derricks, "another great blues singer" who migrated to California. Unfortunately, neither Williams nor Derricks recorded, "which was a pity, for believe me they were the tops in blues singing."[43]

Besides helping down-and-out musicians, Rushing led an active social life. He was in many ways quite a man about town. Writer Ralph Ellison, a fellow resident of Oklahoma City, described him as "a compact, debonair young man who dressed with an easy elegance."[44] As early as 1920, the young Rushing won praise in the *Black Dispatch* for his skills on the dance floor: "Mr. James Rushing displayed much grace as leader and introducer of new dances" at a "frolic" put on by the Sunshine Club at Bethel Hall on East Second.[45] Six years later Rushing once again displayed his versatility and immersion in the music scene by tying (with another couple) for the prize in a waltz contest at the Mardi Gras ball.[46]

Indeed, Rushing was steeped in the popular music and vibrant dance culture of the post–World War I era; it is also significant that he was often associated with what may have been the first Oklahoma jazz band—the Ideal Jazz Orchestra. So he was a part of the Oklahoma City jazz scene from its very beginnings. Significantly, though he was invariably presented as a blues singer with Basie and after, his blues singing is rarely mentioned in the 1920s. Even more, he was often a dance floor manager, a kind of master of ceremonies, who called or announced dances and the beginning and ending of sets. Shortly before Christmas in 1921, Rushing was floor manager at a Slaughter Auditorium dance where the Ideal Jazz Orchestra performed.[47]

Rushing won praise for his role at another Slaughter Hall affair where the Ideal Jazz Orchestra played: "Mr. James Rushing acted as floor manager during the evening and in his usual manner, was at his best" when "by far the largest crowd of dancers that have ever been jammed into a dance hall of the city" entertained themselves "from early evening until the wee hours of Tuesday morning."[48] Then he won the "first gent's prize" on the occasion of the birthday celebration of an Oklahoma City resident in early 1922. This was not an evening of dance, but rather one "spent playing games," which evidently Rushing won, followed by an "elaborate repast."[49]

Rushing's dance interests and abilities as a young man corroborated what Basie said about Rushing: "In those days old Rush was not anything like as heavy as he was later on. He was plump, but not what you'd call fat, and he was also a very good dancer. Sometimes when we were playing somewhere, he'd get a partner and get out there on the floor and dance his old butt off." Much to Basie's surprise, "he was light on his feet, and he could really move." He was also quite "a very fast runner. . . . In the Bennie Moten band . . . somehow when the bus stopped for a break on the road somewhere, he and Bennie, who was about the same size at that time, used to race each other along the highway." This was amazing as "they were both fast" and "sometimes they used to race each other running backwards, [as] Bojangles Robinson was very notorious for doing."[50]

As floor manager, Rushing acquired the kind of experience that was useful for a master of ceremonies during the jazz and swing eras, but he was also, like his father, active in at least one fraternal order —something he never mentioned in interviews. This reveals the degree to which he was an active participant in the social fabric of African-American men—professionals, who were the main officers, along with businessmen, musicians, and those working in jobs that were the lot of these urbanites at the time. The Knights of Pythias and Elks raised funds to provide for the sick, for burials, and for the families of the deceased, and they also included musicians in their midst.[51]

Victory Lodge No. 240, I.B.P.O.E.W. "took the town" one Sunday morning in spring 1922. "The parade of the Elks with their band through the streets of the city was a most gorgeous affair. Brilliant and scintillating with many colors reflected in their gay badges, fez and banners, the huge crowds thronged the streets and watched" them stride to Avery Chapel on the crest of Second Street above Deep Deuce. The *Dispatch* maintained "really, the Elk band did credit Sunday to the race, the city and the organization which it represented" in the parade and the memorial service held for the departed brother. Alonzo Lewis, the Elks' bandmaster, was "one of the finest band directors in the Southwest." Behind the Elks band paraded their leading officers, Dr. I. W. Young, "Exalted Ruler"; Heywood James, "Esteemed Leading Knight"; and James Rushing, "Master of Social Sessions." The Ideal Jazz Orchestra's pianist, T. B. Thomas, was the Elks' organist, and the trustees included A. P. Bethel, owner of the Bethel Hotel, and W. T. Tucker, the Deep Deuce undertaker.[52]

◆ ◆ ◆

It is not clear why Rushing chose the Blue Devils, as it was only one of several possible bands he might have joined. He mentioned the Singer [Singie] Brothers from his first sojourn in Texas around 1919, "then there was the Ideal Jazz Band led by Turk Thomas, a piano player who later played with the Blue Devils. Then another band that could really entertain you with just five pieces was the Satisfied Five... Carl Murphy's band... [and] Lazy Daddy and His Soul Killers." Rushing pointed out that "none of these bands ever got anywhere, but they all played some wonderful music."[53] On the other hand, Troy Floyd's and Alphonso Trent's bands both enjoyed considerable success. Oklahoma's bands included the Happy Black Aces, James Simpson and his KVOO Broadcasting Syncopators, and Payton Glover's Jazz Five.[54]

In Oklahoma City, Payton Glover managed the Aldridge Dancing Academy—at the outset of the jazz decade—and his Jazz Five played for their dancers. The *Black Dispatch* described the academy as "the only first class equipped dancing academy ever in our city."[55] The nationwide influence of the new music, jazz and blues, was very clear at this academy. Jimmy Rushing was in the midst of these changes, which transformed social dancing in the 1920s, but other more pressing matters affected his life at this time.

In autumn of 1921 he married Miss Gene Irene Bunton, from Austin, Texas, shortly after midnight in the home of a friend. Avery Chapel's pastor presided, and the groom's mother and James Simpson were among those attending. Little is known of the bride except that her attending Sam Houston College in Austin probably accounted for Rushing's visits to Texas; as the *Dispatch* reported, "the marriage culminated a courtship that has lasted for a period of over one year." College-educated himself, it is noteworthy that Rushing married someone who graduated from high school in Austin and took a commercial course. As they moved in with his family, the new Mrs. Rushing may have assisted in the businesses of Andrew Rushing, such as the confectionery store.[56]

The new bride was depicted as "beautiful and accomplished," while the groom was "easily the most popular young man among the younger set." Their decision to live in Oklahoma City must have changed at some time in 1922. Perhaps it was the devastating Tulsa race riot that destroyed the Greenwood Street community in spring 1921, or the lynch mob that ran the Singie Smith jazz band out of Norman, Oklahoma, in winter 1922 that assumed the decisive role in the Rushings' decision to leave.[57] A number of Oklahomans headed west for California during these years, however, drawn by the favorable climate and by the economic opportunities of an expanding West Coast metropolis, and it may very well be that the young couple was part of this migration. At least one of Rushing's relatives, an uncle, and possibly a cousin as well, lived in Los Angeles in the 1920s.[58]

No doubt the lure of success in Southern California drew Rushing, the former young man about town, floor manager, singer, and sometimes blues piano player, and his new wife to California. He always mentioned this stint in his interviews, and his meeting the more famous musicians and singers, some of them from New Orleans. He never mentioned that in 1923, when the couple resided at 720 East Fifteenth in South Central, his wife worked as a stenographer while his employment was bootblack.[59] She had a good position, whereas he had one that was open to a Black newcomer without a profession at the time, which must have been a bit difficult for the young couple while he tried to break into show business. This was the only time James was listed at that address, while his wife—who may have stayed in Los Angeles after he left for home—was listed in 1925 as residing at E. Sixteenth.[60] At some point the marriage failed, and we know little about when or why, because Rushing never mentioned it in interviews.

Despite his active life in Oklahoma City's Black dance circles, his hiatus on the West Coast meant he missed certain developments at home, such as the arrival of the Blue Devils with Billy King. Rushing contended that in 1927 the Blue Devils "were the biggest thing in music in the state of Oklahoma, and one night they heard me sing, and that was it." As he recounted their travels, "We toured all over that part of the country and used to run into all the bands."[61] At that time they included some of the original members, not only Walter Page, but Lawrence "Inky" Williams on trumpet, Ermal "Bucket" Coleman on trombone, Smith on reeds, and two who joined soon after Rushing—Basie and Durham. "We were swinging."[62]

Then in 1928 they recruited Hot Lips Page in Tyler, Texas. They heard about "this terrific young trumpeter" playing with Sugar Lou and His Sugarfoot Stompers and convinced him to join them. "In those days he was great with those plungers and other mutes and he played more trumpet than we had ever heard—his intonation was wonderful, and for blues playing and singing, well that was born in Lips." According to *The Jazz Journal*, "As far as blues playing . . . [Rushing] put him on a par with Louis, for Hot Lips Page was one of the very best."[63] After their pianist, T. B. "Turk" Thomas, left the Blue Devils one July night in Dallas in 1928, they "picked up Count Basie," who "was really playing piano."[64]

The Devils battled bands such as Lawrence Welk's, who "wasn't too well known then, except in his own territory . . . up around Minnesota and Wisconsin." One of Welk's musicians played "Tiger Rag" on two trumpets, and others did somersaults, because "most of the bands in those days used to do novelties, because the public went in big for them then." The Blue Devils had some of their own "that would break up any act, but we didn't have to rely on them the way some other bands did, because our music was so good."[65]

The singer dwelt on the hardships and solidarity, and how their joint suffering molded them into more than simply a band, but a band of brothers. Rushing recalled one of the many small gigs they played, this one in Bear Strap, Mississippi, "when, because of bad roads and a rather tired automobile," they arrived too late for the dance. In the center of town a policeman, who asked them if they were supposed to play for the dance, stopped them. When they answered yes, "He attached our instruments!" Next morning the booking agent said they would pass out handbills advertising a dance for that night, but they could not touch their instruments "until we started rehearsing, and then this guy sat there with a big pistol."[66]

He stressed the tremendous joy of playing they experienced, when he explained that "it was a funny thing how that band was organized." It was a commonwealth band, and when they played a dance and no one showed up, leader Walter Page would tell them, "'Well, fellows, come and get it.... We've got enough for a hamburger or something.' And we'd be happy with that ... We'd just take out enough money for gas so that we could get to our next gig." Another time he recalled the sense of solidarity: "We weren't making money, but we were all friends. If one of the boys needed money— like his wife needed coal or had to pay the gas bill—we'd take the amount necessary out of the gross, give it to him, and send him home and split down the leavings among the rest of us." He emphasized that "everybody was paid equal down to the leader."[67]

He also recounted how they toured and how far they ranged in 1927 and 1928: "We traveled in two seven-passenger Cadillacs." A trailer with their instruments followed the cars, and they performed "through Oklahoma, Texas, Missouri, Tennessee, [and] Colorado." In the balance of things, "We enjoyed ourselves, but it wasn't always easy traveling in the South." With some understatement, he recounted how "Some of the boys could take it, and some couldn't."[68]

Rushing related how much the Devils "wanted a battle of music with Bennie Moten in the worst way, but he never would give us one, even though he had heard about our band, and wanted some of our men." The Blue Devils "caught him one night, right in his own territory, and tore him up! We were jumping." Moten's men "were putting gum on their pads, lighting up their reeds with matches, doing everything, but we caught 'em!"[69]

It is interesting that he makes this claim, when other Blue Devils, including Walter Page, denied the alleged encounter ever took place. Rushing did not know much about the Blue Devils' origins either, for that matter; as he recalled it, "In 1925 the Billy King group toured Texas with a show. Some of the boys from this show formed a band called the Blue Devils."[70] Perhaps the reporter made this error in dating the band, but Rushing may have had it wrong because he was on the West Coast when the Devils formed in 1923. His claim that they started in Texas is another mistake, since everyone else insists they originated in Oklahoma City. He maintained he joined them in 1927, which causes one to wonder what took them so long to hear him—as he was working on Deep Deuce in 1926 and 1927—or why they hired a singer at all.

After getting started in 1923 in Oklahoma City, the Blue Devils were quite active when Rushing worked in his father's café next door to the Aldridge. They performed at the Mardi Gras Ball, where Rushing and his partner tied for the waltz contest, and on other occasions in the capital later in the year. The band also traveled to Chickasha and El Reno and nearby towns that summer, as well as into Texas. Perhaps they reorganized there, as Walter Page suggested, and this is what Rushing considered their beginnings.[71]

Nineteen twenty-seven was a high point for the Blue Devils. Either their benefactor helped them or they earned enough to purchase first-class instruments. In winter 1927 the *Dispatch* reported, "Every devil has a brand new instrument—gold, too. . . . Let me tell you that they simply 'strutted their stuff.' "[72] The city's newest society organization, the Twenty Club, hired them for their party in late spring that year.

"According to the club members and the guests the Blue Devils orchestra never played before as they played that night. The music was enthralling as happy dancers flitted through the room under the incandescent glow of lights that peered from bowers of spring flowers. The orchestra was enclosed in a corner of the room by spreading palms."[73] Then the Hotel Boys engaged them to kick off a "lively winter season of socials" at Slaughter's Hall one Monday evening in the autumn of 1927.[74]

Willie Lewis left the Blue Devils, the very band he co-founded, and he was with Alvin Walls's band in late summer of 1928.[75] That autumn five Blue Devils who became legends in their own time were featured in the Kansas City *Call*—Rushing, Walter and Oran Page, Basie, and Smith. They were featured at Paseo Hall on Sunday, and the following Wednesday, which was Halloween, they were touted as the "Syncopation Kings of the Southwest." A picture showed ten Blue Devils standing in line facing Walter Page—five on either side of the leader. Rushing stood on the left end, then Basie, Durham, and two unknowns, then the bassist, with two other unknowns, Smith, Page, and an unknown on the end. The article claimed Walter Page as one of their own, and Kansas City bandleader George Lee had nothing but praise for what he called "one of the finest dance orchestras in the southwest." He also referred to "Oran Page, 'hot lips' trumpeter," perhaps the first time his nickname appeared in print.[76]

The singer/trumpet player, reedman, bassist/saxophonist, and pianist were also featured in another *Call* photo, smiling in their tuxedos under the heading "These 'Blue Devil' Boys Are Plenty 'Hot'." The African-American weekly characterized them as an orchestra that "blazed its not studded way out of the south to please the dance lovers of Kansas City."[77]

A few days later "Kansas City opened its arms Hallowe'en night with a riotous welcome for Walter Page and his sizzling Blue Devil orchestra at Paseo hall." That this took place "in spite of the heavy rain," may have been because the crowd recognized Page as one of theirs. In any case, "1,700 people turned out to the dance." Almost exactly a year before the Great Depression, Kansas City residents dressed in costumes "colorful and brilliant; they ranged from Mexican outfits to Pierrot costumes, and the usual men dressed as girls and vice versa were strongly in evidence." Ever gracious, Walter Page "expresses his gratitude through the *Call* to all the people who supported his first appearance here in his own town." The Blue Devils also performed at the Paseo the following week—on Sunday and Thursday (November 4 and 8). It was two days later that they made their sole record, featuring Rushing singing "Blue Devil Blues."[78]

Later that month the band was still in Kansas City, and they battled in a "dance War" at Paseo Hall. As the *Call* forecast, "There will be war in Kansas City Sunday night." Pitted against each other were Walter Page's Blue Devils and George E. Lee and his Novelty Singing Orchestra. Page's band had a reputation for being "undefeated champions of the southwest," but Lee's "has never lost a fight," the *Call* claimed. To add to the gladiatorial nature of the combat, the Blue Devils' very own "golden voiced tenor," Rushing, challenged Lee to a singing contest. The "punches" he intended to use were popular sentimental songs—"If I Could Be With You One Hour

Tonight," "Way Down South in Heaven," and "Silver Threads Among the Gold"—not the blues. Lee planned his strategy around similar songs: "Guess Whose [sic] in Town," "I Called You My Sweetheart," and "Sweet Sue." The *Call* explained they would take requests, as well, "as both these lads are accommodating."[79]

The two bandleaders also exchanged verbal parries before the battle. Both "generals" admitted they faced "the hardest contest of their lives," and both forecast their victory. Walter Page maintained that his band was "the pride of the south," and furthermore that they "had never lost a contest and we have never run from one." He also challenged Lee: "At last George Lee's crown is in danger. He has at last met an organization that is not afraid to try him." While admitting that his opponents were "a first class outfit and the toughest proposition we have ever had to meet," Lee maintained, shortly after Republican presidential candidate Herbert Hoover soundly defeated the Democrat Al Smith, that his outfit was "ready for them and when the smoke of battle clears away, Mr. Page will think he is the Democratic candidate for president." [80]

One noteworthy thing about the event is that the battle the *Call* emphasized was with George Lee's band, not Moten's, even though Moten's also performed. Though Frank Driggs and others have written as if the Blue Devils battled Bennie Moten, no evidence from the *Call* supports this, and neither does the testimony of musicians, including Basie's: "So far as I can recall, the Blue Devils never tangled with Bennie Moten in any battle of bands while I was with them." Indeed, "All I can say about any of the stories that anybody may have heard or read about the Blue Devils chopping Bennie's band in a contest is that I just can't figure out how I can have forgotten all about something as important as that." Even more telling, "I don't think Walter Page would have forgotten, either."[81] There was, however, "The Greatest Battle of Bands" on December 2, 1929, in Kansas City, at the Paseo Ball Room. The bands included those of Moten, Lee, Andy Kirk, Paul Banks, and Walter Page, but Basie, Durham, and Rushing, as well, had joined Moten by them.[82]

Also significant is the fact that blues were not mentioned at all in the *Call's* articles. Considering the emphasis on Rushing as a blues singer in most jazz journalism, his singing of popular songs is remarkable. In fact, no blues are mentioned in *Call* articles of the time with respect to the Blue Devils or George Lee's or Moten's bands. Even Ralph Ellison typically portrayed Rushing as a blues singer, while also admitting that it was more complicated. As the writer explained, "Rushing is known today primarily as a *blues* singer, but not so in those days." In fact, "he began as a singer of ballads, bringing to them a sincerity and a feeling for dramatizing the lyrics in the music phrase which charged the banal lines with the mysterious potentiality of meaning which haunts the blues."[83]

Yet in his influential reminiscence "Remembering Jimmy," he recalled how "On dance nights, when you stood on the rise of the school grounds two blocks to the east, you could hear [Rushing's voice] jetting from the dance hall like a blue flame in the dark; now soaring high above the trumpets and trombones, now skimming the froth of reeds and rhythm as it called some woman's anguished name—or demanded in a high, thin, passionately lyrical line, 'Baaaaay-bay, Bay-aaaay-bay! Tell me what's the matter now!'— above the shouting of the swing band." This native Oklahoman concluded, "His voice evoked the festive spirit of the blues. Indeed, he was the natural herald of its blues-romance, his song the singing essence of its joy."[84]

Rushing is mentioned as a blues singer only once in the 1920s— at an Elks affair in Los Angeles, where he was relatively unknown. The *California Eagle* reported that an Elk, "Fat" Rushing, "played and sang some Oklahoma Blues" as part of the evening's entertainment at a smoker that the local held shortly before Thanksgiving in 1923. Significantly, this blues performance took place "during the arm crooking session." "To top this gala evening, hot tamales, chili, and the fluid that made Milwaukee famous were served."[85] Blues were sung at a high point in the evening to mark a climax of an evening's celebration, and the food and drink enhanced that climax.

The not-very-common name of "Rushing," the fact that he sang "Oklahoma blues," and even his nickname, "Fats," suggest that the singer was Jimmy Rushing. He had been active as a brother in Oklahoma City, so it made sense for him to continue. In fact, fraternal ties with the local helped to ease the transition in a new city.

Despite their record, "Blue Devil Blues," Rushing and the band performed many popular songs and numbers that pleased white audiences, in addition to their blues repertoire. Even Basie was relatively unfamiliar with blues at the time he was a Blue Devil. Despite the popularity of W. C. Handy and the different blues divas, Basie "hadn't really ever paid any attention to [blues], and I hadn't ever played the blues." He claims not to have gotten his "first real taste of the blues until the burlesque show I first left New York with played in Kansas City that second time," and he went out walking along Troost Avenue "and came to all those joints that started at Eighteenth Street." This is where he entered blues territory for the first time.[86]

Apparently the Devils, like Moten's band, were not primarily a blues band in their prime, as the Basie band became later. In the same way, it was only gradually that Rushing became known as a blues singer, something that was not really a part of his repertoire

Jimmy Rushing and Billie Holiday, circa 1955

until the late 1930s, aside from those semiprivate affairs like the Elks smoker in Los Angeles. He still sang popular numbers, and one must consider that, in the press, any Black singer, even a Billie Holiday, is usually introduced as a blues singer, even those who view themselves differently.

One difference between Rushing and many other singers was that because of his size—his girth, that is, because he was only about five feet tall—he had a comic dimension to him that we often associate with large people. Fats Waller is a good example, and another is singer June Richmond. Dan Burley pointed out that historically, "For time immemorial, fat folk have been associated with humor, with brains and with fortune." In an *Amsterdam News* article, "Fame and Fortune for Fat Folks," Burley contended that Rushing, "Count Basie's Falstaffian vocalist, would doubtlessly be singing in Kansas City beer gardens and house rent parties if he wasn't the rotund gentleman he is." In fact, the former floor manager "stampedes his audiences with his versions of current dance vogues which serve mostly to emphasize his weight."[87]

Less than ten years after enrolling in Wilberforce, Rushing became a professional singer with the Blue Devils. Prior to that, it is difficult to corroborate his explanation that he left college to work as an entertainer. In Oklahoma City his only listed profession was as a bellboy, and even in Los Angeles, he was a bootblack. These jobs acquainted him with the blues life, as well as with racism, and his acquaintance with the poorer folk developed into an abiding love for the underdog. He cast his lot with the Blue Devils and former Blue Devils most of his life, aside from the stint with Moten, but even in Moten's band several former members of the Blue Devils maintained the spirit and traditions of this legendary orchestra.

CHAPTER SIX

Swingin' the Blues

From Circus Boy to Doctor Jazz—
Eddie Durham

Eddie Durham is considered to be "the first electric man" with respect to guitar and also to music generally.[1] As a child he lived with his extended family in his birthplace near San Marcos, Texas, having been born August 19, 1909. Though many times he gave his birth date as 1906—"It really was 1909."[2] San Marcos was a farming and ranching community, halfway between Austin and San Antonio, that had around a thousand residents at the time of Durham's birth. Durham's father, Joe (or José), a "farmer and bronco [buster]"—that is, a breaker of wild horses—as well as "a terrific fiddle player," and his mother, Luella Rabb, a school teacher, raised a family of four sons, Joe, Earl, Eddie, and Roosevelt; one daughter, Myrtle; and two nephews, Allen and Clyde Durham.[3] "Everybody thought they [his cousins] were brothers, so they just growed up in our family."[4]

Durham maintained that his paternal grandfather, who was named Berry, was Irish, and that he married a Mexican and lived in her country for a time. Indeed, the arranger's father was known as José and spoke Spanish, and so did Eddie Durham as a child, underscoring the Durhams' Mexican cultural heritage. Also, Eddie maintained that his father's aunts were "all Mexican," and that his father "wore a waxed moustache all the time . . . always a waxed mustache." He claimed that his mother was Native American, further compounding the Durham brothers' racial identity. He recalled that when he was a youngster, he wore his hair long and plaited—"two big plaits . . . [with] a ribbon on the end." In fact, all the brothers looked "Mexican and the girls were real light-skinned" suggesting the boys were dark-complexioned.[5] Proving his claim that his grandfather was Irish is more difficult. The only things the Manuscript Census data revealed is that his father's parents, Berry and Patsey, were from Mississippi (or Tennessee) and Kentucky, respectively. They were both literate and were born around 1840—shortly after Texas became a republic, and possibly even before. They had seven children born between 1857 and 1872. Mary and Joseph, the two youngest, were born after the Civil War ended, and named almost as if they were heralds of a new order.[6]

The Durhams personified Texas musical traditions. José, or Joe, Durham had quite a reputation because "he could play fiddle enough for a hundred people to dance by rhythm."[7] He did not read music, however. In fact, "he didn't want to even see music. . . . He figured that people couldn't hear you read; they heard you play."[8] Young Eddie's introduction to performance began with a unique role: he leaned over his father's shoulder while he fiddled, using long hat pins to beat rhythmically on the fiddle strings "not too far from the bridge." The tapping that he made "sound like a drum . . . come out just as loud as he is."

His father and other musicians also constructed violins out of cigar boxes, cutting them and shaping them to their satisfaction. There was another innovation that foreshadowed the experiments that Durham made in the 1930s with the electric guitar. They hunted rattlesnakes, shot them, cut off their rattles, then dried the rattles and placed them inside the violin, and "that fiddle would sound like an amplifier" when played.[9]

Most important for the family's music education, Joe, Eddie's oldest brother, born in 1894, was assigned to the 24th U.S. Infantry "which merged with the 10th Calvary," where he became adept at playing not only violin but trumpet, and, in fact, "all instruments," and then he taught his younger brother Eddie "from the beginning." In addition, Earl, the second brother, born in 1898, was "a terrific clarinet and saxophone player." Roosevelt, one of the youngest of the four boys, was a pianist, while the cousins, Allen and Clyde, were trombonist and bassist, respectively.[10] In the 1920s the four brothers and two cousins were joined by Edgar Battle, who was "very young" when he lived with the Durhams, and the seven made "a pretty good-sized band."[11] Eddie Durham and Edgar Battle were thereafter a team, composing music, writing lyrics, producing shows, and recording together until Battle died more than a half-century later. His daughter, Rudine, maintained that her father and Eddie Durham met in their teens, in the 1920s, and that "usually whatever Dad was involved in, Eddie was involved in it. They made sure of that."[12]

It is noteworthy that Durham related little about his father and still less about his mother. He mentioned that the bronco buster was never thrown (so far as the son knew), made fiddles, played magnificently, and loved to gamble. "He died in the early stage,"[13] so in interviews Durham devoted more time to his brother, who taught him not only different facets of music but how to shoot, ride horses, and hunt rattlesnakes. He also mentioned visiting his brother's army friends at the post near the Mexican border, but there is nothing comparable about either his mother or father. One is left to conclude that his oldest brother's influence was paramount.

Under his diligent tutelage, Eddie Durham learned how to read music and to write scores, as well as how to play both trombone and guitar. He claimed that he started learning trombone at the age of eight.[14] From the beginning of his introduction to music, he learned to play two instruments, trombone and guitar, and neither was the main one: "They both come along about together." He also "kept a banjo."[15] His brother's military experience resulted in a thorough musical education that was passed on to other members of the Durham family. "And ... when he came out of the Army ... he kept books and he stayed deep into the music." Eddie added, "and then I was deep into getting experience from what I got off of him."[16]

During his childhood, "we always had a family band playing a lot, in school and everywhere. ... Weekends, [we would] take gigs and like that." "We had the whole band except drums, and we always used an outside drummer." In his first band, the Durham Brothers Orchestra, he co-led and played guitar and trombone—when he was in the fourth grade. Years later Eddie Durham explained, "We were making peanuts ... but any kind of money was money back then. Fifty cents was a lot of money in those days; if a guy had ten dollars he was rich."[17]

The Texas frontier heritage, combined with a powerful family music tradition, prepared them well for a life in traveling road shows. Probably the oldest brother took charge of the others as a matter of course after the father's death. The four brothers went with the Doug Morgan Dramatic Show in the late teens or early twenties. "It was a white show, but he had the black guys in the band." Eddie Durham said he played guitar at this time. In fact, Doug Morgan bought him his first guitar.[18] Before then, "I'd always borrow them and use them, borrow and travel and give it back." He also played trombone in this show.[19]

Durham also studied under the tutelage of a bandleader and schoolteacher, probably in Terrell, Texas, in the early 1920s. The family very likely moved to this small town about thirty miles east of Dallas after the father died. Terrell was "a musical town."[20] Eddie Durham stayed there until he entered the seventh or eighth grade. "I was living in Terrell, going to school...it was a musical school."[21] His brother, Roosevelt, also attended school in Terrell for about two years. Eddie Durham revealed a bit more about his early music education when he explained, "They had a teacher there named Professor Barnett [William H. Burnett], and it was one of those schools out there where the principal, anything he wanted to do, the whites backed it...he had everything going on in that school."[22]

William Henry Burnett was born in Ellis County, south of Dallas, in 1872, attended Lincoln University in Pennsylvania, where he obtained an M.A., and was principal of the Black high school in Terrell for forty-four years. A "lover of music" as well as a "natural musician," this educator "had the best band in Texas in that school there. And the best of the musicians came out of that band." The school provided musical and military training in addition to the usual curriculum. The student body included girls as well as boys.[23]

Burnett and the other teachers, all of whom played instruments —usually trumpet—recognized Eddie's talents. When he was in the fourth grade, they had him participating in musical presentations with seventh- and eighth-grade students. He also assembled three or four others, and they played recorders—flageolets, they called them—at concerts and student assemblies. So even when Durham was not traveling with road shows, he was honing his musical skills with his brothers while attending school, probably late in each year, as Texas school sessions were usually only a few months between cotton crops. Perhaps it was different under Professor Burnett. Durham recalled that he left Terrell for the 101 Show.[24]

With his brother Joseph on trumpet, he joined the 101 Ranch, named after a huge spread in the southwest. "It was a big circus... like the Ringling Brothers Show, only they had a bigger ring, because in some of the acts they had three or four tribes of Indians." Chief White Cloud was in the show, "and they'd perform just like they do in a movie... a big [tented] arena with a lot of hay, and the settlers would come out in three or four wagons... and the Indians would ride out on the horses, maybe 15 or 20... with arrows... and sometimes rifles."[25] He was with them for two seasons and left after their last show in Yankee Stadium in New York City in 1922. "Then they tore down that year after that. They went to Europe with the show."[26]

The Wild West Shows that emerged in the heyday of Buffalo Bill, in the last decades of the nineteenth century, foreshadowed the emergence of vaudeville with different kinds of staged entertainment for the masses. In addition to dramatizing settler-Indian gunfights and other forms of entertainment depicting the Wild West, the 101 Ranch show had two bands, "a great big [white] band and they had about 15 pieces of black band, and then they'd break the black band down to about nine pieces for the minstrel show."[27] Minstrels were actors—white or Black, but in this instance Black—who, forced to adhere to this U.S. stage tradition, blackened their faces and presented ridiculous scenes that caricatured and degraded African-American life. Whites started minstrelsy before the Civil War, blackening their faces to sing, dance, play musical instruments, and perform in dialogues and skits that ridiculed Black folk and their culture. Within a few decades African-Americans entered minstrelsy and continued the blackface tradition, satirizing white minstrels as well as Blacks, and it remained a vital part of Black show business until the early 1930s.[28] The 101 Ranch bands followed the strictures of segregation in still other ways: the white band headed the parade every day, "and then later on the minstrel band would be further back in the parade playing jazz type of stuff." The minstrel show, consisting of "five or six fellows and five or six girls and about a nine-piece band on the stage," also included "comedians on the wagon" and was presented in the midst of the nighttime's entertainment. Indeed, "it was two different types of show." In other words, the first band played straight, and the second clowned and jazzed; in a way the two bands complemented each other. Durham explained, "So that's how I got into the [101] ranching deal."[29]

At a relatively young age—he was in his early teens or mid-teens at this time—Durham was quite entrepreneurial as well as versatile. After an evening of playing trombone in the 101 Ranch band, "then I started giving dances myself, and then that's when I used the guitar."[30] Through this experience, he "learned to voice above three-part harmony, because after the show break at 9:00 at night, we'd always go someplace where you could give a dance, charge 50 cents to get in." The old timers, "all the old guys play the French horn and all those things, they always was glad to get the chance to play some music I wrote."[31] In those days they only used three-part harmony, "so I figured, with my guitar I could find more than that."[32]

After the 101 show, around 1922–23, Durham and his longtime friend and collaborator, Edgar Battle, performed with Mamie Smith, the legendary blues queen. "They had about 70 some people on that show." And this was "when Battle was kind of shining with the band."[33] Eddie Durham's cousin Herschel Evans was in this band ("It must have been about a nine-piece band."), and they put him on tenor saxophone rather than the alto he usually used. Durham "went all over the country with that show," so in his teens he was better traveled than the average adult.[34]

Around 1922 Durham visited Chicago with the 101 Ranch, and he obviously liked it because he settled there after the 101 went to Europe. He was in Chicago "about a year or two," and like Rushing and Oran Page, heard Armstrong and Oliver; "they played a ballroom and it cost about fifty cents to get in." This allows us to date these years. The former circus boy maintained that he stood outside the club where his heroes played because he did not have the money for admission: "I didn't have any money, and I was one of the younger guys that would line up on the windows, listening."[35] However, in the same interview, he emphasized that he made good money with the 101 show "about $25 a week." With some pride, he claimed, "I was rich when payday come."[36] He was also successful in saving his salary "put it right in the bank," so the excuse that he had no money does not jibe with what he stated later. It is more likely that in the early 1920s he was still too young to enter such a resort and was very likely still in short pants when the event occurred, before Armstrong joined the Henderson band in New York City in 1924.[37]

Durham insisted that in Chicago, "That's when I really went into the business heavy."[38] There are three bits of evidence that he revealed concerning his Chicago years. He studied at the U.S. Music Conservatory, he worked in Starkey's Bakery, "a German bakery,"[39] and he also worked for a Dr. Dorsey. The conservatory was very probably the American Music Conservatory at 306 South Wabash, amidst Chicago's tin pan alley of music stores and publishing houses. He claimed that his brother "told me to find it."[40] A number of musicians studied here. At the conservatory Durham "learned a little bit more about . . . well, I would say dynamics and correct wording for this and that." For the native Texan, the "correct wording" was a foreign language—"they was using a lot of Latin terms in music, like tempo and wait a minute, I forget the words [*accelerando* and other Italian terms]." Durham concluded, "so that's what I learned there. It got so they couldn't offer me much and (unintelligible) what I got here, I got a foundation, so I went creating for myself."[41]

The Starkey's Bakery where he worked probably belonged to either Lee R. Starkey or Samuel Starkey, both of whom lived on the far South Side in white neighborhoods. Another possibility was that it was the Starks Do-Nut Shop at 5013 South State, on the border of, or at least closer to, the African-American district.[42]

The Dorsey connection yields far more that explains Durham's development as a musician. Durham recalled, "my brother knew a doctor there named Dr. Dorsey, and I lived with Dr. Dorsey, he owned a drugstore . . . I worked a little at the lunch counter and I would go down to this trade school. You'd work your way through it. . . ."[43] Dr. Dorsey's nephew, Thomas A. Dorsey, a more recent migrant to Chicago, lived at the same address on Giles Avenue in Chicago's Black Belt, and was deeply involved in popular music. After playing at the 101 Theater in Atlanta and at rent parties and various spots in Chicago, "Georgia Tom" toured with Ma Rainey, and eventually became better known as Tommy Dorsey, the Father of Blues Gospel, one of the most renowned African-American composers of the twentieth century.[44]

It would appear rather unlikely that Durham worked for Dr. Dorsey and had no contact with his musician-nephew who boarded with his uncle and future wife, the sister of Dorsey's nurse. Indeed, as a musician, arranger, composer, and master of the blues idiom that was the staple of Ma Rainey, Bessie Smith, and the blues divas, Dorsey was very likely an inspiration for Durham. It is very possible that Durham was taught by Thomas Dorsey or worked with him, learning about composing and arranging.

Chicago, at this time, was a major site in the history of this music, as other Blue Devils noted. Four recording companies had studios in this Midwestern city.[45] Besides Armstrong and Oliver, who first recorded in 1923, Jelly Roll Morton made Chicago his home that very same year, recorded duets with Oliver, and published his compositions with the Melrose Brothers. Ma Rainey first appeared in the Windy City in 1923, followed by Bessie Smith in her first Chicago appearance in 1924.[46] The city's significance for the Blue Devils, who felt the powerful urge to travel there, suggests that its music scene was of singular importance in the inspiration and history of the band, along with Duke Ellington and Fletcher Henderson.

Durham was vague on the periods when he toured with different territorial bands, just as he was with his dating of the road shows. He mentioned performing with the Alabama and also the Georgia minstrels and belonging to several bands in and around Kansas City in the late 1920s, including Edgar Battle's Dixie Ramblers, Gene Coy's Black Aces, Jesse Stone's band, and then Chauncy Don's Rinky Dinks, which was "the next best band in Kansas City [after Moten's]."[47] He was a member of T. Holder's band ("not . . . over two or three weeks") and Walter Page's Blue Devils before joining Moten. "I didn't stay within those bands long enough, though. Maybe just a few weeks."[48] His joining and quickly departing from various bands in the 1920s became a blur in his memory, unlike his recall of the 1930s. In this way he was a proverbial rolling stone, sometimes hoboing with Edgar Battle from one place to another.[49]

One bit of unity in this peripatetic existence was provided by the fact that he often teamed with his brothers, with Edgar Battle, and with other friends. In the Rinky Dinks, there was "Eddie Tompkins, Paul [Webster], because we formed a clique, which was the two trumpets and myself and Keg Johnson...[and another musician]...there was five of us." This quintet "all went into Jesse Stone's band, the same way."[50] He liked these musicians "because they could execute more. Yeah, Paul and I, we could play it free." They liked Stone because "Jesse would throw anything on the paper and we liked that."[51] Durham considered him to be a master of writing fine arrangements at this time and admired him. A few years later they went to Jimmy Lunceford, a leading swing-era bandleader.[52] These territorial bands were all cooperative bands, he claimed, even Moten's. They collected the money at the end of an event, took out what they needed for expenses, and divided the remainder equally among the bandsmen. As Durham explained, Moten "thought that the men was worth just the same thing he was. Any musician in his band, he felt like a...side man was worth the same thing as the leader."[53]

The trombonist-guitarist joined the Blue Devils in 1927 or 1928, but was somewhat uncertain on how: "probably through Buster Smith and Booker," members of the Blue Moon Chasers at the time. He observed that after a stint with such a band, "You get hungry and you go to the Blue Devils." The band's name was meant to convey the message that it was a Black band, like the Black Aces and the Dark Clouds of Joy.[54]

As Buster Smith played a role in his joining, he explained how he met him in Terrell, while attending the music school headed by Professor Burnett. He used to travel the thirty-two miles to Dallas, "go over there on Sundays with a girl and ride." He met Smith and they started performing together for "dances with some of the little groups, even with Buster's little band."[55] For Durham, Smith "was the greatest," and self-taught, at that. Durham maintained, probably from his own experience, "you can teach yourself from books."[56]

Walter Page was the Devils' leader at the time, and this suggests that Durham joined after the other originals departed. Page was playing bass on his baritone sax. "It'd be more like string bass. In between. It's like the tuba, but it's in between."[57] The leader "didn't have too big a band" at the time. Durham listed the sidemen: Lips Page, Walter Page, Buster Smith, Jimmy Rushing, Dan Minor, "who they never mention," and who came in from the Moten band, and Alvin Burroughs, but he could not recall the others. Durham was, once again, however, a rolling stone: "I didn't stay there too long. The money was light."[58] Moten's Kansas City band was far more attractive. He told them, "I'm going—I went up there and got with Moten. Big pay, say let's all the rest of us go. That's how they started drifting away."[59]

Actually the story is more complicated, because in the summer of 1929 Durham, together with his brother Joe and Count Basie, performed with Elmer H. Payne and His 10 Royal Americans in a Kansas City club, in fact, the largest in the city.[60] That autumn they recorded in Chicago with Moten's orchestra and performed at the Ritz in Oklahoma City, and then at the Eltorren ballroom in Kansas City. They also broadcast over Columbia's KMBC station three times a week. Eddie Durham continued to work with his brother Joe, even when Eddie was with Moten.[61] Durham's entrance into the Moten band preceded Basie's. The pianist "must have come in [to Moten] a little after me."[62] The two wrought a transformation in the band's music as they sought to enlist more Blue Devils. "The [earlier] Moten style," Durham recalled, "was set by Thamon Hayes' trombone; Woodie Walder's clarinet, which he would take apart and play in sections; Harlan Leonard's alto sax; Vernon Page's tuba, and Bennie's brother [*sic*] Ira doubling on piano and accordion."[63] Durham's arrangements, in particular, and his compositions, along with the arrangements of Eddie Barefield—who became a Motenite in 1932— and the addition of Blue Devils like Oran and Walter Page, produced the legendary 1932 New Brunswick recordings. These included the classics "Toby," "Prince of Wails," "Moten Swing," (foreshadowed in Durham's 1929 composition "Oh! Eddie," as well as in "Here Comes Marjorie"), "Lafayette," and other arrangements that presaged the big band music of the swing era. These are considered by music critics to be the first swing recordings.[64]

Durham described the changes in personnel that occurred late in 1929 and the increase in the size of the brass and reed sections that presaged developments in other swing bands. Moten "only had two trumpets and a trombone, Ed Lewis and Booker Washington and Thamon Hayes. But when I came in, then that made four of us [brass]. Then when Lips came in, that made five. Then they added another trumpet, it made six."[65] The enlargement of sections also occurred with the reeds: "The reed section went from three up to four."[66]

Durham claimed that Walter Page made a difference all by himself when he became a Motenite in winter 1932: "He could master tone or filler. He could be heard without amplifying. Big hands and arms, I don't know how he hit those notes, but when he would hit a note, the vibration would vibrate in any room, and the stage would sway."[67] A big strong man, Page would hug the bass when he played, "and he said his body and things had a lot to do with the tone of the bass, too."[68] His sound was at the heart of the rhythm section in the Blue Devils, the Moten band, and the Basie orchestra. Durham explained it was "the way he'd hit the note. . . . Like a lot of guys pick it like this? He used to hit those notes. Big, like that. That was the style then."[69]

The budding composer played guitar and trombone when he was with Moten. In all the bands in which he performed, "We play one [instrument] awhile, and if it's something I like, I'll switch to guitar in most of the arrangements." As he himself admitted, his solos in the Moten band were usually on guitar. This was "because we had a trombone player and I didn't see much to playing trombone." On guitar he soloed on the 1929 recordings "Rumba Negro (Spanish Stomp)," where the castanets resemble Eddie Durham's tapping on his father's violin strings; "The Jones Law Blues"; "Band Box Shuffle"; "Small Black," where with just a few notes his guitar ends the piece; twice on "Every Day Blues (Yo Yo Blues)," Durham and Moten's composition; "Boot It"; "New Vine Street Blues" and "Sweetheart of Yesterday," both at some length; and "Here Comes Marjorie." His guitar introduces "I Wish I Could Be Blue."[70]

He also immediately began arranging with Moten. The trouble with the old band was that "they had a funny, peculiar sound, due to the tone. . . . But it had to be changed." Their 1932 New Brunswick recordings revealed the difference. " 'Lafayette' and 'Toby' and all those things. Barefield was with me on 'Toby.' He had created some of the things. And some of the things he played, I wrote them down, because he was a writer, too. All those are my numbers there." Though Barefield assisted, Durham was the main arranger. "Nobody wrote anything after I got there."[71]

Among his arrangements were "Boot It" or "Tiger Rag," "New Vine Street Blues," "Band Box Shuffle," "That Too, Do," "Won't You Be My Baby" ("I think I did that"), "Blue Room," and "Prince of Wails."[72] Durham helped compose "I Wish I Could Be Blue," "Every Day Blues (Yo Yo Blues)," "Oh! Eddie," "That Too, Do," and "You Made Me Happy." Moten and Basie were credited with "Rumba Negro (Spanish Stomp)," "The Jones Law Blues," "Band Box Shuffle," "Small Black," "Rit-Dit-Ray," "New Vine Street Blues," and "Mack's Rhythm."[73]

Durham recounted who influenced him at this time: "Mostly, my influence come from a guy like Duke Ellington. Sounded like he had something . . . music and creating. And Fletcher Henderson . . . He had another type of thing going."[74] And Moten's arranger added a new bit of information about Count Basie's title when he continued, "And the 'New Moten Swing,' 'The Count'—I named Basie the Count, so that's when they started to call him Count." Moten used to say of Basie, "Oh, that guy ain't no 'count. . . . So I wrote that tune and gave it to Bennie to play. And we'd say, play the Count, Bennie. Everybody would laugh, you know? Basie didn't know what it was all about . . . [inaudible]." Durham contended, "That's how he got his title."[75] He explained how Moten would tell the new recruit, "Basie, play this for me" and Basie would respond, "Man, I can't read that." When Basie helped with the arrangements, Durham would ask him, " 'Basie, set down and make up something,' because he'd make up a little something, I'd write it down." Durham told him, " 'Man, you've got terrific ideas,' but he wouldn't stick with it." Basie would leave saying, " 'finish it . . . finish it.' And that's all he'd want to do." Moten would ask, "Where is that guy? He ain't no account." And that was the expression always. So that's why I named that tune 'The Count.' "[76]

The Moten band depended upon written arrangements, unlike the Blue Devils or the Reno Club combo, which used "head" (memorized) arrangements based largely upon riffs—rhythmic motifs.

"They didn't do much heading then...Bennie Moten couldn't head."[77] This changed when Durham, Basie, and other Blue Devils became Motenites. They shifted from the two-four beat towards the four-four, adding a powerful swinging and a singing aspect to the band's orchestrations.

Prior to his experiments with electrical amplification, Durham became familiar with others methods in the circus, an institution whose influence on jazz and popular music cannot be overemphasized. The megaphone was vital to the big bands: "You'd get a megaphone about 12 inches long for the trumpets, and they would hold them up by the hand and play them like a mute, then they'd get one about 24 inches long for the trombones." Jimmy Rushing used a megaphone about three feet long when he sang. They made stands for these devices, "and you could set them up on the stand and you could turn and put your horn in there and the trombones would sound all over the place."

Megaphones were hardly practical for the guitar, however.[78] Durham began his experiments with guitar amplification when he recorded with Moten late in 1929. For these four years he performed on acoustic and steel guitars, switching back and forth as he experimented, and as he recalled years later, "The [big] bands'd drown you out...so I'd take a straight guitar and get into the mike, put it right in the sound-hole of the guitar so it could be heard." He did not recall anyone doing this before him: "I had never seen anyone do it."[79] He used the club's PA system at first, but in 1932 he started to use a mike plugged into his own amplifier and system. He had to innovate in a new area. His experiences with electricity as a youth were no doubt invaluable.[80] At first, "I made a resonator with a tin pan. I'd carve out the inside of an acoustic guitar and put the resonator down inside there." The resonator was the size of a breakfast plate, and he had to fasten it to the instrument. "And when I hit the strings, the pie pan would ring and shoot out the sound." Before long he adopted the National guitar that had a resonator built in and "was used as a steel guitar with a bar." Durham removed the bridge and replaced it with a bridge from an acoustic guitar, "because the other bridge held the strings up too high." He also experimented further by attaching "a metal clothes hanger to the bridge, [and] hitting it from time to time to achieve a separate vibrato."[81]

His experiments continued as he "tried converting radio and phonograph amplifiers and even drilled into the body of the guitar." "We had to have them [amplifiers] made up. It was my idea, but I don't know who else had the idea or if there were one or two at the same time. All I know is that I had my own idea because I'd never seen one before."[82] Durham explained he would get an amplifier and tell a craftsman, " 'Make me a box,' and then set it in it." The box was very heavy and hard to move around. "Now they have some perfect ones—very near perfect, but the sound isn't the same." When he plugged into "the big house set . . . you'd get the effect of a pipe organ in the church. You'd make it loud and the people'd look all around and say, 'Where's that coming from?' "[83] His fellow musicians made fun of him, calling his amplifier a "starvation box." They laughed at him, calling him "circus guy because I learned in the circus." Eventually this changed: "Then when I started playing publicly so much, they had to quit teasing." Durham summed it all up with, "But I was a pretty good creator."[84]

By 1935 he was playing electric guitar, as "pickups had made their appearance." He was one of the first to use a D'Armond pickup when they came out. "I made an attachment where I could play into the sound system."[85] He only soloed, he recalled, because the sound was too loud for playing rhythm. When he started to perform using his amplifier, "the proprietors would throw up both hands and say, 'Man, don't let this band blow out my lights with that stuff!' " His setup did sometimes "fuse all the lights," and "electric shocks were a common occurrence, too."

Before long musicians were waking him up asking him to sit in on jam sessions: "Get up and get your guitar and get on down here to this jam-session so you can break it up!" At that time, he claimed, "I didn't know anybody playing guitar, when I was traveling round in the early stages with Lunceford [1935] and Moten." With both of these bands, he sat in the trombone section while the guitar was positioned down in front of the band, and when his time came to play, he would walk to the front. Lunceford directed his band in front, so when Durham soloed, the bandleader "knew what spot I was going to hit, so he'd get the microphone and poke it right in there so you could really deal something with the band. You can hear some of that ensemble on numbers like 'Hittin' the Bottle.' "[86] This particular record is often regarded as "the first recorded example of an amplified guitar," but it was not an electric guitar, as some have thought. Durham played an ordinary guitar with a metal resonator or plate set inside. Acoustic guitars that use a simple microphone are amplified, but are not, strictly speaking, electric guitars.[87]

Lunceford's other arranger, Sy Oliver, considered Durham to be "probably our best jazz arranger at the time."[88] Yet he was perturbed by the guitarist's experiments and lack of concern for the band's proper execution of his arrangements. Basically, Oliver claimed, Durham lost interest in them after writing them. "When someone, at rehearsals, made an error in playing the chart, Eddie would just sit there fooling with that gismo [the aluminum resonator]. . . . It was up to me to straighten out the guy who made the mistake." But Lunceford, Durham explained, "was crazy about the resonator" and encouraged him to write "amplified guitar solos into the arrangements as well as trombone trio parts."[89]

As Durham traveled the country and popularized the amplified and electric guitar on recordings, he was a veritable pied piper, influencing other guitarists. He told how, traveling with the Lunceford band in 1937, he met Charlie Christian in Oklahoma City, where Christian played piano. "He wasn't playing guitar" but insisted he wanted to play like Durham. Christian came to a jam session on Deep Deuce with "an old, beat-up wooden guitar that had cost him $5."[90] When he heard Durham play, Christian "had big eyes to sound like a saxophone, and I showed him how, by using down strokes, we could get a sharper tone and how, on a down stroke only, the player could get a more legato effect while the strings were bouncing back as the hand was on its way back up."[91] Guitarists usually alternated up and down strokes on the strings up until then. This was all the fledgling guitarist needed. As Durham recalled, "Man, I never saw a fellow learn so fast, nor have I ever seen anyone rise to the top so quickly. The next thing I knew Christian was a star with the Benny Goodman band" by 1939.[92] In one interview, Durham indicated that Christian was interested in more than guitar technique. "He asked me to give him some pointers, like what to do if you want to play with class and go through life with the instrument."[93] This is reminiscent of Oran Page's statement that he learned about life from Armstrong.

There is only one problem with Durham's account: the Lunceford band went to Europe in 1937, but not to Oklahoma City. But when Durham was with Basie in 1938, the orchestra stopped in this city, and furthermore, the *Black Dispatch* reported that when Basie came to Oklahoma City in early 1938, he had two guitarists, Durham and Green.[94] So Christian's sudden ascent must have taken place in a year's time, since he joined Benny Goodman in the summer of 1939. If Durham had recalled the year correctly, he would have been even more impressed by Christian's ability to master the electric guitar.

Christian's reputation soon overshadowed Durham's as the premier electric guitarist, and some fans think he was the first to play or record on electric guitar. Actually, it was George Barnes in early March 1938.[95] Yet the quiet, unassuming Durham deserved credit for his early experiments with amplification and electrification, for popularizing the electric guitar in performances and on record, and for leading bands while playing this instrument. He was certainly the first to play what he called his "starvation box," an early version of electric guitar, in the swing bands of the early 1930s. Also, the mid-March 1938 records with Buck Clayton, Freddie Green, Walter Page, and Jo Jones, and the September records on which Lester Young was added, were the first to feature an electric-guitar-led band. But in ten years the electric guitar supplanted both trumpet and saxophone as the coming instrument in popular music.

Durham also gave the Basie band its sound in his arrangements and by writing its standards—songs for which it would be known forever, and compositions that epitomized both the swing era and the Kansas City sound. He still had a major role to play as a composer, arranger, and instrumentalist after leaving Basie and with numerous other swing orchestras.

CHAPTER SEVEN

Swing Maestro

Oran "Hot Lips" Page

Born in Dallas, Texas, on January 27, 1908, Oran Alfonso (not Theodore) Page was the first child of Alfred Page and Maggie Veal, who married in 1907.[1] His father was a teamster and driver who worked in Dallas, and his mother, a school teacher, also taught music. His father died in 1916 when Oran was eight, and his mother, who lived until the 1950s, raised him in Dallas and then in Corsicana, Navarro County, "one of four principal cotton counties in Texas," just fifty miles to the south.[2] In 1914 Alfred Page resided at 1400 Orleans, south of Deep Ellum (near Elm Street), the Black music district that was east of downtown and straddled the railroad tracks that ran through town.[3]

In the first decades of the twentieth century, Dallas's Black residents experienced intense racial discrimination, labor unrest, and repression. As a youngster in a vicious Jim Crow society, the young Page attended segregated schools whether he lived in Dallas or Corsicana. His mother no doubt saw to it that he mastered his lessons in school, and she was his music teacher, too. If she introduced him to European classical music, he never mentioned it, and no one has noted its influence in his playing.

He undoubtedly received much of his music education in the streets of Dallas, where musicians performed, especially around Deep Ellum. Blues guitarists Blind Lemon Jefferson and Huddy ("Leadbelly") Ledbetter performed for listeners and pedestrians on street corners and for dancers in saloons and at "frolics" and picnics.[4]

One of Page's songs memorialized someone he might have recalled from the vibrant Dallas street scene: "Moanin' Dan . . . was a blowin' man. . . ./Took a tin can—played it like a saxophone."[5]

Interestingly, critic Dan Morgenstern claimed that young Oran's first instrument was clarinet. At age twelve, the youngster switched to trumpet and, in the tradition of many musicians, joined a children's band.[6] Page had been running errands and doing odd jobs to help out, after his father died, but when he discovered that "he could make more money blowing a trumpet than shining shoes," he made music his profession, joining the children's band led by Lux Alexander. Alexander was a bass drummer who "could play all the different instruments, and he used to form kids' bands to play for weddings parties, picnics, parades, fire sales, and lodge meetings." Sometimes the band comprised as many as thirty-five or forty children.[7]

Around 1923, Page became too old for the children's band, so he had to leave. He maintained that his first professional engagement was two years later with the French New Orleans Orchestra. He also performed with Goog and his Jazz Babies in Shreveport, Louisiana. When he was young, he also toured the Midwest, sometimes with famous blues singers such as Ida Cox, Ma Rainey, and Bessie Smith, and in various other road shows, going as far as New York City and Atlanta.[8]

Page's mother was his major influence as well as his first music teacher. In the 1920s the young trumpet player attended the G. W. Jackson School for African-Americans on the east side of Corsicana. The principal, G. W. Jackson, advocated the course of industrial education advanced by Booker T. Washington, head of Tuskegee Institute. The school added high-school classes in 1916, but resources were limited by the segregated system. "The high school department was in name only as the principal was required to teach all classes in all branches from seventh grade through high school."[9]

Maggie Page had high aspirations for her son: "When I was a boy, my mother wanted me to be a doctor, and I went to college with that idea in mind, but I never finished. I was much more interested in music. I had always liked music. My mother gave me my first lessons."[10] She saw to it that he completed his schooling, and he not only graduated from high school in 1926 but attended Texas and then

Butler colleges, circa 1926–27, shortly before joining the Blue Devils.[11]

Page appears to have grown up fast: as early as 1924, at age sixteen, he had made music his lifelong career and was listed as a professional musician in the *Corsicana City Directory*.[12] He and his high-school sweetheart, Zenobia Harris, ran away to get married one day in spring 1926, the year that he graduated. A daughter, Ora Lee, was born into this union late that year. The young couple lived with the bride's parents, John and Rosetta Harris, at 1100 East Sixth Street in Corsicana, in 1926.[13] It is not clear how long the marriage lasted, but by 1930, Oran had joined the Oklahoma City Blue Devils, taken up residence on Deep Deuce in that city, and also appears to have remarried.[14]

Page explained how, when he was starting out, Gertrude Pritchett—the veteran performer of the blues age better known as Ma Rainey—"took an interest in my playing, and did what she could to encourage me, with the result that I got a chance to play with her when she worked at the Lincoln Theatre in New York City." A few years later he toured with a dance act in Texas known as Sugar Lou and Eddie. Years later in interviews, he discussed his various influences: "Of the men who influenced me on trumpet, Louis Armstrong was the most important. . . . The first time I ever heard Louis was with King Oliver. I had heard of the Oliver band, and once I went all the way to Chicago just to hear them play." He added, "Up until then, I thought I had heard everything!" Then he told how the next time (perhaps the next night) he took his fifteen-dollar Sears and Roebuck trumpet with him, hoping to sit in. When he began to play from his table in the corner of the club, the bouncers appeared to throw him out, but singer Bertha "Chippie" Hill intervened from the bandstand, protecting the youngster and insisting they leave him alone.[15]

Dating the musical episodes in his life that he mentioned in interviews—such as his stints with these blues queens of the 1920s, and the time when he went to hear Oliver and Armstrong and was saved by Hill—presents some interesting challenges. His mentioning Chicago, New York, and Atlanta causes us to focus on the presence of Oliver, Armstrong, Rainey, Smith, and Hill in these cities. A series of coincidences in late spring of 1926—when Rainey was in

Chicago—allows for the possibility that the cabaret event occurred then. The story of Armstrong's teaming up with Oliver in Chicago in the summer of 1921 is well known, as is the fact that he left for Fletcher Henderson's band in New York City in the summer of 1924. However, Armstrong returned to Chicago in November 1925— when Page would have been seventeen.[16] (He also recorded with Ida Cox at this time.) This was a likely age for a youngster to travel from Dallas to Chicago on his own, as Page claimed. Chippie Hill, from Charleston, South Carolina, arrived in the Windy City around 1924 or 1925, played with Armstrong and Oliver at the Plantation and Dreamland, and stayed for a few years.[17] This may very well have been when Page came to hear his hero, Armstrong—1924 to 1927.

It may be possible to pin the date down more accurately than these three years. Hill's recording "Kid Man Blues," on the Okeh label, was advertised in Chicago in spring 1926, and she sang at Chicago's Vendome Theatre about the same time.[18] Earlier that winter, Oliver and Armstrong played together at the Chicago Coliseum, and late in 1926, Oliver, who was playing at the Plantation, sat in with Amstrong at the Sunset. A repeat of the Coliseum assemblage of musicians occurred in June 1926, about the time Hill was appearing at the Vendome.[19]

A French reporter wrote that Page visited Chicago in 1926, verifying the possibility that the event took place in the middle of that year.[20] The "Cabaret and Style Show" of Okeh Records involved a fashion show, a Charleston contest, and eighteen hours of music from Oliver, Armstrong, Hill, Erskine Tate, Clarence Williams, and many other Okeh recording artists. This early jazz festival took place on Saturday night June 12, 1926, from six in the evening until noon the next day before an audience of about eighteen thousand, and was "the most extensive . . . ever . . . conceived for a like event in Chicago."[21] A benefit for the musicians' union, it was advertised in the *Defender* two weeks in advance (late May), enough time for word to reach Texas and for an enterprising young trumpeter to find his way to Chicago. The incident Page described might have taken place about this time if not at the benefit itself, as this is the only time the three principals—Oliver, Armstrong, and Hill—could be found in Chicago during the summer.

Page mentioned other influences besides the New Orleans performers; trumpet player Harry Smith, from Kansas City, was one, and another was Beno Kennedy, who "specialized in the upper register, and he could play the most perfect high 'C' you ever heard." Kennedy also hit much higher notes than others could, and rumor was that he had a "trick lip" that enabled him to play this way. Page was well on his way as a professional musician by 1927 or so, when the Blue Devils discovered him in Texas. He recorded with them in 1929, soloing on "Blue Devil Blues" and "Squabblin'."[22] In 1931 he joined Bennie Moten, as had several other Blue Devils, and in 1932 made the Brunswick, New Jersey, recordings that included such classics as "Toby" and "Moten Swing."[23]

The Dallas tenor saxophonist Budd Johnson places Page with the Southern Serenaders around 1927, a band that included three Blue Devils—Bill Owens on reeds as well as Walter Page and Jimmy Rushing. At the time, the trumpet player "was playing . . . everything Louie Armstrong ever put out, note for note. If you put one in one room and one in another you could hardly tell them apart." Johnson concluded, "What a great trumpet player!"[24] Page was clearly the star of the Moten band by early 1933, when the *Oklahoma City Black Dispatch* pointed out that Page could always be counted on to take a "hot" chorus, "but the way he's handling a sweet solo impressed the writer most." By this time he had developed his versatility in playing well on different songs.[25]

Page used to practice on a piece of music titled "Hot Lips," and before long he acquired his nickname. By the early 1930s his playing was legendary. When Count Basie led the Moten musicians (having temporarily taken over a group of them), the *Black Dispatch* mentioned how "Hot Lips" Page was one of the "star performers" along with James Rushing. When Basie's Kansas City Stompers performed at Slaughter's Hall, the patrons, "jubilant, and kept in a rollicking mood" by the band, "were stopped cold by trumpeting Oran 'Hot Lips' Page, sensational Louis Armstrong impersonator." Page "staged a show 'all by himself' and surprisingly undertook a breathtaking solo, plentifully bespattered with high C's, through a score or more choruses."[26]

Page and former Blue Devils gigged around Kansas City clubs in the mid 1930s. Hot Lips Page and Eddie Durham performed with

Pete and his Little Peters—probably Pete Johnson's band—in fall 1934.[27] Late in 1935, Page was featured in the Rhythm Ramblers orchestra that furnished music for the floor show at the Rhythm Rendezvous club on East Twelfth Street.[28] In 1936 he served as M.C. at the Reno Club, playing trumpet while James Rushing sang with the band led by Basie and Henry "Buster" Smith. As they reorganized the band, they followed the maxim "Once a Blue Devil, always a Blue Devil," and recruited such band stalwarts as Leonard Chadwick, Lester Young, and Walter Page. By the time John Hammond decided to offer a contract to this sensation band, its trumpet star had secretly signed with Joe Glaser, taking away the band's leading soloist. By summer 1937, he performed with his own swing band in a "gala premier" on Sunday night, August 22, 1937, at Small's Paradise in Harlem.[29]

The Kansas City *Call* reported on Page's debut in New York City because he was a "home boy"—one of their own despite his Texas origins and Oklahoma City connections. The weekly referred to the young trumpeter as "the musical flash from Kansas City." Page was regarded as "a great stylist with vast potentialities."[30] At first he had to wait until he satisfied the union's residency requirement, and for two weeks he was featured as a guest with Andy Kirk's orchestra. Eventually he was able to assemble his own band, consisting of Bob Schafner, trumpet, George Stevenson and Harry White, trombones, Bennie Waters, tenor sax, Joe Haynes, alto sax, Jimmy Reynolds, piano, and Yank Porter, drums. With Joe Glaser, the manager who made Armstrong one of the highest paid performers, backing Page, and the direction of Rockwell-O'Keefe offices in Radio City, how could he not succeed?[31]

In early spring 1937 he went into the recording studio with tenor saxophonist Leon "Chu" Berry's Stompy Stevedores, including George Matthews, trombone, Buster Bailey, clarinet, Horace Henderson, piano, Lawrence Lucie, guitar, Israel Crosby, bass, and Cozy Cole, drums. They cut four records: "Now You're Talking My Language," "Indiana," "Too Marvelous for Words," and "Limehouse Blues." It was a year before he was to record again with a studio orchestra.[32]

Coming late in the summer, his premiere at Small's was an important milestone in his career. It was his official welcome to Harlem, in a manner of speaking, as Small's was either the top club or one of the top clubs in north Manhattan. His band opened at the famous nightspot August 17, and, according to the *Amsterdam News*, "will remain there as the headline attraction in the new show, which goes into production next month." Page's past Kansas City association was part of his identity in Harlem. At "a gala premiere celebration" held on Sunday August 22, he was introduced as "the former Count Basie ace trumpet man" to "celebrities of stage, radio and screen," who were at Small's "to welcome the talented young trumpet star." His importance was signaled in the remark that Page was "now regarded by music critics as being among the foremost stylist[s] of the present era."[33] Of course he was also compared to his trumpet inspiration: "Page, a new sensation a la Louis Armstrong…toots a mean horn and will…be stealing the show away from Louis."[34]

Archie Seale, the *Amsterdam News* columnist, reported around that time, "It's really becoming smart to be seen at Small's Bar." Since it opened, "until today, this cozy and warm spot has been enticing the celebrities, playboys…sportsman [*sic*] and any number of visitors to its door." At any time one might enter and find, as Seale had the previous Sunday night, "several well known bending elbows, sitting at booths and just lingering about laughing and talking." They included "the Bill Robinsons…Sunshine Sammy…[and] Stepin Fetchit, while exiting from the cabaret was the eminent Dr. Marshall Ross and wife, along with Dr. Jenkins of Columbia, S.C., and party…." Seale compared Small's to the famous Lindy's of Broadway.[35]

As was typical of cabarets at the time, Page's orchestra swung "out in sizzingly style to provide an adequate tempo" for the production, "Harlem Jamboree," the new fall show, whose "capacity crowd" included not only regular Harlemites, but "a very liberal representation of whites." The *Amsterdam News* reporter recommended, in particular, "the Jungle number in which Dotty Seamond lifts an ordinary 'shake' dance from its ordinary level to that of a work of art." He also praised "the inimitable tapping of the veteran Derby Wilson" as well as the comedians Rastus and Kitty. Different aspects of the total show had their moments: "Insurance against a fall in temperature is provided by the introduction of 'Sausage' and his Tramp Band...and this ragged but roisterous aggregation takes over in earnest with scorching scatting and sweltering swing which just about completes the evening."[36]

Page was sufficiently important to be singled out in the *Amsterdam News*'s pages repeatedly, especially if he provided a sharp visual portrait like the one depicted around Thanksgiving 1937 in "Scenes of A Rounder": "Hot Lips Paige rushing to work, all out of breath, only to find himself more out of breath after hitting those high notes on his trumpet..."[37] (His named was spelled "Paige," a not uncommon spelling for him at this time, though it is unclear why it changed.) In many ways 1938 was a very good year for the new trumpet sensation, as he often held billing with the top Black swing bands. At Small's, New Yorkers witnessed "his popularity for delivery of true cabaret swing music, missing in a lot of the spots where it is claimed to prevail." His twelve-piece band broadcast over WRNS opposite the show "Harlem Jamboree," in which "to cap it off, the corps of singing, dancing waiters came on in both finales on the first and second halves of the show to wow the evening patronage with a first-class exhibition of tray-spinning, 'chirping' and the etceteras that go with a novel presentation."[38]

In early spring he was touted as one "who trumpets mean and low like Wingy Manone and Louis Armstrong." Page "guest-starred at the Hickory House" one Sunday afternoon, "the occasion being the regular Sunday 'Swing Concert,'" where "the jitterbugs were there in honor of the suntanned gentleman from Kansas City."[39] In April he was an "honored guest" with Louis Armstrong, along with Fats Waller, Gene Krupa, Lionel Hampton, and other celebrities, at the Rockland Palace.[40] Again the love of this music by dancers was evident, as the Rockland was described as a place "where all of the jitterbugs will be." The affair was a "gala pre-Easter prom and celebrity show" presented by the Harlem Joy Makers late one Palm Sunday evening.[41] Page may have played a role as M.C., as well, as the Harlem weekly mentioned "Maestro Page will be on hand to help dish out some swing times and otherwise help the festivities along."[42]

In May, Page was described by the *Amsterdam News* as the "sizzling trumpet man" who opened with his orchestra at the Plantation Club and then four weeks later was still a starring attraction.[43] In the summer of 1938 he performed for a week as "a new swing sensation" at Harlem's famed Apollo Theatre on 125th Street. He was "a new and sensational trumpeter—classed as Louis Armstrong's closest rival." "A great revue cast" and "Streamline Sue, [a] fast stepping shake dancer," were featured with him, along with a new song and dance act, Spizzie and George, the comedy acrobats the Stanley Brothers, comedians "Dusty" Fletcher and Sandy Burns, and "sixteen brownskin beauties."[44]

The next week he was billed along with "nine of the leading colored orchestras" in the swing world, Count Basie, Andy Kirk, Luis Russell, Cab Calloway, Willie Bryant, and others at the "Bandfest Benefit [for] Blind Musicians" at Randall's Island Stadium.[45] It was expected that the "joint will jump," and the roles of dancers and the audience were noted when it was observed that "each and every Harlem jitterbug will get his chance Thursday night to hear and compare the music and ability of the various bands in Harlem."[46] This was one of many benefits for which Page performed regularly, underlining his social commitment and sense of responsibility for the less fortunate.[47]

Archie Seale, in his column "Around Harlem," ranked Page with the leading swing bands, evidence that, while he did not compare to Ellington or Calloway, he was clearly among the top swing band contenders. The columnist sketched a brief history of the music. After mentioning the era of Bessie Smith and Adelaide Hall, Seale observed that "the band craze" followed with Ellington, Henderson, Armstrong, Calloway, Basie, Chick Webb, Earl Hines, and Page. Then came the female singers with bands—Billie Holiday and Ella Fitzgerald among them.[48]

A part of the trumpet player's reputation resulted from his association with Basie. In December 1938, for example, Page was featured with the Basie band at Carnegie Hall on the song "Lips Blues." A French writer described his performance as "eight choruses of trumpet in medium tempo, of inspiration blazing but tender (tenderly blazing), containing a quintessential ringing sonority and a powerful serenity. His vibrato, attack, and inflexion, his sharp and at the same time solid sonority has never been better displayed than on this occasion. It is perhaps his most stunning performance on record."[49]

This event was meant to signal that jazz was welcome in such a venue as Carnegie Hall, even though this was not the first time it had been featured. What was unique here was that the history of the music was presented, with its roots represented by country singers Sonny Terry and Big Bill Broonzy, and religious songs by Mitchell's Christian Singers; urban blues were sung by Joe Turner, while Sidney Bechet and the New Orleans Feetwarmers symbolized the origins of jazz; James P. Johnson demonstrated the Harlem stride tradition, and Benny Goodman performed as the representative of modern swing.[50]

The next year, 1939, Page seems to have suffered from the politics of the music industry. For one thing, he is rarely listed in the *Amsterdam News* that year. In one of these rare references, in spring, he was mentioned as appearing with his orchestra and two additions—guitarist Slim Gaillard and bassist Slam Stewart—at the New Onyx on Fifty-second Street. A photo of him blowing trumpet is enhanced with text explaining his absence from the scene: "Paige was inactive for quite some time because of attempts to 'freeze' him out on the good bookings." Without any further explanation, the caption added, "However, he's back in the business again and swinging on down."[51]

In the *Amsterdam News,* disgruntled Black musicians discussed the problems they faced as union musicians. One of the Harlem musicians complained that he only paid his dues to keep the medical and death benefits, "but as for a job, well, that's a joke." Indeed, he had not been able to work for five years. In many instances Black bands auditioned for Broadway jobs, but white bands always got them. He concluded, "As usual, no one can put his hand on the union official and say that's the way it looks to me and to the rest of the colored musicians. We sure get a rotten deal every time."[52]

Racism was at the core of the problem in still another way: "That whites have invaded the field of hot jazz, or swing music if you prefer, in large numbers is no secret, nor is it kept under cover that a good many dusky bands are currently finding it difficult to obtain regular employment." Poet-journalist-activist Frank M. Davis, writing for the *Amsterdam News,* pointed out, "if the truth is wanted, then the old standard issue of race has caused this increasing freezing out of our bands" as Charlie Barnet, Tommy Dorsey, Benny Goodman, Artie Shaw, and Gene Krupa's orchestras moved to the fore. He pointed out the fact that this followed a historical pattern in popular music: "Will Marion Cook had given a 'syncopated concert' in one of Gotham's most conservative music halls a good many years before Paul Whiteman introduced to the elite a synthetic hybrid called 'symphonic jazz,' but Whiteman, being white, got credit for the innovation and set the style in dance music for more than a decade."[53]

Joe Glaser, Page's manager, does not appear to have been the reason for the trumpet player's lack of work. When the former Chicagoan opened his suite of offices in the RKO Building on New York's Sixth Avenue in spring 1938, his roster included not only Louis Armstrong but the Mills Brothers and the Andy Kirk, Noble Sissle, and Willie Bryant orchestras, among others, and their careers prospered at the time.[54] Armstrong, Glaser's star performer, earned $1750 weekly at the Connie Club in 1939.[55]

By fall 1940, Page and his band held forth at the West End Theatre on 125th Street. The *Amsterdam News* contended that the event was "one of the greatest tributes to a colored musician," because there were to be thirty-minute jam sessions with guests such as drummer Gene Krupa, pianists Teddy Powell, Teddy Wilson, and Big Joe Turner, "and most of the top notch instrumentalists in the country," if they were in town. The weekly heralded the Texas musician as "the man who blows a trumpet loud and long, with his band of scorching serenaders," and continued, "needless to say, with Paige and his crowd on the bandstand this week's ... production will be 'Sweet and Hot.'" Page was to present "the sweet vocalizing of Romayne Jackson," whose popularity soared after joining the band; former Cotton Club dancers Honi Coles and Dynamite Hooker also performed, while Sandy Burns and other comedians saw "that the laughs [were] well dished out."[56]

But the Basie orchestra and his alleged Kansas City background continued to claim him, despite his roots in Dallas and Corsicana, Texas. In December 1940, he shared the bandstand opposite Count

Basie, as well as bandleaders Earl Bostic and Vernon Andre, at the Third Annual Bar-Grill Popularity Contest, held at the Renaissance Casino, at 138th Street and Seventh Avenue, from 10:30 p.m. to 6:00 a.m. The breakfast dance benefit was for the "Harlem Christmas Basket Fund," and tickets could be purchased in advance for seventy-five cents at local bars and grills. All of Harlem's taverns and nightclubs were said to be participating, expecting to win a trophy if named the most popular nightspot. A special permit for the occasion had been acquired, in this effort to reestablish the breakfast dances of the Cotton Club days. Different nightspots were not the only Harlem institutions involved; the Elks Rendezvous show was featured, and Blyden's Bookshop on Seventh Avenue (named after the late nineteenth-century emigrationist minister Edward W. Blyden) was the headquarters for the event.[57]

There were other indications of Page's success at this time. He began to record regularly for the first time since he was with Moten in December 1932. The early 1937 recordings have been mentioned. In late winter of 1938 he recorded "Good Old Bosom Bread," "He's Pulling His Whiskers," "Down On the Levee (Levee Lullaby)," and "Old Man Ben," followed by "Jumpin'," "Feelin' High and Happy," "At Your Beck and Call," "Rock It For Me," "Skullduggery," and the Ellington hit "I Let A Song Go Out of My Heart" in April. Five of these songs were composed by Page, one with a co-composer, and "Old Man Ben" was very similar if not identical to "West End Blues," an Armstrong hit of the 1920s. That summer he was in the studio again and recorded "If I Were You," "(A Sky Of Blue, With You) And So Forth," "The Pied Piper," "Small Fry," and "I'm Gonna Lock My Heart and Throw Away the Key." Former Blue Devil Abe Bolar played bass on these selections. The popular and sometimes nonsense songs suggested he was trying to appeal to the public's liking for such hits as Ella Fitzgerald's "A Tisket A Tasket."[58]

He recorded in a trio format with guitarist Teddy Bunn and bassist Ernest Hill for Bluebird in 1940. His love of blues was evident in the selections, "Evil Man's Blues" and "Do It If You Want." Reviewer Frank Marshall Davis wrote that Bunn's guitar and singing, "plus Page's muted obbligato and open horn solo," were, in the idiom of African-Americans, "something to write home about."[59]

The trumpet player settled into domestic life in Harlem. In the late 1930s he married Myrtle, from Montgomery, Alabama, whom he had lived with in Kansas City, and a son, Oran Jr., was born to the couple in the summer of 1939. His new family gave Page a sharper focus in his life and motivation to increase his salary with better jobs. His growing prosperity is evident in the fact that in 1940 he moved from 226 West 136th Street, a three-story Harlem flat, into an imposing apartment building at 105 Edgecombe on a corner near today's Mahalia Jackson School. Page lived in a fifth-floor apartment at this address for the remainder of his life.[60]

These records, the benefits of touring, and his newfound fame launched his career, and by 1941 he performed in some of the major Fifty-second Street nightclubs. At the same time, the singer-trumpeter never forgot his upbringing and his love of blues and Black culture in general—especially its Southern roots. He was modest, though he could be assertive, and seemed always willing to forgive and forget. As noted, he frequently played at benefits, such as his scheduled appearance for the Mother Cabrini Society of Sacred Heart Chapel at their annual dance in 1941.[61]

Most important, following the migration of jazz from Harlem to midtown, was his playing on "The Street," as Fifty-second Street was known. In June 1941, Dan Burley, *Amsterdam News* columnist, pianist, and compiler of the classic *Handbook of Jive*, reported—using the jive slang that he loved to promote—that "Hot Lips Paige is breaking it up slightly at the Stables where he's featured."[62] Burley published the handbook himself, and in its first run it sold more than three thousand copies in five days.[63] The Stables were Kelly's Stables on Fifty-second Street, where Lester "Pres" Young performed in the spring; its special atmosphere and props suggested an equestrian or Western setting. "Swing is the thing at Kelly's Stables with Hot Lips Paige...and his musical crew, 'Stuff' Smith, Billie Holiday, Billy Daniels," and the trumpet player was said to be packing them in nightly, featuring an arrangement of "Maria Elene" which was met with "repeated encores."[64]

The trumpet player's sense of justice and fair play was evident in an incident that may have taken place shortly after he began playing at Small's Paradise. Page walked into the Monterey Bar, near 137th and Seventh Avenue for a drink on his way to work one November evening around 9:30 p.m., carrying "a brand new shiny trumpet, with a fancy case." Selmer made the instrument especially for him, and it was worth more than two hundred dollars.[65] "Trumpet man Page rested his instrument case on the floor, but it didn't remain there long, as Mr. [Leroy] McDaniel was at one end of the bar, 'licking his chops' as Maestro Page gulped down that long drink of Cutty Sark, and he grabbed the musician's trumpet and dashed out the door."

Page was just as quick and, that evening, even faster. "Other than being a hot trumpet player, Mr. Page can pick 'em up and lay 'em down, because he caught his man within two yards of 135th street, and that doing 95 yards almost as fast as Jesse Owens," the famous track man and Olympic gold medallist. They went to court, but Page recommended a suspended sentence because all he wanted was his trumpet and case. He was quite forgiving in this instance and in others. With this story, Page became a part of Harlem folklore as one who understood the importance of Christian forgiveness.[66]

The "big break" that became available to a number of African-Americans, such as Billie Holiday, Teddy Wilson, Lionel Hampton, and Roy Eldridge—the opportunity to play with a name white swing band—beckoned to Page in late summer of 1941. Trumpet player Max Kaminsky was recruited by Artie Shaw and, ever loyal to his friend, recommended that the bandleader hire Page. "'If I were getting a big swing band together, I'd get Lips Page.' 'Who...is Lips Page?' Shaw asked. 'Only the greatest trumpet after Louis,' I responded softly. So Shaw hired Lips for his new band, along with me and Dave Tough."[67]

As his friend explained, Page amazed people with his inventiveness, his drive, and his sheer stamina: "He could play chorus after chorus without ever repeating himself." Kaminsky added with caution, "They have said that about other musicians, but Lips was the only one I have heard who could actually do it." On a good day he "could do thirty or more choruses, each one different." His generous spirit always shone through. "One night after the show [in the deep South], a cracker came up to the bandstand and said he thought Lips played so great that he wanted to meet him. After shaking Lips's hand, the Southerner said, '...and Ah want you to know this is the first time Ah ever shook the hand of a colored man.'" Kaminsky recalled how his friend "flashed one of his wide, happy grins and said in his wonderfully pleasing way, 'Well, buddy, it didn't hurt, now, did it?' "[68]

Shaw had the idea of doing something different with his swing band; originally he had planned to enlarge it to fifty-two musicians but had to abandon the idea because they could not find auditoriums large enough to make it profitable. So he had to be content with hiring thirty-two musicians, including fifteen on strings, five saxes, seven brass, and four rhythm. Kaminsky was, in fact, one of a number of ex-Shaw sidemen who returned, including Ray Conniff, George Auld, and Johnny Guarnieri. Page's photograph was featured in the *Metronome* article on the band, as his singing and trumpet playing would be when they started performing before the public. They rehearsed in New York City studios, and in late August they embarked upon a string of one-nighters in New England.[69]

The orchestra's repertoire was rather broad, "everything from jazz to classics." Significant for some contemporary composers was the fact, *Metronome* added, that "much attention will be given to works of modern Americans, such as William Grant Still," the famous African-American classical composer.[70] They toured in a caravan of three vehicles, the bandleader's Lincoln Zephyr, a bus, and a truck, and landed in Oklahoma City, Page's former stomping ground, that fall.[71]

Jimmy Stewart, the community activist and longtime *Black Dispatch* columnist, informed his readers that Page had joined Shaw and reminded them that "Lips was at one time the husband of Theresa Young, Douglass high graduate," and that he joined Bennie Moten, and after the bandleader's death, played with Basie for a while before going to New York on his own. "His orchestra was never a sensation in New York but he has managed to stay on several different jobs with small combinations." Stewart wished him luck with the Shaw band in late summer 1941.[72]

Several weeks later, Stewart announced with anticipation, "Sepias [African-Americans] will get a chance to hear Artie Shaw and his 32 piece orchestra at the Muny [Municipal] auditorium October 18. 'Hot Lips' Paige, former local cat with the Original Blue

Devils," would be "remembered by music fans of the late twenties as
the boy wonder trumpeter with Willie Lewis and His Original Blue
Devils, and later one of the hipped cats with Bennie Moten's Kansas
City orchestra" and was returning "to the scene of his early days to
show the homefolks, just what a homeboy can do in the big show."
Stewart told readers that Shaw, who in 1938 had signed Billie Holiday with his band after she left Count Basie, was "quite popular in
Harlem and on Central Avenue in Los Angeles because of his liberal
attitude towards sepia artist[s] and his readiness to jam with sepia
cats at anytime." In this segregated city, several hundred seats at the
Municipal Auditorium were reserved for African-Americans. In particular, Stewart praised Page's trumpet playing and singing on Shaw's
record "Blues in the Night." "A local welcome committee" was planning "to give 'Hot Lips' a warm reception during intermission at the
Auditorium Saturday night."[73]

Segregation threatened the band's future performances, however, as the bandleader canceled a Southern tour of thirty-two dates
because he insisted on equal treatment for Page, the sole African-
American in his band. "Shaw made the move rather than weaken
his band by temporarily keeping Orin 'Hot Lips' Page ... out of the
lineup." Significantly, "Shaw could have gone ahead and played
the southern tour, getting a fat guarantee of nearly $2,000 a night,
but he preferred not to endanger his brand of music with Page out of
the picture." Also, "Artie admitted he probably could have used Page
in the South, but that any anti-Negro comments likely to arise would
prove embarrassing to Page and to Artie himself." The bandleader
opted not to gamble. The problem was exacerbated by the fact that
the trumpet player was "Shaw's number one sideman in popularity,
according to reaction of the crowds which have poured in to watch
the group."[74]

The next week, Stewart praised the performance of the former
Blue Devil: "Shaw was just partly right when he said that his band
would be weakened if he had to drop 'Hot Lips' on the Dixie dates.
He should have said that his band would be killed without 'Lips.'"
On the previous Saturday night, Page was "the center of attraction
at all times and even [stole] number one position from Artie, his
leader." Indeed, Stewart added, "my feeble utterances are far short

of the deep sense of appreciation that one gets when he sees a sepia musician doing his stuff head and shoulder above all others in the band."[75]

Then too, Page divulged sentiments to the reporter at intermission that he might not have shared with anyone but his homies: the Shaw orchestra "was not playing music as he would like but will shortly start playing arrangements by Jimmy Mundy and Eddie Durham that will send the toughest of non-believers." Stewart agreed with Page that Durham and Jimmy Mundy, another African-American with considerable experience as an arranger, would produce results that would make a difference: "I'll agree with you Lips, those boys are hard to shave."[76]

On the eve of World War II, Black arrangers such as Mundy, Durham, Sy Oliver, and Fletcher Henderson had for years imparted an African-American tone to their productions, with an emphasis on blues, on "hot" solos and riffs, and voicings from the Black aesthetic. As Durham pointed out, superior arrangements were as much as 50 percent responsible for a swing band's success.[77] Even William Grant Still, the African-American classical composer, arranged "Frenesi" for Shaw, who used it in recordings in summer and fall 1941. Both "Blues in the Night" and "Take Your Shoes Off, Baby," both of which featured Page, exemplified this blues-based influence.[78] These developments resulted from white bands' use of Black arrangers, indeed, but also from the integration of white bands with one or two Blacks, and from the interracial jam sessions that excited fans so much in the swing era.

"Blues in the Night," mentioned by Jimmy Stewart, was recorded at the Hollywood Palladium in late January 1941; B. Challis did the arrangement on this Johnny Mercer and Harold Arlen song, while Page sang and played trumpet, starting out with the waw-waw mute, then scatting for a few bars, and then singing the lyrics about two-faced, worrisome women who will leave you singing the blues in the night. As Page sang, "My momma done told me" about these blues. Strings accompany his singing on the bridge, Shaw's clarinet is heard for a few bars, and Page resumes singing. Then the band performs, the strings come in, and Page closes with a searing solo while the band plays the melody, there is a break when the trumpet plays a coda, and the full ensemble ends the arrangement.

As Stewart pointed out, Page played "head and shoulders" over other members of the band, even Shaw himself. On "There'll Be Some Changes Made," featuring the clarinetist, Page plays a prominent role, soloing on trumpet just after a tenor sax solo. The drumming changes, emphasizing the beat on bass drum and cymbal, heightening the tension, and brass and sax riffs back Page as he soars above the ensemble. More riffs without Page, and then Shaw's clarinet is followed by the full ensemble, which ends the piece. On "Nocturne," Page leads with the melody, *Metronome* observed, "with a wonderful edge to his tone." Eventually the song descends into a pastiche of strings and horns playing melodic fragments—a forerunner of the "Third Stream" music of Gunther Schuller, perhaps.[79]

The entry of the U.S. into World War II ended this version of Shaw's band. Band members were recording at the Victor studio "when Artie's manager handed him his letter of greetings from Uncle Sam. The band was immediately given its notice."[80] Interestingly, *Metronome* gave other reasons for the band's demise, stressing Shaw's throat ailment and his need to recuperate, forcing the band to take a six-week vacation after having two weeks off in early January 1942. It did mention a rumor that he had been drafted, but the journal noted that he was not eligible for the draft because he was the sole support of his mother. Page was said to have moved on over to Charlie Barnet's band.[81]

This was a high point in Page's career, or at least, he considered it to be.

The polls also suggested that this was a high point for Page as well. In the hot jazz poll that the Associated Negro Press conducted in autumn 1940, his band was voted the second most popular swing orchestra.[82] Early in 1942 he was ranked thirteenth on trumpet, just behind Rex Stewart (Louis Armstrong was ninth) in the *Metronome* poll, and tenth in *Down Beat*.[83]

Within Page's life and career one can review the history of early jazz and the emergence of swing. As jazz historian Dan Morgenstern noted, Page "went way back to Ma Rainey and the deep Texas blues, and far ahead with the boys at Minton's before bop was a concept."[84] He was also a composer who contributed to the idiom while sometimes using the melody of established selections, such as when he borrowed Armstrong's "West End Blues" for his own "Old Man

Ben." He also helped to compose "One O'Clock Jump," which is usually attributed to Count Basie, but which Buster Smith and Eddie Durham wrote.[85]

He loved jam sessions and was recorded with Charlie Christian and others associated with bebop at the famous Minton and Monroe's nightclub sessions in Harlem, where bop is thought to have originated.[86] One has to ask, if someone associated so closely with swing, and then with the New Orleans revival of the late 1940s, could play with the originators of bop, and swing at that, how could swing and bop be antithetical? The fact that Goodman's and Basie's swing bands had small combos within them—Goodman's Quartet, and Basie's Kansas City Six, with their reliance on swinging riffs—provides clues as to how bop grew out of swing, if not out of the music of King Oliver, as Armstrong maintained.[87]

Page's love of jam sessions, in which musicians battled and tested each other's stamina and creativity, was legendary. This was another aspect of what was known as the Kansas City tradition. Page was never known to turn down a competitor's challenge; he was like "Little Jazz"—Roy Eldridge—in that both throve, or rather feasted, on challenges. These sessions allowed him to showcase his artistry. "Fellow musicians often commented that they had never known him to play a solo the same way twice."[88] As early as 1935 at the Reno Club, he was not a regular member of the orchestra, but was rather the club's M.C.[89] He was respected and adored for his gift of words, his ability to engage the audience, and to banter and joke with them and the musicians. As noted, radio D.J.s loved him and often invited him to their programs. He was, for example, "in charge of the Negro entertainment for the first 'Bundles for Britain' all-night WNEW programs."[90]

Page spearheaded interracial assemblages of musicians similar to Norman Granz's Jazz at the Philharmonic. In 1946, before President Harry Truman ordered the integration of the U.S. military, Page led an interracial "Travalcade of Jazz" at Boston's Symphony Hall a few days after Christmas. Musicians included Mary Lou Williams, Don Byas, Charlie Ventura, Chubby Jackson, and Woody Herman's rhythm section.[91] The next year he was head of a "jazz cavalcade" on a cross-country tour. They gave their first performance in March that year, and the cavalcade included "top entertainers" who performed "special concerts" on college campuses in addition to dances for the public. The artists included Eddie Durham, Jack Teagarden, Charlie Ventura, Don Byas, Sid Catlett, and Chubby Jackson, among others, and the tour ventured to the Midwest before heading for Canada. The *California Eagle* contended, "Hot Lips seems sure to soar to the top in this venture just as he is doing with his latest recording, 'Open the Door, Richard.' "[92]

Late in 1947 his orchestra toured with rhythm and blues singer Wynonie "Mr. Blues" Harris in Hillsboro, Delaware.[93] In December 1947 he recorded with this very controversial entertainer, "a larger than life character in the history of black music," and their collaborations included "Good Morning Mr. Blues," "From Bad to Good Blues," and Harris's hit "Good Rockin' Tonight." About the same time, Page also recorded "Too Tight Mama" and "Dirty Deal Blues" with Mabel "Big Maybelle" Smith. He fit right in with these artists, and in fact paved the way for them with some of his own recordings, beginning in the late 1930s. These artists—Harris, Smith, and Louis Jordan—were pioneers, forerunners of rock and roll, the movement that displaced many jazz musicians.[94]

In spring 1949 Page achieved what would become the dream of many musicians, a chance to play in Europe at a jazz festival. The event was the 1949 International Jazz Parade in Paris, which Page viewed as, and quickly termed, paradise—much to the joy of the French audiences and press.[95] Promoter Billy Shaw selected several musicians to represent the U.S. at the Jazz Parade, including Sidney Bechet, Charlie Parker's combo, Tad Dameron, Max Roach, Kenny Clarke, and others. Expatriates James Moody, Rex Stewart, Bill Coleman, and Don Byas were also slated to participate.[96]

The Week of Jazz took place between May 8 and 15. Michel Boujut, writing for *Jazz Magazine,* observed that Paris had never seen such an assemblage of jazz musicians.[97] All the various and allegedly contradictory elements were represented—New Orleans (Bechet), swing (Page and Coleman), and bebop (Dameron, Davis, Parker) during the week.

The *Courier* noted that Page "knocked them out with his trumpet stuff during the [Paris] 'Jazz Festival.' " Evidently Page wrote

Billy Rowe that "he didn't get the big money, but walked away time after time with the honors." He saw Armstrong open at the Lido, and also heard singer Inez Cavanaugh, and "King of the Twelve String," Huddy "Leadbelly" Ledbetter, among others who toured Europe or had taken up residence there after the war.[98] Europeans "treated them [Black musicians] like gods" in the war's aftermath, and Page thoroughly enjoyed the sharp contrast with stateside.[99]

Before heading overseas, he took on a job that was evidence of his versatility. He agreed to serve as "technical jazz advisor" to *Life* magazine. The photojournal was planning a special layout on Americans in Paris at the time of the festival.[100] As he looked forward to another

Elizabeth, Oran Jr., and Oran Page, just before the trumpeter headed for Europe

visit to France, Page, like Buck Clayton, studied French. Though he boasted he never in his life had a singing lesson, he planned this language study as well as voice lessons in order "to articulate in the best Parisian manner."[101]

Nineteen forty-nine was a good year for him for other reasons, besides the Parisian jazz festival. He recorded a bestseller with singer Pearl Bailey, "Baby, It's Cold Outside," and also "The Hucklebuck" in June. The former was said to have been written by Page, according to family members, and it consists of a duet in which the gentleman attempts to convince his girlfriend to spend the night because of the weather.[102] Significantly, it involved as much dialogue as it did singing, and there was also much bantering and joking between the two. Pianist Ray Tunia, Tony Mottola on guitar, bassist Al Hall, and Specs Powell on drums accompanied them.[103] The second song was based on Charlie Parker's "Now's the Time," and represented the rhythm and blues version of this song, an instance when a popular song paralleled a jazz instrumental. The Hucklebuck was also a dance, and the song attempts to teach the beginner: "Wiggle like a snake/ Waggle like a duck/ That's the way you do it when you do the Hucklebuck." Page and Bailey were so popular that Joe Glaser put together a tour for them later that year.[104]

Late in summer Page and his band opened at Jimmy Ryan's, one of the famous Fifty-second Street clubs. Sidney Bechet headlined before him, so he was in some ways the rival of this grandmaster of jazz. He was doing so well that he signed up with Columbia's Harmony label to record some follow-ups to "Baby, It's Cold Outside."[105] His band included his old friend Walter Page, in addition to the former Basie saxophonist, the Texan Buddy Tate.[106] A few months later he was at the Village Vanguard and was being considered for a television show.[107]

His success, his overwhelming popularity, and his fame are evident from the Royal Crown Cola ads that featured him in the 1940s.[108] The pianist Hank Jones, who joined Page's band in 1945 for about a year, and then played with him again in 1949, contended that Southern audiences loved the trumpeter/singer, and he loved them.[109] Up North, Columbia University students awarded him a scroll, "acclaiming Page 'their choice as the top record star of tomorrow.'"[110] Morgenstern commented on the general attraction between his audiences and Page: "Wherever Lips went, the people loved him. . . . And whatever the groove, he fitted."[111]

These fans were very much his people, reflective of his tastes and loyalties—the folklore and sly humor and pathos of his blues and his love songs, and the "jump" quality of his band's driving rhythms, which pleased dancers so during the heyday of the jitterbug and jazz dancing. Though bebop excited some Northern musicians and a few of their fans in the 1940s, Southern Blacks found it unappealing, preferring the blues, in particular, and popular songs and dance music. Jazz journalists, most of them Northerners or European immigrants, and most of them white, did not readily understand Page, who was a Southerner at heart.

His Southern proclivities were evident in his language as well as his behavior. He liked the Southern tours where he played in the dance halls and barns of the rural and small-town South despite the problems of racial segregation that convinced some musicians, such as the Michigan-raised Hank Jones, never to return South. As further evidence of his loyalties, all three of his wives were Black Southerners—from Corsicana, Texas, Montgomery, Alabama, and Salem, Virginia.[112] Then too, Page often visited his mother, brother, sister, nieces, and nephews in Dallas during the summer, and sometimes he took his son, Oran Jr. ("Spike" to family and friends from childhood) with him.

The tragedy of a blues life, which meant so much to Southern audiences, was not foreign to him, either. His second wife, Myrtle, the mother of Oran Jr., died in childbirth in 1946, and in December that year he accompanied her body to Montgomery for burial. His attachment to family as well as the region is suggested by the fact that he sent his son to live with his deceased wife's mother in Birmingham after Myrtle passed, and then, about the time when he remarried three years later, he went to court to obtain custody of his son. Spike came to prefer the South, considered himself a Southerner, attended schools in this region (Morgan State at Baltimore and Howard University in Washington, D.C.), and settled there after law school. He lives in the Deep South to this day.[113]

The warmth that Oran Page generated in white and Black alike was remarkable and indicative of his special relationship with fans. As Morgenstern, who was introduced to Page by a white trumpet player and protégé of the bandleader, reflected, the entertainer "was one of the warmest, kindest and biggest men I have ever known."[114] A loyal and truer friend would be hard to find, and in this way he showed how much he cherished the bonds that Southerners held dear. He felt deeply indebted to fellow trumpet player Kaminsky, and he let everyone know it. His friend explained how "Forever after, I was Buddy to Lips, and years later, whenever we ran into each other he would relate the story to everyone within earshot." Page's eyes shone as he recounted, "I was never so happy in my life [as with Artie Shaw]...and this is the man who got [the job] for me." He also complimented "Buddy's" playing. According to Kaminsky, Page "was always saying I was the best lead trumpet man, but I always felt Lips was the most underrated of the jazz greats."[115]

Page's loyalty to his friends was exemplified by his behavior in Chicago when the manager of the club where he played attempted to keep a friend of his from entering. The *Pittsburgh Courier* mentioned how Page came to New York City's Famous Door "after some trouble in Chicago."[116] About the same time, this newspaper also mentioned how "Hot Lips Page came out of that Chicago job with his band feeling like Joe Louis after a few rounds with the jernt's manager."[117] Joe Sherman, owner of the Garrick Stage Bar, tried to prevent Page's friend from listening to the band. "Sherman...is alleged to have reached for the unwelcome guest's jaw but Hot Lips intercepted Sherman's punch and landed one of his own rights." Later, when the owner tried to get Page with a sucker punch, the musician was faster and knocked him out.[118] Obviously he was more than simply an admirer of boxers—as his son recalled, his father followed boxing very closely. Miles Davis has a reputation for fighting, having been embroiled in a fight with police in front of Birdland one night, for instance, but Page engaged in similar behavior fifteen years earlier.[119]

The trumpet player was evidently a Black musician with a political conscience and an intense sense of right and wrong, who was impassioned with the desire to help the underdog as well as women and children. When he came back to the U.S. after a trip to Europe, he remarked in a letter that he was back behind the "Iron Curtain," referring to the totalitarian state of race relations in the U.S., and, of course, suggesting comparison with the Eastern European nations dominated totally by the Soviets.[120] His son remarked that his father was the first Black nationalist he ever knew, and that, unlike the typical jazz musician, Page read constantly and encouraged his son to do so, as well.[121]

Page's career can be traced in his music. His Texas heritage is celebrated in his compositions "Corsicana" and "Big D" ("D" for Dallas). His life on the city streets as a youngster is evident in "Small Fry," in which he sings:

> *Here comes that good for nothing brat of a boy,*
> *He's such a devil I can whip him with joy,*
> *He's been carousing at the burlesque,*
> *Just watch me teach him with the soul of my shoe.*
> *Oh, small fry, dancing for a penny,*
> *Small fry, counting up how many*
> *My, My, just listen here to me,*
> *You aint the biggest catfish in the sea.*
> *You practice peckin' all day long,*
> *On some old radio song,*
> *Oh yes, oh yes, oh yes.*
> *You'd better listen to your pa,*
> *And some day practice the law,*
> *And then you'll be a real success.*[122]

His other songs—blues and love songs—can also be interpreted in light of his life, with its ups and downs in marriage and in music, and that of the people with whom he identified. This is not to say that the songs were strictly autobiographical, but rather that he drew inspiration from life all around him, not from just his own. He delivered a variety of songs, and this accounted in part for his widespread appeal. Some of his records were blues, and among them were "I Keep Rollin' On," "Uncle Sam's Blues," and "Double-Trouble Blues" —all by Page.[123] ("My woman's hollerin' murder, and I ain't even raised my hand," he sang on "Double-Trouble Blues.") Some songs were folksy and humorous, "Willow Mae Willow Foot," "You Need Coachin'," "Gimme, Gimme, Gimme," "Ain't No Flies on Me," "Open the Door, Richard," "You Stole My Wife, You Horse Thief," and "I Never See Maggie Alone." Others tendered advice to the lovelorn, and some were simply gems, such as "Bottom Blues," used by Chester Himes in one of his Harlem novels, and his hit with Pearl Bailey, "Baby, It's Cold Outside."[124]

Through the 1940s, Page signed with a number of different record companies and had quite a few hits and near-hits. "Rockin' at Ryan's" and "Good for Stompin'" (both 1944) were among the flag-wavers that demonstrated his devotion to dance music.[125] Notably, before and during the Cuban and Afro-Latin music craze, Page recorded a few such pieces. His son recalled that he loved Mexican trumpet players, and this feeling may have been inspired by West Indian, especially Cuban, musicians in New York City. His masterpiece in that style was "Harlem Rhumbain' the Blues"[126] (1940), but there was also "Dance of the Tambourine" (1944) and "La Dance" (1947). "Sunny Jungle" was another exotic composition, Ellington-like in its reliance on muted but raw and powerful trumpet and a very prominent role for the drums' special effects. Not surprisingly, the maestro's drummer on "Jungle" was Sonny Greer.[127]

On "Fish for Supper" (1944), several musicians sang, as in Louis Jordan's Tympani Five, and anticipating some of the group singing of Dizzy Gillespie's band in the late 1940s. They sang, "We've got fish for supper, First one thing and another," and "Last night we had bread and fish, Tonight we've got fish and bread." "Main Street" illustrated Page's ability to chronicle the exploits of ordinary African-Americans, fun-seekers at night on Main Street, and "They Raided the Joint" was quite similar. In the latter, police come in as if it were still prohibition:[128] "They raided the joint, took everybody down but me/.... and I was drunk as I could be."[129]

He was versatile in still another way, as he often jammed, played, and recorded with New Orleans musicians, or in that style. He thus participated in the revival of this music, playing not only one of the songs for which he was particularly known, "St. James Infirmary," but also "When the Saints Go Marching In," and "Muskrat Ramble." On the latter, Peanuts Hucko, clarinet, and Ralph Sutton, piano, joined him. Child's Paramount and Stuyvesant Casino were among the nightspots featuring the older songs—Bennie Moten's "South," "Sweet Georgia Brown," and "St. Louis Blues."[130]

While his songs and music provide a key to interpreting Page and his career, so do the articles that appeared under his name, or as interviews with him in jazz journals, and the testimony of his family is especially valuable. In articles and in his personal life, he was constantly advising the younger musicians. In this respect, he was continuing the tradition of mentoring that he experienced in his younger days from his heroes and heroines, like Ma Rainey and Louis Armstrong. He told how generous Armstrong had been with him in the early 1930s: "While I had met him before, he had always been like God to me, and it never occurred to me that he would ever spend a whole afternoon with me, giving me pointers on this and that."[131]

As versatile as he was, playing several different types of jazz, and anticipating Ray Charles in some of his songs, he tried to convince younger musicians that the distinctions were meaningfulness. As a *Down Beat* article contended, Page "is trying to put into practice what a lot of people have been saying the music business needs: a breaking down of the tight barriers separating Dixie, swing, and bop and using an amalgamation of the best facets of each." Page's music was modern in that what "Lips' group produces keeps moving along all the time."[132]

He also shared his views on phrasing with musicians in a jazz journal. "Phrasing is like an artist painting a picture. Your phrase should be colorful, pretty, melodic variations, built up to a climax."[133] Like Armstrong, Henderson, and others, he was critical of bebop. "Bop is just a short cut for the kids who didn't serve their apprenticeship playing the real jazz. They came up the easy way."[134] It was Page's opinion that "the public doesn't like bop...and never will because it doesn't paint any picture." He shared Harry "Sweets" Edison's opinion that "you must give the public something it can understand; something it can sing or whistle."[135]

Despite his reputation and his successes, in the early 1950s he continued to alternate between summer gigs in Europe—France, Belgium, and Sweden, in particular, where he was lionized—and struggling in the U.S., where he felt he was behind an iron curtain. He continued playing clubs, touring, leading his band, and singing on the eve of the rock and roll era, unrecognized by many youngsters but adored by jazz stalwarts of the swing era and the New Orleans revival.

CHAPTER EIGHT

The Phoenix Rises

In 1928, a number of Blue Devils—most of its founders, in fact—left the orchestra, and these included Willie Lewis, pianist and the "brains" of the band, trombonist Ermal Coleman, and drummer Ed McNeil; Lawrence "Inky" Williams apparently left around the same time, if not sooner, and in 1930 was an usher at the Aldridge Theatre.[1] Then after Durham, Basie, Rushing, and Oran Page exited for Moten between 1929 and 1931, founder Walter Page continued to find new recruits and lead the band until early in 1932, when he, too, left for Moten's outfit.[2] But these were glory days for the band, from the perspective of the new recruits—Chadwick, Whyte, Hudson, and Bolar. The Blue Devils traveled through the territories and up into Nebraska and Iowa, and the band was often praised in the Kansas City *Call* in much the same way as its chief rival, Bennie Moten.

Besides those who went on to become famous, such as Basie, Durham, the Pages, and Lester Young, numerous lesser-known musicians passed through the Blue Devils. It has been claimed that tenor saxophonist Ben Webster was a Blue Devil, but this has not been verified. He did, however, live in Oklahoma City in 1930.[3] Trumpet players James Simpson, Harry Youngblood, Le Roy "Snake" Whyte, Leonard Chadwick, Abe Bolar (who replaced Walter Page), Reuben Roddy, Reuben Lynch, and others played in the band, or, in the case of Simpson and Whyte, actually led it for a period of time.[4] What is so remarkable is how the band managed not only to survive but even to thrive with lesser-known musicians.

As Buster Smith frequently explained, the Blue Devils performed at the Cinderella Dance Palace, "an ofay [white] ballroom"
in Little Rock, Arkansas, during the summer months, and then at the
Ritz Ballroom in Oklahoma City in winter, with only a few days off
each year.[5] They also barnstormed through the Midwest and northern prairies under the National Orchestra Service. Contemporary
reports indicate a degree of success nearly comparable to Moten's
band. In at least one report, the Chicago *Defender* confused the
band with its Kansas City rival. Late in 1929, the Blue Devils were
described as "a Bennie Moten unit."[6] After their summer stint at the
Cinderella Dance Palace, the Devils went to Oklahoma City, where
they performed at the Japanese Garden. The band members included James Rushing and Oran Page, who are often thought to be
with Moten at this time; Walter Page, as manager; Alvin Burroughs
on drums; Reuben Lynch, banjo; and Charles Washington, piano;
the reeds were Henry Smith, Bill (or Thomas) Owens, and Reuben
Roddy; brass were Oran Page, Druie Bess, trombone, and James
Simpson.[7]

Their love of sports, and their close involvement in community
affairs, were evident that fall when they attended the Black college
football classic and performed at the victory dance in Dallas. This
was part of the 1929 Texas State Fair.[8] The next month the band appeared in Detroit backing Billy King, whose show, "Moonshine,"
launched the Blue Devils in 1923. He performed at the Castle theater, and his show included a cast of fifteen, "not including the Blue
Devils orchestra which will supply the music for the show." His recent appearance at the Koppin theater produced sufficient laughs "to
indicate that the old master is still among the first ranks of American
rib ticklers."[9] It is noteworthy that no Blue Devils mentioned this
event or reuniting with Billy King in interviews. This appearance
took place within a week of their record session in Kansas City.

◆ ◆ ◆

The Blue Devils played at the Ritz late in 1929 before going on the
road for a month. They also had a radio spot, broadcasting over KFJF
from 10:30 until midnight. Walter Page, who came back to his band,

lived on Second Street in Oklahoma City, as did Oran Page, but interestingly, he listed his address as the Ritz. This is evidence that he might have been leaving the band at the time, or in transition before joining Moten.[10] Changes in personnel were made in 1929, 1930, and 1931, with Walter Page, then James Simpson, and Page again, and Buster Smith and Ernie Williams, working together, as well as Le Roy Whyte, leading the band. After wintering in Oklahoma City, the band returned to Cinderella Gardens, a resort, the next summer in Little Rock. Personnel changes had taken place: James Simpson was the leader, Theodore "Doc" Ross had joined the sax section, Leonard Chadwick was on trumpet, and Ernie Williams, drummer, singer, and M.C., was another new member, while Rushing and Owens had departed.[11]

Walter Page left from the autumn of 1929 until the middle of the next year, for family reasons, and during that time he was in the Bill Lewis Orchestra with Wesley Manning, Ermal Coleman, Abe Bolar (who eventually replaced him when he finally left the Devils for good), and James Rushing. Leonard Chadwick, a pre-dental student fresh out of Fisk University, was also in that band in late 1929. Walter Page took him under his wing, schooled him some, and then returned with him to the Blue Devils.[12]

The Bill Lewis band held forth at Mitchell's Oak Cliff Night Club. Outside Oklahoma City, its patrons were white workers from the newly discovered oil fields. This was a boom time, so pay was good for a young man like Chadwick, as well as for veterans Walter Page and James Rushing. At first Chadwick took the regular pay of five dollars per night rather than depend upon the "kitty"—the tips that the musicians split nightly. Then he quickly changed his mind, forgoing the regular salary for the fifty dollars—his cut from the kitty—that he earned for his work every night for the rest of the week. Chadwick recalled, "Because people were coming in out of the oil fields and the wells come in, they were very generous with their tips. . . ."[13]

Every day, Chadwick explained, "They picked us all up in a bus early in the evening, and we'd go out there and Page [taught him music]. . . . He had trained me and I made it. He took me back to [the Blue Devils] band as the first trumpet player even though I couldn't read that well. I played all the hard parts and Lips . . . Lips played the difficult parts." He meant that as lead trumpet, he played the written parts, while Lips was the "hot" trumpeter who soloed. This was late in 1929. Evidently Rushing did not return to the band but went to Moten.

Chadwick shed light on the band's repertoire: "that's when Buster began to write four parts and five parts. . . . Buster's arrangements were a little different because he knew the capabilities of his men and he wrote for that effect. And they were *very* good. He started writing four and five part harmony." Like Jesse Stone and Eddie Durham, two other Southwestern arrangers, and their eastern counterparts, Smith began writing for larger sections of four and five saxophones and brass.

> Most of the stock arrangements and things were in three part harmony—that's one, two, three parts. A regular chord. One person plays one note, another person plays another note, another person plays another note, and that makes the chord. . . . Buster began to add the sixth part to the chord. He began to experiment, and I think that's one of the things that made our band so unique, because we were one of the first bands in that area that was carrying five brass. We had two trombones and three trumpets. . . . And then we only had three saxophones . . . Doc Ross, Buster, [Reuben Roddy] and then later on we added Lester Young for the fourth saxophone.

The trumpet player explained, "Buster was spreading the harmony throughout the band, and I think that's one of the uniqueness, plus the ability of our people to solo so well."

Smith was the brains behind the band's music insofar as he did nearly all of the arrangements. "We didn't have any outside arrangements. Most of our arrangements were done by Buster." Once in a while someone else would do one for the band. The soloists were all swinging. "We'd play those [stock arrangements], then branch off it something we could feel as though it had a little jump to it, and we'd do some solos, then go back to the ensembles." Whyte, Smith,

The Blue Devil reed section, 1932: Theodore "Doc" Ross,
Lester "Pres" Young, and Henry "Buster" Smith

Young, and drummer Al Burroughs were the soloists at the time. As
first trumpet, Chadwick did not solo.[14]

Leroy Whyte also made a contribution to their repertoire.
"When Snake joined the band that was the days when 'Ring Dem
Bells' were [in the bands' repertoire (recorded July 1930)]...and
Snake took the arrangement off the record just like it was on
there.... He took it off for us and we played it, just as it sounded on
the record, and Snake had more musical background I guess than
most of [us] so he would like to go ahead and play things that he
would...try to create...."

He was full of praise for band members. "In the early days of the

Blue Devils, we had some tremendous musicians." Charlie Washington was a "pretty good piano player." Of Eddie Durham, Chadwick insisted, "he was tremendous," and as for Al Burroughs, "he was from Chicago, he was a heck of a drummer, done a lot of drum solos" —something that was unique at that time. Their new tenor saxophonist was original and very exciting. "Lester played everything different. It wasn't the soulful type of thing that you used to hear.... He did everything different, and everything he did was exciting, because it was a contrast to what you had been hearing."

Chadwick distinguished Young from other tenors. Rather than a balladeer, "Lester was rough and totally explosive.... There was nothing that he tried to be pretty about." Moreover, "when Lester came along, why he played nothing like ... [Chu Berry], or he didn't try to play like that. And as ... [a] result he attracted attention because what he was doing he was doing it well. Doing it exciting. He was more of an exciting player. When Chu and them got real moanful.... But Lester, he was just all over his horn."

While Chadwick was a Blue Devil, they played mainly the small towns in Texas, like Tyler, and for events such as the dance after the Langston-Wiley college football game. Under the National Orchestra Service, they traveled north into Iowa and the Dakotas. "We were on the same tour that Lawrence Welk was on." They played dances for whites in these states. Their repertoire was quite diverse in the nation's heartland: "We played everything." They performed for Blacks on Monday nights, and Chadwick recalled, "we had a little more feelings into it when we played for the Blacks, and we got more when you look out and see your brother."

While there was a strong spirit of brotherhood among the Devils, there were also cliques. "Well, we had two or three groups in our band. Doc Ross was [in] a society group. We had fellows who ... [when they] hit town, they looked up the official people. They were a group of Doc [and] Charlie Washington. Then there was a group that took up [with] the drinkers and party-goers. Then there was a middling group that just—I liked to meet the people at the restaurant, the waitresses, and things.... So we were close, we were organized, cause we nearly starved to death, there was a loyalty within the band."

This strong sense of loyalty functioned "to hold the band together, because we knew there was a better day ahead. We enjoyed playing, enjoyed playing. Now there were incidents where, when everybody didn't agree, you know, but all in all, there wasn't a lot of changing of men."

The touring life of a bandsman was a hard one, however, and even more so if he had started a family. Chadwick related, "You didn't have a chance to do much resting, and it was really a Godsend when we got two or three nights in one place.... But most of ours was road work." The newlywed trumpet player left the Blue Devils in 1932 and joined King Oliver's band at the Ridge Inn in Nashville, Tennessee. He stayed with Oliver for a time, but like Snake Whyte, he had his family on his mind, and his son, Leonard Jr. was born in 1933.

In the depths of the Great Depression, he played music to support his family: "I saved $3 a night to send home." Finally, in Bristol, Tennessee, he had had enough of being away, and he caught a bus to Fort Smith, Arkansas ("that's all the money I had"). There, he pawned his suit and a pair of shoes for three dollars for a ticket to Oklahoma City. For the next few years he led a band, the Rhythmaires, which included former Blue Devils as well as Charlie Christian, at the Ritz Ballroom in Oklahoma City, while he worked washing dishes at a twelve-hour shift in a local waffle house.[15] Spring 1931 found the Blue Devils in Kansas City, where the *Call* maintained that Walter Page "needs no introduction to Kansas City," and that, furthermore, the band had "improved a great deal" and had some surprises for the "home folks."[16] At the 1931 May Musicians' Ball, the Devils were last on the program. "They took care of 'Lonesome Road' like nobody's business" and "quite properly received an ovation from the crowd."[17] Under the auspices of the National Orchestra Service, they immediately went on the road in May 1931. They performed at the Rigadon Ballroom at 712 Pierce Street in Sioux City, Iowa. Advertised as "Walter Page and His 13 Blue Devils," the band played primarily for whites, and "gents" paid forty cents while "ladies" paid half that much.[18]

In a rare letter to the *Black Dispatch*, Walter Page described the successful tour as including "the principal cities of Oklahoma, Arkansas, Kansas, Missouri, Nebraska," and then Iowa. Next they headed for Kansas City and St. Louis. The members were Theodore Ross, Reuben Roddy, and Henry Smith, reeds; Leonard Chadwick, James Simpson, Harry Smith, Dan Minor, and Chappie [Druie] Bess, brass; Charlie Washington, Reuben Lynch, Raymond Howell, and Page in the rhythm section; and Ernie Williams, M.C. and singer.[19] Touring dance bands familiarized Iowans with the latest in popular music. In late spring, George E. Lee was advertised in Sioux City, and then the next week Ben Bernie and His Orchestra performed. Dancers paid $2.50 to $3.00 per couple for the latter band, indicating that it was an elite affair.[20] Lee and the Blue Devils battled one another in Sioux City later in the month, continuing the rivalry among the best territorial bands.[21]

Eight bands were to appear at the Musicians' Ball in Kansas City the following September. While "word has been received from Walter Page and his Blue Devils, an excellent band, by the way, that they will come in for the affair if there is any way to do so," this was not possible. Yet a month later, as some indication of their loyalty to the locals, Page and the Devils promised to perform at a charity sponsored by the Kansas City Young Matrons.[22] After their swing through Iowa, Nebraska, Minnesota, and the Dakotas in spring and summer, and while they missed the September Musicians' Ball,[23] in fall they entertained the dancers at Paseo Hall, and the *Call* reported, "Page's band is a new organization now in point of melody, arrangement, speed, and smoothness, to the group that Walter first assembled." When complimented on his new outfit, Page responded, "Well, it takes plenty of practice, and that is what we have been getting."[24] Referring to their recent tour, the Devils were advertised as "the toast of Minnesota, Iowa, Dakota, and Nebraska." Their repertoire was also quite diverse. They were at least four bands in one. The weekly's ad promised, "Walter Page will answer the demand for a pleasing change. He has a sweet band, a smooth band, a hot band, a stomp band."

Because of their leader's roots in Kansas City, locals regarded the Blue Devils as "essentially a home town band."[25] In November 1931 they performed at the Labor Temple and for a Break O' Day dance on Thanksgiving Day. As the name Break O' Day indicated, the Blue Devils entertained Kansas City dancers from 1:00 a.m. until early morning.[26] For a Musicians' Ball in early December 1931, the *Call* promised, "Walter Page's Blue Devils are expected to walk on the water with [their?] part in the dance program." "A galaxy of stars" in the bands of Andy Kirk, George E. Lee, Troy Floyd, Zack Whyte, and Bill Little were to perform.[27] "Walter Page and his Blue Devils started the ball rolling with a brand of syncopation which has made this band a byword for hot music all the way from here to the desert. They started hot and ended the same way." The Devils' rendition of "Sweet and Lovely" was also praised by the *Call*.[28]

The day after Christmas, they gave a benefit for the boys at the Jackson County Home, just as they had earlier in the year for the Kansas City Young Matrons. This benefit manifested their loyalties to the community and their belief that they should seek to contribute to the well-being of the less fortunate. At this event, Walter Page was praised as a Lincoln High graduate, indicating that he was still with the Blue Devils late in 1931, even though others place him with Moten at this time.[29] Dance was so much a part of the social life of Black Kansas City that "That Mighty band the Blue Devils" performed on a Sunday night late in January from 10:00 p.m. to 2:00 a.m. at Forest Park, "Oklahoma City's largest dance pavilion."[30] As this was a farewell dance, obviously they were going on the road again. Early the next month, the *Dispatch* reported that they were "back home again" to perform at Forest Park. The Devils had expanded to fourteen pieces and were led by James Simpson, indicating Walter Page's departure. Rushing's replacement, Ernie Williams, "our own home town boy," was to sing "that famous song 'Blue Devil Blues.' "[31]

By April they were back down to thirteen again for a "big cabaret fete" at the Ritz Ballroom. The personnel were: Leonard Chadwick, James Simpson, Le Roy White, D. (Druie) Bess, Jasper Jones (brass), Theodore Ross, Lester Young, Henry Smith (reeds), Charles Washington, Reuben Lynch, Raymond Howell, Abe Bolar (rhythm), and Ernest Williams.[32] Their fans heard the Devils over the radio on stations KFJF and WKY in Oklahoma City, WFFA in Dallas, and KTHS in Little Rock.[33] That spring they participated in the Kansas City Musicians' Annual Ball sponsored by the musicians' union (local 767) at the Labor Temple and were advertised as Simpson's Blue Devils.[34]

The Blue Devils were a band for all occasions, whether for the Yo-Yo Ball at Forest Park, where a prize was awarded to the best yo-yo performer,[35] or a dance sponsored by local radicals. They appeared and performed at "the first interracial dance ever staged in Oklahoma City." Mixed couples "of both white and colored laughed and enjoyed themselves without any sign of friction during the entire evening." White women danced with Black men, and Black women danced with white men, "and the novelty of such an occasion in the South was apparently being enjoyed."[36]

In the summer of 1932 another leadership change occurred when a local Kansas City bandleader, Bill Little, head of the Little Bills, took over the Devils. Little went to Minneapolis to complete negotiations and his takeover of the band. It is unclear whether he was acting on his own behalf or as an agent for Bennie Moten, because his Little Bills were "a Bennie Moten unit" in 1930. This may have been why some considered the Devils a Moten band at this time.[37] For the next few weeks the band and its new leader were praised. Little contended "there is no doubt in my mind that this band is one of the best anywhere in this vicinity, bar none. They have everything a band needs—rhythm, melody, punch, and clever arrangements." He predicted "a very bright future," and they played after the baseball game at the Kansas City Monarchs Victory Dance early in August, and at the Musicians' Annual Labor Day Ball in September, but Little's association with the band did not last long.[38]

Then another change in management occurred. Either Little's expectations were not met or he left the band for some other reason, and he turned it over to another band member. The *Call* announced in early September that the Devils' trumpet player, Le Roy Whyte, born in Buxton, Iowa in 1907, "is in charge."[39] Whyte was a close friend of Eddie Barefield and Lester Young, musicians with whom he performed in Minneapolis and the outlying regions in the late 1920s. In fact, he played a key role in convincing Young to join the band in early 1932. Whyte replaced Hot Lips Page, which allows us to date his joining the band as winter 1931. His father—a coal miner, railroad worker, minister, and musician—taught him to read and write music, and he did some arranging for the band. Whyte was known for his high notes, as he had filed his mouthpiece or altered it in some way to enable himself to hit them.[40]

The trumpet player explained how he became a Blue Devil:

"I had been with the bands around here [Iowa], Omaha, and the band was in Des Moines and what not. And...one band...took us to Kansas City and I run into the Blue Devils....Then we went on from there to Oklahoma City. I jumped whatever band I was with, and joined the Blue Devils. And...then I stayed with the Blue Devils...a long time."

Whyte's memories of the band's glory days were ecstatic:

That was heaven. I thought that was the greatest band in the world, which even in the jazz...even in the books that I've seen, where it was mentioned, they run into Buster Smith and they said that if that band had ever hit New York at that time...the situation would have been a lot different as far as.... 'Cause we were really...we had a banner said, "The Band that Never Lost a Battle." We...we didn't care nothing about Bennie...Bennie Moten who was supposed to be great in Kansas City at that time. But when we got that band...we headed east. We headed east. And [I] got as far as Cincinnati.

Whyte related how "We really built that band up and added [to it]. It was beginning to add men to the band, instead of having two trumpets, three trumpets, yeah. See, when I joined them, Leonard Chadwick was playing first trumpet. And another...Simpson, was playing second trumpet. And I had to write.... See, they were using stock arrangements, and I had to write all of the third parts because stock arrangements was made for two...for two trumpets and the one trombone." He teamed with Buster Smith on the band's arrangements.

"Buster Smith and I started making arrangements where we added a fourth trumpet. I think we had four trumpets. Well, that's how that started. Because up in that...up in that time...every band in the country, they had stock arrangements. You bought them for 35 cents. And had...two saxophones and a tenor, two altos and a tenor, two trumpets and a trombone. See? Then we started to adding to the saxophone section." Speaking generally of later developments, rather than the Blue Devils specifically, Whyte recalled, "Then they added to the brass section till we got four trumpets, four trombones, five saxophones, and that's...that's a, you know, full chords you know."[41]

He told how Buster Smith learned entirely on his own to write arrangements:

> Buster used to make an arrangement, and he'd have three saxophone parts laying here, and two trumpets and the trombone parts laying here, and the rest.... And the piano, and the bass. Rhythm section. And he'd write on the first trumpet player, his part. He played piano...he'd put that down. And then he'd reach in and get the second trumpet, he played that.... That's the way he was taught to write.... he had never seen a score pad, where all the instruments is on the score pad, you understand?.... Where you write everything.... That's the way he did it. Took him a long time too. I...I came there, I had the first score pad he'd ever seen.

Prior to meeting Whyte and learning about score paper, Smith used "Just manuscript [paper].... So the first time I walked in I seen all the music scattered on the floor. (laughs) Said, 'What are you doing?' [He] said, 'I'm making an arrangement.' I said, 'You making it on the floor?' He said, 'Well, that's my way of writing.'" As Whyte explained, "It took him about three, four times as long.... But he had some powerful ideas."

The trumpet player also introduced their self-taught arranger to the correct names of chords. Whyte recalled, "And, you know something, he didn't know what the chords was. He'd hit something, I'd say, 'Hey, Prof,' we called him Prof, 'Hey, Prof, what was that you hit?' 'That was one of them there (unintelligible).' And then I'd say, 'What was it again?' 'Oh, that's a so-and-so. That was an F-13.' 'A what?' Or whatever it was.... He knew them! [intuitively, but]...I taught him the [correct] names of them."

Nonetheless, Whyte marveled at Smith's superior soloing: "Buster was a clarinet fool, see. Plus alto." Smith "was something else. I could shut my eyes and...seems like his horn would be talking. He could...he...he was something." The observation that he sounded as if he was talking recalls the significance of the oral tradition in blues—in this instance, in jazz—and is noteworthy because this "talking" quality is usually attributed to Parker and the avant-garde saxophonists of the 1960s.[42]

The new leader eventually quit the Blue Devils because of his family—in addition to his intense dislike of traveling through the South, something he had learned about on his first tour into that region. In "the Blue Devils, we carried our wives with us, most of us, all the time. See? You know what I mean. And . . . so when my kid got to the age where he had . . . my wife said, 'Roy, I can't go no further. Junior's got to go to school.' "[43] So he left the band around November 1932, in Cincinnati, and joined Zack Whyte in 1933.

From here the band evidently went on its disastrous Southern and Eastern tour, because they do not appear in the *Call* after late October 1932 or in 1933. The *St. Louis Argus* was the last newspaper to report the band's performances in 1932, when they numbered fourteen band members. They joined in the "greatest battle of music ever offered" against Eddie Johnson's Victor Recording Orchestra at the Peoples Finance Building in November. Later that month they were featured in "another great jazz" festival with the St. Louis Crack-A-Jacks at the Dance Box. Then they disappeared from the newspapers.[44]

Whyte explained how and why this disastrous last tour happened:

> And . . . this guy had . . . he had booked Benny Moten's band first . . . [for a] long time. Well, Benny went back to Kansas City and was going to stay. And this guy talked to Buster Smith and them boys that was from down south . . . talked them in to going over Benny Moten's route. Going through the south, you know . . . Anyway, when they got to there, I said, "Well look. I'm not going down . . . I'm not going to the south. Not with my wife." . . . And . . . I said, "Well, we got a chance . . . we booked in to go to New York and that's what we should do." And all of them [inaudible], "Oh no. We want to go to down south like Benny Moten." Benny Moten was "king" down south at that time. And . . . so they . . . you know, out talked [me], and I just left. That's where I joined Zack Whyte. See? I joined Zack Whyte's band in Cincinnati.

Le Roy Whyte explained years later, "I know I wasn't going south, that's what . . . that's what was the end of my Blue Devils thing." The band "should have went east, kept east, instead of them going south."[45]

Buoyed by the successes of Bennie Moten during his tours, and perhaps unaware of the number of times his band had been stranded, the Devils headed for Newport News and other Virginia towns. Perhaps the fact that Ernie Williams was from North Carolina and Reuben Lynch hailed from West Virginia gave them confidence that they could survive the hardships of the Depression in the South and the difficulties that came with being far from home. Then Lynch became ill and went home to Bluefield; he worked in the Weirton, West Virginia, steel mills and never played professionally again.[46]

Smith recalled that in Newport News, "I guess it was the wrong time of year or something, and we were in a little speakeasy joint, and we couldn't do any good in a place like that." During such times the commonwealth form of organization was a disadvantage, because "we couldn't go anywhere or accept a job unless we had a vote on it." The problem was that "nearly always, seven of the boys would pull one way and five or six would pull the other way, and we would end up doing nothing and staying where we were."

Then Fats Waller offered them a chance in Cincinnati to play with him on radio station WLW, but the band split as usual. "He offered us eight hundred dollars to play for him on an hour and a half show and some of the boys thought it wasn't enough."[47]

Abe Bolar blamed Ernie Williams for their problems. At that time bands depended upon road managers who called ahead to make bookings. "Ernest Williams was managing when the band broke up," but he "didn't know anything about management. He didn't know the road like a road manager." As the bassist recalled, "We were playing mostly colored down in the Carolinas. The Virginias." In these places, audiences "liked the band! Once they heard it and come on in, why I mean they were sold! But they had never heard nothing like it."

On the other hand, he thought they "didn't have any business that far away from home base." Their former colleague, Hot Lips Page, was with Bennie Moten at the time, "and he called and said he knew a guy that could get a lot of work for us, you know." Nonetheless, "that petered right out ... we had three or four gigs and that was all. However, the Depression was just setting in and it was really bad. ... In '33 it was rough. You can't fault anybody for anything because there wasn't no money."[48]

They went to Martinsville, Virginia, to play in a dance hall owned by Dr. Dana Baldwin, a local physician, businessman, and booster of the African-American community in that town. The Baldwin Block, newly built in 1932, consisted of a shopping center, theater, barbershop, drugstore, restaurant, and social club. They stayed "a few weeks." Smith complained, "We didn't like it but we were broke and couldn't leave." Then a young man came to see them, promised them work, and lured them to Bluefield, West Virginia.[49]

They performed at a white night club, but it was the usual chicanery: "He had quoted us a straight price for the job and then turned around and took a big cut out of our salary for himself."[50] Angered, the Devils were helpless, because the culprit was under twenty-one—too young to make valid contracts or be sued. Zack Whyte came to recruit some, but not all, of the Blue Devils—who thought he should take all or no one—and the taxi drivers who drove them to the job became impatient for their money and suspicious, fearing that band members would leave without paying them. Then the Traveler's Hotel where they stayed put them out.[51] Their instruments were attached to ensure that they would not suddenly leave town without settling their debts.

The Blue Devils' 1932–1933 tour ended in disaster and the band's gradual dissolution, until it finally broke up in Bluefield. A Black lawyer put up the money to get their instruments from the court that had attached them in lieu of outstanding hotel and taxi bills, and he told the band members he would hold them until they sent the money for them. So on Easter morning 1933 Buster Smith, Lester Young, "Doc" Ross, George Hudson, Abe Bolar, and a few others hopped aboard a Mountain Jack—a train with two engines to enable it to climb the steep mountain grades—heading toward Cincinnati.[52]

The stragglers selected a coal car and covered themselves with the coal to keep warm that night. In the Ohio River city, they camped in a hobo jungle where they enjoyed the hospitality of the unemployed, who were quite generous, looked out for one another, and welcomed newcomers to food and a refuge during the Great Depression. Young borrowed a horn to make a local gig to get some money for the group, and—in about a week's time—they finally made it to St. Louis, where someone came from Kansas City to pick them up, and some joined Bennie Moten.[53]

Significantly, new bands known as the Blue Devils emerged. Late in 1932, Eddie Randall formed his band of Seven Blue Devils in St. Louis.[54] Edward Christian's Blue Devils were photographed in 1935, and James Simpson's Blue Devils held forth in 1937.[55]

Abe Bolar thought the Blue Devils' uniqueness was due to a certain feeling that was not easily described. "You don't just play with feeling cause you got a band. You got to have somebody in there putting the feeling in there. Somebody that plays with feeling. Some one or two or three in there that puts the feeling in the band. Band within itself doesn't just have a feeling."[56]

Buster Smith, he maintained, made a major difference in the band. Not that the band lacked a certain feeling before him. Before Smith, the Devils "had a different feeling." In the same way, he maintained that he got a different feeling on the tuba than on the bass, and unlike many other bass players, he preferred the brass instrument. "I can't express myself on the string bass. I never could. That's the reason I never did like it. But on the tuba, I could play anything I wanted, anytime, without thinking. String bass is something else."

Bolar believed that the feeling the Blue Devils and other Southwestern musicians possessed was something innate, and that it was lost after a few decades. At first Basie's band had the feeling, but then lost it. "He added this feeling, from out here. . . . He had a southwest feeling. So you . . . change and get eastern musicians, get what you call real polished musicians, you going to get a different sound, cause they don't have the feel. The feeling feel. They have the feel for correctness, polish. . . . They just don't know the feel, cause they haven't got it . . . and practically haven't been around it." As Bolar explained, "All this stuff was born in them. That's the reason I told you I don't know what the white folks talking about when they talk about jazz, and I don't think they know."[57]

CHAPTER NINE

Moten Swing

Kansas City Dance Traditions

Ironically, in trying to succeed like Bennie Moten's band on their tour through the South, the Blue Devils floundered and ended up in the Moten camp—though not all of them and not immediately.[1]

While the former Devils are usually presented as joining Moten in the aftermath of the Blue Devils' breakup, in fact their activities in 1933–1934 were a bit more complicated. Alto saxophonist Theodore Ross, for example, who joined the band around 1930, was reported to be "now beating it out nightly at Ben Wilson's night clubs with one of the hottest small bands we have" in Minneapolis, late in 1933. This was the very same Minneapolis band that Lester Young joined and played with at the town's Cotton Club the next year.[2]

A year later, Ross, "formerly of Bennie Moten's band," claimed that the music business was so good in Billings, Montana, that he performed there for six months, and late in the year he reported that he was headed for Tokyo, Japan, for a year's stint. Ever interested in staying in touch with his Blue Devil section mates, he asked that Buster Smith and Lester Young contact or write him.[3]

Nor did Young go immediately to Bennie Moten. After the Blue Devils, he joined King Oliver for a few months late in 1933. In late 1933 or early 1934 he was with the Moten-Lee combination, and he and Herschel Evans, who was with Basie's band, used to switch jobs from time to time.[4] Eventually he moved back to Minneapolis, where he stayed with his wife, Beatrice, until he became a member of Count Basie and Buster Smith's Reno Club combo in Kansas City early in 1936. Also, Walter Page, who became a Motenite early in 1932, played with the Jeter-Pillars Orchestra in St. Louis in 1934 instead of staying with the Kansas City bandleader.[5]

In a little less than ten years' time, Bennie Moten had established himself and his bands as the model for dance bands in the Southwest. His reign lasted from the early 1920s until his death on the operating table in spring 1935. Eddie Durham was one of the musicians who regarded him as "king." Drummer Jo Jones claimed that "Bennie Moten was the greatest bandleader that ever lived." Furthermore, "Whenever you saw... a Fletcher Henderson; whenever you saw a Cab Calloway; whenever you saw a Duke Ellington... that's Bennie Moten. You see Basie, that's Bennie Moten."[6]

Oran Page had nothing but praise for Moten and his business and political acumen. The bandleader was "a business man first and last," who had "a lot of connections... and was a very good friend of [Tom] Pendergast, the political boss." Through this and other contacts, "he was able to control all the good jobs and choice locations in and around Kansas City." In Page's opinion, Moten was "stronger than MCA [the booking agency Music Corporation of America]." He rated the bandleader's musicianship quite highly: "A real old-timer, he was an excellent ragtime pianist and he could play along with the best of them."[7]

In 1931 and 1932, Moten's band was at its height in popularity and possessed dazzling arrangers—Basie and Durham, mainly— and outstanding soloists—Hot Lips Page, Eddie Barefield, and Ben Webster. The *Call* reporter E. W. Wilkins visited the band backstage at a Kansas City theater "which doesn't cater to colored people" in order to report "how Herr Moten and his cohorts looked when they were doing their stuff for the palefaces." Accompanied by a Broadway producer who arranged the Moten date, the journalist went to the band members' dressing room and commented that they were "all dressed up and look[ed] good enough to take a spot on anybody's program." Visiting with the Motenites backstage, Wilkins witnessed stage managers and "prop" men who rushed about, and he noted that "everything looks like one big jumble... but it's not, never fear."[8]

After the act onstage finished, the rear curtain rose and the lights shone on the resplendent Moten band members, "and they cut loose with a hot number which is guaranteed to take the roof off. And it darned near does!" The audience clapped as the second number began, with Bus Moten (Bennie Moten's nephew), "dapper as always, cutting with that baton, pressing the band to better and better efforts." When they started "Travelin'," Jimmy Rushing came out of the wings wearing blue overalls, a red bandana about his neck, and an old gray hat, and he held "a stick with a bundle tied in an old handkerchief" over his shoulder. The *Call* reporter described how Rushing "sidles across the stage as he sings the number," finishing with a skip off into the wings. The house roared its approval. The Motenites played three shows a day, except for Saturday and Sunday when they did four shows.[9]

◆ ◆ ◆

The Moten band was dominant in Kansas City and won considerable recognition in the Eastern U.S. They were awarded first prize in a band competition in Chicago in 1928. They ranked third and fourth among jazz bands judged by African-Americans in public surveys four years later. They were touted as the only Black band to play in the Hotel Statler's dining room in New York City and at the Twentieth Century Club in Buffalo.[10]

Wilkins delighted in focusing upon the dancers' responses to music: "From the gong, the crowd cavorted about in a way to let everyone know it was having a good time. It was all dressed up, and that dance was 'really some place to go.'"[11] At a Moten dance, one of George E. Lee's musicians, and brother of Moten bandsman Woodie Walder, was praised for his dance prowess: "tall and immaculate Herman Walder... who is always politely suave and who dances with ease and grace."[12]

In its heyday the Moten band made local tours in Missouri and Oklahoma, and longer junkets into the South or East. In Kansas City they played nightly at white dance halls and amusement parks, and then for African-Americans on their nights off, usually Mondays, and on special occasions, such as national holidays, Labor Day music festivals, Thanksgiving and Christmas dances, and so forth. What was remarkable was that they maintained both their popularity among white audiences and their close relationship with Black Kansas Citians.

In Kansas City, Missouri, in 1930, more than twenty thousand African-American residents—Black Kansas Citians between the ages of fifteen and forty-four—were potential dancers[13] at the dawn of the swing era.[14] Admittedly most stayed home or worked at night or lacked the money for admission, but still Black swing-era dancers and fans often numbered as many as eight to fifteen hundred at the musicians' balls and welcome home dances for touring bands. Social clubs frequently sponsored dances as well, for pure enjoyment as well as for community causes, and other groups also held dances for charities. Like Harlem or Chicago's South Side, Kansas City's east side was without doubt one of the dance meccas in Afro-America, and it had many bands and musicians to cater to the needs of the fans.

On the first Sunday night of 1930, Moten's band performed at Labor Temple from nine until one. "I want to open the New Year right," he told the *Call* readers. "I've got some numbers to turn on for the folks Sunday night that will surprise them. Come, ready for a good time."[15] As evidence of the band's popularity, the week before about fifteen hundred fans—mainly, if not entirely, African-Americans—"stormed Paseo Hall...to hear a dance contest between two of Kansas City's best known and best liked orchestras." Motenites battled George E. Lee's band, and while "there was no decision given... everyone seemed to have a good time."[16]

At a farewell dance before leaving for a tour, Moten once again expressed his desire to please his fans. He proposed to play all requests from the audience. "We won't be back for a long time," Bennie said, "and we want to leave a good taste in the mouths of the hundreds of friends we have here." They would begin early and continue "until the last person is satisfied." Ever the diplomat, he thanked his Kansas City friends, promising, "we'll be back after a while, working all the time to be better than ever, to seek their favor again."[17]

Moten not only gratified, but also challenged his audiences. Shortly before a Labor Temple dance, the bandleader warned: "Don't come to this dance unless you are prepared to reel and rock to some of the hottest music this town has ever heard. The band is hitting on all six and is ready to bring some real entertainment to the lovers of the dance. It will be a stomp frolic from midnight to the crack of day."[18] His style of banter suggests that the give and take between bands and dancers was at the heart of their celebrations, like the verbal sparring between different bandleaders. The popularity of Moten and his band members with their Kansas City fans was evident at their homecoming dances when they returned from road trips. At Paseo Hall in winter 1932, about thirteen hundred "rabid fans, starved since last September for the brand of syncopation which the Moten band has made famous stormed the hall as a part of the welcoming ceremony." They were so entranced that for much of the dance, they "simply stood around the platform watching the men in the orchestra go through the old familiar motions." The onlookers chided band members, "I thought you birds would never get back from out East!"[19]

Their joy was unbounded. It did not stop with the "gay exchange of conversation.... Young chaps ... gave way to the inner spirit and did impromptu tap steps as they milled about the edges of the floor," and "Girls, on the way out to dance, pirouetted a bit before settling down in their partners' arms." Bennie Moten summed it up when he entered, looked around, and exclaimed, "The East is all right, but heck—Kansas City is home!"[20]

Jimmy Rushing thought it was the rhythm of the band that was so distinctive, and this may have been what enchanted listeners. Rushing recalled, "When I first joined the Moten band ... I couldn't get with that beat at first." The Motenites' "accent was on the first and the third although they played four. It sounded almost like a train coming." Rushing was ambivalent at first: "I liked that rhythm, but I didn't did [dig?] it too good." After a month he was able to get used to it. Moten's rhythm was irresistible and captivating: "You couldn't get away from it. It had such a terrific beat. You couldn't move from it." The singer "used to see people bouncing to it. I've been on that beat ever since, and now I can't get with the other." In his hometown it was different: "The beat was more even. And New Orleans was more or less even when they used a four." Eight years later the singer insisted, "It's the same beat that Basie has today."[21]

The popular bandleader delighted his fans with innovations such as Break O' Day Frolics, dances that started around or after midnight and lasted until dawn. He introduced this custom and often played them when he was in town.[22] Bill Little was the promoter, and admission was a modest fifty cents at the Labor Temple frolic in spring 1930.[23] These "colored dances, beginning after midnight, have become an institution eagerly looked forward to and catering to constantly increasing numbers." The following year, 1931, his fans asked that he "resurrect these after-midnight dances" following a lengthy cross-country tour. Perhaps this custom marked the origins of "one o'clock jump," the phenomenon that not only epitomized the high point of the dance, but became Basie's theme song.[24]

Summers were always uncomfortably hot and humid in Kansas, and in Kansas City, black entertainment spots installed cooling systems, as Paseo Hall did in 1930. It also redecorated the famous dance hall, surrounding the orchestra pit with latticework, extending rose-entwined trellises from the sidelights to the walls, to give the effect of a rose arbor, and strategically placing palm fronds and plants around the hall. The idea was to create a cool garden atmosphere to refresh Kansas City celebrants out for a night on the town. Even the upstairs balcony was painted "Ginger Blue," and tables and chairs were added to "give it the appearance of a roof night club."[25] This refurbishing took place in time for the battle between the Duke Ellington and George E. Lee bands.[26] The same week Moten's band performed at the new Paseo, giving a Break O' Day dance from 12:30 a.m. to dawn.[27]

At summer's end, in 1930, Paseo Hall was the site of a "Monster Labor Day Celebration [and] Musicians' Ball and Battle of Bands," when "eight crack bands, the cream of Greater Kansas City's orchestras" performed in competition with one another. Grant Moore's band members from Detroit were out-of-town guests. Moten, Page's Blue Devils, Jasper Allen's Famous Casa Loma Orchestra, Andy Kirk's Clouds of Joy, and Julius Banks and the Red Devils were scheduled to regale dancers from 8:00 p.m. until 2:00 a.m. These and other local bands battled early in May and on Labor Day every year in the early 1930s. Such spectacles were often benefits for the musicians' union.[28]

A parade invariably preceded the celebration, advertising the special event and showcasing the bands that would perform that night for nearly two thousand patrons. In 1930, Wilkins reported, "I went to the parade and I got an eyeful. I had the good fortune to see all the musicians in action. I mean walking action." Their impact was noteworthy. "One little girl, who had been accustomed to seeing Bennie, Harlan [Leonard], Rushing and Bassey [*sic*] in automobiles, said, 'Well, you could have fooled me. I didn't know those men could walk.'" At the dance, Moten's band included a new cornet player, Paul Webster, and tenor saxophonist, Ben Webster (no relation) [29]

The musicians' balls were quite gala affairs, and the excitement of anticipation always preceded the actual dance. One September evening "cars were parked double all along the Paseo, filled with people, white and colored, who wanted to hear the bands in action." On this very special occasion, "The green light at the corner held its meaning but lost its effect. It said 'go,' but the music said 'stop,' and the passersby obeyed the commands of the tantalizing musical strains which poured through the windows." Reporter Wilkins waxed ecstatic when he described the effect of Moten's band: "He kept the flame of joy glowing in the hearts and feet of those who danced and listened." The revelers did not always dance, "many choosing instead to watch the antics of Bus and Rushing."[30]

Occasionally members of the crowd were carried away with excitement. At the Labor Temple in spring 1932, "In the eyes of the spectators," Wilkins noted, "there were several happenings ranking on a par with the large attendance and the truly excellent music." "These extracurricular divertissements" included "two fist fights, the turning off of the lights for about five minutes at 1 am, the fainting of a woman in the balcony, and the appearance of the winner of a recently conducted bathing beauty contest." Fans continued to dance during the blackout, and one "old boy" on the dance floor was heard to murmur, "What a break for me, baby." That night, dance fans "got their money's worth and more."[31]

The band's ascent peaked when it was scheduled for a downtown Kansas City engagement at the Mainstreet, a member of the RKO circuit, early in 1931. It performed for a vaudeville act. In addition to being lucrative, the job meant they had broken into the big-time white circuit, which boded well for the future. The Motenites in early 1931 were: Bennie Moten, piano; William Basie, arranger;

James Rushing, entertainer and vocalist; Buster Moten, director and accordion; Harlan Leonard, Jack Washington, Woodie Walder, reeds; Willie Washington, drums; Leroy Berry, banjo; Edward Lewis, Booker Washington, trumpets; Thamon Hayes, trombone; Edward Durham, arranger, trombone, and guitar; Vernon Page, sousaphone.[32]

Oran "Hot Lips" Page joined in 1931 and enlarged and enhanced the brass section. In the spring, the *Call* observed that "He was a sensation on Bennie's recent eastern tour" and a hit with local fans. His comedy work as well as his cornet playing were praised. The band now numbered fifteen.[33]

Moten increased his audience and delighted his fans with radio broadcasts on WDAF. One Friday evening in 1930, a few weeks before Thanksgiving, the band presented a special dance program for an hour and a half. Their repertoire included "Passin' the Time with Me," "Dinah," "Go Home and Tell Your Momma," "Jeanette," "Somebody Stole My Gal," "The Count," and "Zella Mae."[34]

Because of the growing popularity of Harlem jazz, after an Eastern tour, the Moten orchestra performed at "A Night in Harlem," a Kansas City cabaret party possessing "all the essential details of a true cabaret, down to the tables on the edge of the dance floor, and dancing and singing entertainers." Balloons, confetti, "several paid entertainers," and "some fancy tap dancers, a songbird or two," promised to recreate the atmosphere that showcased Harlem jazz. "Just how the Harlem atmosphere is going to be transplanted to Paseo hall is a secret that has not yet been divulged," the *Call* teased.[35]

Moten also innovated by combining Break O' Day and "flashlights only illumination" dances. The *Call* felt obligated to explain this new affair: "A flashlight dance, *mes enfants,* is a dance where the only illumination in the hall is the light cast from flashlights carried by the dancers." It promised "good fun." The custom was new to Kansas City, but was reportedly enjoyed in other areas of the U.S.[36]

Moten combined another innovation with the Break O' Day revelry—the pajama dance, where dancers wore colorful sleepwear. Because the dance had been rained out the Saturday before, the rescheduled event was to be "larger and better." After all, "Women love pajamas. A lot of them brought special ones for the dance, and by Jimmy, they are going to make a chance to wear them!" The *Call* promised, "They will be at the ball in all their glory and don't think they won't." Of course they turned out in full force.[37]

Moten's band also introduced the Lindy Hop to Kansas City dance folk. Woodie Walder, Moten's clarinetist and Herman's brother, demonstrated how, in the Lindy "the dancers part, whirl around, and get together again somehow."[38] Its name was both a commentary on and a kind of satire of Lindbergh's recent solo flight across the Atlantic. Walder was "some great shakes when it comes to waggling his feet," and his partner was "a local artist of enviable reputation in the dance." Another couple also demonstrated the new fad, the woman having learned it at the Savoy Ballroom in New York City.[39] The dance was again displayed at a Saturday night Break O' Day dance later in 1931, at Paseo Hall. "This dance," Wilkins explained, "has also been called 'The Collegiate,' and has swept the east by frenzy."[40]

The very language and images of Moten's advertisements underlined his close connections with down-home as well as elite Kansas Citians. In one ad he boasted how he would present "some numbers to turn on for the folks Sunday night."[41] Another depicted a rather large porker and the statements "you will cut an awful hog if you don't attend the Beau Brummell big Tent Friday" and "There ain't gonna be no flies on this party!" This latter saying was taken up in Oran Page's song years later, "Ain't No Flies on Me."[42]

Moten was a businessman with a strong sense of public service, and, as he was concerned with the welfare of the less fortunate, he made certain to contribute to local charities. The band performed at an Elks Annual Charity Dance around Christmas 1930, and proceeds went to helping five hundred needy families. This was the eighth year the fraternal organization had sponsored an event to raise money to give food baskets to the poor. Moten promised "some especially hot numbers" for this charity dance. "This year," the *Call* reported, acknowledging the Depression's seriousness, "the need is even greater."[43]

Like the Blue Devils, the Moten band performed for the inmates of the Jackson County Home. Guest artists—a soloist and pianist— were also featured. Such an affair had been arranged the previous summer, as well. The band members and entertainers were served dinner, "after which they engaged in games."[44] The day before the general election in November 1932, the Moten band was one of the nine outfits scheduled to perform at a pre-election festival for unemployment relief and charity.[45] In fact, typically the musicians' union balls were for the benefit of the musicians' union if not for some other charity.

In summer 1930, the band's good fortune was highlighted in the *Call* when it announced a Moten all-night farewell dance at Paseo Hall. They were heading for Oklahoma City and then on to Hollywood. It just so happened that while "playing at Fairyland this summer Bennie's music caught the ear of a high mogul of movie land and it is rumored that they will be offered a contract." If this had happened, Moten would have preceded Duke Ellington and Cab Calloway, both of whom went to Hollywood with their bands to appear in films a few years later.[47] The Hollywood contract appears to have fallen through, however, because late the next month the Motenites played at a homecoming dance and a Grand Halloween Ball. No mention was made of California.[48] Each time the band left town, nonetheless, they held a farewell dance and, upon their return, a homecoming dance, and their exploits in the East or South were celebrated by their fans and throughout the region.[49]

The band recorded a number of hits in the 1920s, and late in 1930 the tedium of the process was detailed for the *Call*. "Bennie and his men spent five hours on one number alone and three and four hours on several others." Placement of mikes, equalization of volume, and, of course, producing a good version of a song were crucial to an acceptable recording. Victor Records was quite confident of Moten by this time, and it recorded, among other selections, "New Moten Stomp," "Somebody Stole My Gal," "High and Dry," "When I'm Alone," and "Jeanette." Rushing sang on "Liza Lee," "Now That I Need You, You're Gone," "When I'm Alone," "Jeanette," and "Baby Mine"—at most two, and possibly only a single blues number in the group. Popular songs along with originals by Basie, Durham, and Moten, such as "Zella Mae," by Basie and Durham in honor of Bennie's daughter, "Oh! Eddie," "Elsie," and "Marjorie," figured in the mix.[50]

Early in 1932 the Motenites went on a two-month tour to perform in "all the larger cities in the east" as they had once before, and the band "received warm welcomes wherever it went." Band members promised "to keep close touch with the home town dancing public by regular correspondence" with the *Call* journalists. Thanks to these letters and the columns of Earl Wilkins, we have some details of the band's travels.[51]

◆ ◆ ◆

Their new prosperity was evident when they purchased a bus, thus "eliminating the necessity for using [the bandsmen's] cars." Private autos worked on shorter trips, but for a journey to the East Coast, a bus permitted band members to travel all together. "And the bus will make for convenience as well," the *Call* contended.[52] The day after a Monday night farewell attended by twelve hundred fans at Paseo Hall, the Motenites gathered in front of Moten and Hayes' Music Shop on Eighteenth Street where they said their good-byes. With driver Lyman Darden at the wheel, they headed for Columbia, Missouri, for a Tuesday dance and left immediately afterwards for a St. Louis performance the next night.[53]

Trombonist Thamon Hayes penned several letters describing the tour. About one hundred white students from the University of Missouri, an institution that barred African-Americans, attended the Columbia date. As Wilkins of the *Call* observed rather wryly, "Those students can't learn anything about young colored people because Negroes are barred from the state university, but they learned plenty about hot jazz from colored artists that night—dog bite 'em!"[54]

In St. Louis, African-Americans jammed the Pythian Temple to hear Moten's orchestra. A number of white musicians attended their performance. Next the band rode to Indianapolis and played at the Madame Walker building, named after the pioneer hair stylist who became the first African-American millionaire. They were warmly welcomed at their first performance in this Midwestern city. In Dayton, Ohio, they observed local racial restrictions by performing two dances—one for whites and one for African-Americans. Here they added Oran Page to their ranks. In his *Call* column, "e.w.w." pointed out, "for the consolation of wives of the orchestra men who may read this," that the band members spent the night in the local YMCA.[55]

At the next performance, in the famous Greystone Ballroom in Cincinnati, they played opposite the Edward Collegians. Four thousand fans attended, and the two bands also broadcast over the radio. The management invited them to return, a sign of their sure success, and they continued on their journey, stopping in Zanesville, Ohio, and Lexington and Louisville, Kentucky. If this schedule appears irregular, it was because they had to set up bookings as they went. Sometimes these dances were rough affairs. In Louisville, "there was many a fight, with plenty of whiskey bottles in evidence and the who-struck-who which follows too free imbibing." The Moten bandsmen were prepared for such outbreaks.[56]

The Motenites were heading for the big time. Darden, the driver, was "wrestling with that bus like a veteran" and sported a new uniform with "Bennie Moten" written on the cap and across his chest. Making the two-hundred-mile trip from Zanesville, Ohio, to Fairmount, West Virginia, over "a mountainous road with a flock of sharp curves and yawning valleys waiting beneath [was enough] to make everybody nervous."[57] A further detail reminded Moten's fans of the sacrifice involved in a road life: "The men are lonesome for their wives." With tongue in cheek, Wilkins offered to console the spouses and to allow them to weep on his shoulders as they read the letters sent by band members.[58]

From Fairmount, where they performed at the local armory, they traveled to Pittsburgh and Harrisburg, Pennsylvania, and Washington, D.C. Over the next week only two letters arrived, and they described the band's performance in "the most beautiful hall in America owned by Negroes, the Masonic hall." The crowd was hard to please, but the band eventually succeeded. The Motenites went sightseeing to the Washington Monument and Howard University and proclaimed D.C. one of the most beautiful cities they had seen. In Wilmington, Delaware, they broadcast over the air and played requests that listeners made over the phone and by wire. Here the Motenites encountered the new dance, the Lindy Hop.[59]

Philadelphia's Pearl Theatre, where they followed the famous Fletcher Henderson Orchestra, was the next stop. The Motenites were billed as "The Hottest Band this Side of Hades." Featured on the stage, they played two shows a day for two weeks. The *Call* reported that "The hades idea was carried out even to the decoration of the music racks with little devils." Fans were lined up for a block to get tickets, and the theater's aisles were packed with listeners. The Pearl's owner claimed that "Bennie's orchestra was the best that had ever played the theater." During this stint, Basie and Durham wrote and introduced "Moten Swing," although Bennie and Buster copyrighted the instrumental.[60] Harlem's Lafayette Theater and Savoy Ballroom were next, and band members felt that this was indeed the big time at last.

Kansas City's most famous band hit New York City on Easter Monday, the very week that McKinney's Cotton Pickers played at Paseo Hall. The Moten outfit was touted as "something new in the line of [a] dance orchestra...something so different from the ordinary run of outside combination that this town...has suddenly set up to take notice." They came quietly into town to perform at the Lafayette Theater, one of Harlem's oldest spots, in *Rhythm Bound,* an Irving Miller production. After hearing the band in Philadelphia, Irving and his brother, Flournoy, two show business veterans, insisted, "They are greater than Duke Ellington's Orchestra."[61]

Before long, Harlemites were asking "Who is this Bennie Moten?" The band was said to lack a Cab Calloway or Sonny Greer "to give it personality," but "notwithstanding this, there is something about the alternating soft harmony and crashing resonances which they specialize in that holds the listener in a trance." Their rendition of "Rocking Chair," one of Rushing's specialties, was described as "about the best thing heard in these parts." Irving Miller claimed that "Bennie's band was one of the best that ever played the Lafayette."[62]

Moten's band then played at the Savoy, "home of the happy feet," in Harlem, opposite two other bands. They performed for a weekend at this dance palace when they visited the Empire City again in the fall of 1931. They were also offered a position where "one of the oldest and most established orchestras in the city" held forth. It is not clear which club this was, or why the band did not accept the offer.[63]

Band members went sightseeing in the Big Apple and acquired greater appreciation of the variety in the nation's urban areas and of the complexity and depth of African-American culture. During their stay in New York City, they could hear Horace Henderson and his band at the Rockland Palace and Jelly Roll Morton at the Checker Club.[64] Given their growing reputation as a new jazz band, they also got a chance to interact with Harlemites. Earl Wilkins wrote, "the band while in New York took plenty of strolls up and down Seventh Avenue so that Harlem could get a good look at the tump-tumpers from Kansas City." The next day they went to Baltimore for another Miller production.[65]

◆ ◆ ◆

When they toured in autumn that year, they visited East Coast cities in Pullman buses with leading swing bands and performed against them in music battles. Their adversaries were Blanche Calloway and her Jazz Boys (Blanche was Cab's sister; both were from Baltimore), Chick Webb and His Chicks from the Savoy, Johnson's Happy Pals from Richmond, Virginia, and Zack Whyte and his Beau Brummells out of Cincinnati. In effect, "the Savoy Ballroom's mammoth caravan of jazz" was a touring jazz festival a full fifteen years before Norman Granz's more famous program, *Jazz at the Philharmonic*.[66] Having arrived in the big time, they toured in the company of the bands of Duke Ellington, Noble Sissle, Blanche Calloway, and Fletcher Henderson when they broadcast over WJSV out of Mt. Vernon Hills, Virginia.[67]

Of course, after these tours, band members fully understood that there's no place like Kansas City, and on returning home, they particularly enjoyed the welcoming dances. Moten's band played one in early May, but stayed for only one night before leaving for Sioux City for a week's engagement. May 18 was their "first stomp for the home folks" in Kansas City at Paseo Hall in 1931. The bandleader told *Call* readers that they "were anxious to do our stuff at old Paseo hall." He added, "You can say that far from having lost our stroke, we have added a lot of new touches which we think the folks will like." He warned his fans, "Stand by for a rip-snorting homecoming party!" After this Monday night dance for African-Americans, they spent the summer of 1931 playing at Fairyland—one of the city's amusement parks—for whites.[68]

While the Motenites, like the Blue Devils and other territorial bands, played for African-Americans, this was often on Monday nights, on holidays, and on special occasions promoted by various social clubs. Mondays were their nights off from the whites' amusement parks and ballrooms. These bands were among the first swing orchestras in the U.S. who were adept at pleasing different audiences—whites as well as Blacks. African-American audiences liked blues along with popular songs, but the only blues number that whites liked was the "St. Louis Blues."[69]

Whites danced differently from African-Americans, according to the *Call*. Moten's band performed at Fairyland one summer evening "for a floor full of wiggling bobbing white dancers out for a big Saturday night." The band drew very large crowds to this amusement park, and when they began to play, the concession stands were deserted and the dance floor filled. "Dancers weaved in next to the platform calling greetings to the band and asking for special numbers; others hopped up and down and skittered about in a vain but admirable attempt to fit Nordic stiffness to jungle rhythm." When the music stopped at midnight, the dancers clamored for more. The Motenites withdrew, went to Paseo Hall, and performed for African-American dancers, whose movement, Earl Wilkins confessed, "was much easier on the eyes and nerves."[70]

In the 1930s, Kansas City bands performed for African-Americans at Labor Day, Halloween, and Thanksgiving dances, often battling one another in marathons that lasted until dawn. The Motenites and McKinney's Cotton Pickers were billed as the "Greatest Band Battle Yet Staged" and a "Fight to [the] Finish." Both leaders anticipated victory. Moten explained that, before their East Coast tour, the band members had lacked confidence in their abilities, but after their reception in New York City, they felt ready to handle a band with a reputation like McKinney's.[71]

Then Moten's band faced off against Andy Kirk's at the Annual Labor Day Musicians' Ball at Paseo Hall. Eight bands were supposed to participate, performing all night long, but "the real fireworks won't get under way until after midnight," when Kirk and Moten's outfits would take the stand. Competition between the two was especially fierce because they played at rival Kansas City amusement parks that summer.[72]

Nineteen thirty-two was the last good year for the territorial bands. The Blue Devils struggled under one manager and then another, as we have seen, and even Moten's outfit evolved as they acquired new members. Some personnel changes were perhaps reflected in the headline "Bennie Moten Not to Break Up Band" early in the year. Rumors about this came out of Chicago, but the Kansas City musicians' union denied the report.[73]

Moten did make some rather important changes that winter, and when he came to Kansas City after several months in the East and Midwest, he was asked about the new developments. He responded that the personnel changes constituted "a move for the better. It is my intention to keep ever striving for greater and greater perfection." He explained, "Only by following that course can I keep faith with the hundreds of friends this band has—friends who expect us to keep going up the ladder of national recognition."[74]

The new members included some Blue Devils that Durham "stole"—his and Basie's terminology. The old ones who stayed were Moten and his nephew, Bus, Basie, Rushing, Durham, Oran Page, and Buster Berry (banjo). The newcomers were Ben Webster, the saxophonist and former pianist and violinist; Eddie Barefield, a reedman originally from Iowa and a boyhood friend of Snake Whyte who was picked up in Chicago; Walter Page, just from the Blue Devils; Ed Crumbly, trombone; Joe Keyes and Joe Smith, cornets; and Willie "Mack" Washington, drums.[75]

Ed Lewis, Woodie Walder, and Thamon Hayes, the mainstays of the old Moten band, departed. Hayes was, in fact, Moten's manager for a number of years, and he was also his business partner, as they owned a music shop on Eighteenth Street. In February 1932, Hayes announced that he was no longer associated with Moten and would form his own band. He took five Motenites with him: Ed Lewis and Booker Washington, trumpets; Vernon Page, sousaphone and bass violin; and Woodie Walder and Harlan Leonard, saxophones. From George Lee's band he recruited Samuel "Baby" Lovett, drums; Jesse Stone, piano and arranger; and Richard Smith, trumpet. He intended to have an orchestra of twelve topnotch musicians.[76]

◆ ◆ ◆

The new Moten band made a tour in fall 1932 and performed in West Virginia at a Cotillion Club dance before arriving in New Jersey a few weeks later to make their most famous recordings.[77] These records heralded the start of the swing era as much as anything by Ellington or Calloway. "Moten Swing" became an anthem, but it was a swing version and takeoff of the popular song "You're Driving Me Crazy." Then there was "Toby," named after TOBA, the Theater Owners' Booking Association (or "Tough on Black Acts" and less-quotable variations on this), the Black vaudeville circuit known familiarly as "Toby." Other recordings included "Prince of Wails," celebrating the visit of English royalty in 1924, and "Lafayette," after the Harlem theater where they performed.[78]

When they played "Moten Swing" at the Pearl Theatre in Philadelphia, the audience went wild, demanding seven encores! The theater management liked it so much, they said if the clamor continued, they would open all the doors to let everyone come in and hear the band. This is just how popular "Moten Swing" was when introduced, Durham recalled. He said the public knew there was something different about this band and this song.[79]

◆ ◆ ◆

The former Blue Devils—Durham, Basie, Rushing, and both Pages—made the difference. Durham and Basie were highly talented songwriters and arrangers, one of the most successful swing duos in the history of jazz; Oran Page was a soloist par excellence; Rushing sang popular songs as much as, or more than, he sang blues; Walter Page's bass playing was central to the rhythm section of the Moten, and later the Basie, sound. In their own way, these musicians, along with Barefield and Webster and the more famous East Coast composers and arrangers, charted the development of swing and the music's future.

The personnel at the end of 1932 were Bus Moten, director and accordion; Rushing, vocalist; Dan Minor, trombone; Basie, piano; Jack Washington, saxophone and later a Basie stalwart; Willie "Mack" Washington, drums; Durham on trombone, guitar, and occasionally banjo; Webster and Barefield, saxophones; Joe Keyes, saxophone; Durward Stewart and Oran Page, trumpets; Walter Page, and, of course, Bennie Moten. For various reasons, Moten did not keep these band members, except for Durham, for much longer. Basie emerged as a leader in his own right, and so did Oran Page, while Barefield and Webster went on to other bands.

Upon returning to their hometown around Christmas in 1932, Moten announced that the band "has learned many things during its sojourn in the east." Moten was one of those cosmopolites who introduced East Coast styles and fads to the Midwest, and he promised that "All the latest numbers which are the rage out East will be played for local fans, giving them a taste of the metropolitan atmosphere right in their own back yard."[80] Having taken their distinctive sound to the East, it was only appropriate that band members bring back the latest songs, dances, and dress styles of that region.

At the outset of the swing era, Kansas City stayed abreast of new developments in the night-club business by opening its own venues, the Castle late in 1932, then the Cherry Blossom, which replaced the Eblon Theatre in 1933, and then Piney Brown's Sunset.[81] "Lavishly decorated," the Castle was formerly the Dreamland, and was remodeled "along the same lines of the smart night clubs in eastern cities." The management promised "Excellent food at moderate prices.... Hot music, a great floor show, good eats and [that] every other item has been considered in order to give the patrons real entertainment." The Castle opened at 8:30 p.m., and "frollicking" lasted until dawn. Thamon Hayes's band was featured opening night. The newly refurbished Cherry Blossom near Eighteenth and Vine was decorated with a "Japanese god" and "Japanese dragons and monsters."[82]

Eddie Durham shed some light on the atmosphere in such places. He saw the notorious gangster Pretty Boy Floyd at the Cherry Blossom, and later at a nearby pool hall, a few days before he was killed. Gangsters ran Kansas City, and fugitives could count on the police to warn them: "You better get out of here, the police [federal agents] are looking for you!"[83] Despite these underworld connections, both Buster Smith and Durham maintained that the gangsters never bothered the musicians, who minded their own business. Smith went so far as to claim that the gangster was the musician's best friend. "They give you a job, and something to eat, and work regular. We didn't know nothing about their business, they didn't know nothing about ours, all they want us to do is play the music, and keep the crowd happy."[84] In his way, he was alluding to the fact that the underworld supported them when the universities and respectable world shunned them. As Durham explained, the gangsters protected the musicians, and not just them: "Those gangsters would always treat everybody right. If you touched a musician, or any of the girls, you'd go out on your head. Nobody ever harassed musicians."

Gangsters and racketeers provided places different from the Cherry Blossom, such as the Sunset, the Yellow Front, and Piney Brown's, where illegal whiskey flowed and gambling was one of the main items in the back rooms, while risqué shows and jam sessions reigned in the main room. Ellis Burton, of the Yellow Front, "was the kind of guy that just liked musicians, and he had music round the clock." He was a bootlegger, "and never looked a man in the eye. He always had his hat down so that he's looking at your lips and nose...and you can't see in his eyes." Some men were bothering Sam Price, and Burton told them, "If you interfere with Sammy Price anymore, forget those favors I used to do for you." Price's problems went away.[85]

Piney Brown, his associate Felix Payne, and Ellis Burton "were like godfathers actually for most musicians." Count Basie saw Piney as "sort of a gentleman about town" who "was good to all musicians." Reedman Eddie Barefield recalled, "Piney was like a patron saint to all musicians. He used to take care of them."[86] These were places where musicians congregated and enjoyed themselves after their jobs at the Cherry Blossom and elsewhere. Durham recalled, "Kansas City bands come off the stage at 8:00 and 9:00 in the morning for people to go to work. And that's the way it was all night long, because they had liquor stores that stayed open 24 hours in Kansas City."[87] Then, "after all the jobs was over, all the musicians would meet right on 18th and Vine, and the meeting place was right in the middle of the street." The street was the crossroads that are so significant in African, Caribbean, and Southern religion and folklore.

Durham got off from work at some nightspot around 2:00 or 3:00

or 4:00 a.m., and "I'd go down to Piney Brown's or down there where Joe Turner was bartending. When I'd walk in, I'd have my guitar throwed around my neck."[88] Then he would "go there and I'd jump up on the stage there and sit up on the bar and get the guitar, and Joe Turner would wipe his hands, and he'd come there and he'd sing, see, and Joe Turner would sing and Jo Jones would have his snare drum, he'd come in—no, with his sock cymbal, and it'd be about three of us. And that was another job. We used to work there until about 7:00 the next morning."[89]

◆ ◆ ◆

When they once again left Kansas City, touring the South in winter 1933, Motenites played four venues in Memphis and performed in Vicksburg, Shreveport, and Birmingham. (In fact, Moten's theme song, "South," became a swing standard and was written by trombonist Thamon Hayes and Bennie Moten.) Around this time, Moten once again added "quite a few new faces" among the familiar ones; besides Bennie and Buster and Basie, Rushing, Durham, both Pages, Jack Washington, Dan Minor, and Willie "Mack" Washington, the band included E. Ewing, banjo, Earl Bostic, and Herschel Evans, saxophones. Aside from the new banjoist, the change was mainly among the saxophonists.[90] By October, Joe Smith returned, but all others were gone except the Pages, Rushing, Washington, and Durham—eight had left.[91]

The Depression affected musicians as much as other workers, and as it worsened, band members became increasingly desperate. Barefield maintained that just before the 1932 recordings they were stranded in Columbus, Ohio. "We were stranded all over the U.S.," Barefield stated, "we were stranded in Zanesville, we were stranded in Columbus, Ohio, we were stranded in Cincinnati." "Everywhere this band—we had a lot of fun but we never really made any money." "Sometimes the guys would run off with the money after the intermission and leave us." Then they went to the Pearl Theatre in Philadelphia, and "we were stranded in Philadelphia."[92]

On arriving at the Pearl Theatre, they felt "this is it"—the big time—but a debtor attached Moten's profits, and they were des-

perate again. Barefield pawned his clarinet and a suit to get by. A
benefactor showed up with a "big ol' raggedy bus" that took them
to Camden, New Jersey. He also provided a rabbit stew with bread
(Barefield suspected it was an alley cat), and thus fortified, they went
into the recording studio.[93]

The Motenites faced other serious problems. There were only so
many night clubs and theaters to maintain big bands, especially outside of the largest cities like New York and Chicago. It is well known
that Kansas City bands continued to prosper under the Pendergast
machine, but beneath the folklore some significant changes were
taking place. In his autobiography, Basie related how "our financial
situation got so bad that we almost had to give up the bus" in 1932.
At one point, when jobs were scarce, and "since the band wasn't really working steady, some of the guys went out on other gigs from
time to time."[94] The Blue Devils also suffered in 1932—a prelude
to what happened to them the next year. Though it is commonly
thought that Basie took over the Moten band after Moten died in
1935, the actual story is somewhat different. There was a split between the Moten and Basie factions some time before his death.

In early autumn 1933, Moten and his band reached a decisive
turning point, according to the *Chicago Defender*. "The story,
signed by Oran Page, says Moten has been dropped and the name of
the band changed to 'Count Basie and His Orchestra.'" When the
Defender's representative attempted to contact Moten, they learned
that he was out of town. The band had a job at the Cherry Blossom
performing for a floor show featuring Rufus and Billie White.[95]
Lester Young recalled that "Moten was stranded, too, and all
the men put him down." Basie squabbled with the bandleader, "so
Count cut out and took over most of the band while Bennie Moten
and George Lee formed another group." Young went with this
contingent.

As we shall see, the Basie band members played local clubs and
dances and traveled about the South in 1933 and for the next few
years. Moten also had to adapt to the changing music scene, and he
did this by joining forces with George E. Lee. In spring 1934 the
new combination, known as Moten and Lee's Harlemites, opened
the show at the Labor Temple ball. A Harlem night club floor show,

M.C.'d by Maceo Birch—a dancer and local pharmacist interested in show business, and later a manager for the Basie band—was featured after the Moten-Lee band. Count Basie's orchestra also performed at this ball, indicating that the New Jersey musician had reached a level equal to that of other Kansas City bandleaders. Representatives from several labor organizations were slated to speak, suggesting that in the darkness of the Great Depression even entertainment affairs had some very sober moments.[96]

Once a Blue Devil

The success of the Basie band is often attributed to good management or the sterling musicianship of its members, and while these factors no doubt played a role, so did the practical and business experience of the bandsmen. That is, as former Blue Devils and Motenites, and as members of numerous other territorial bands, they had acquired a world of experience that they drew upon when they became Basie-ites. Histories of jazz rarely discuss such intangibles as their shared opposition to racism and segregation, and their belief that they were at least the equals of whites in terms of certain core values. Their strong sense of professionalism and loyalty to the profession was another notable feature. Together, all these characteristics amounted to a distinctive legacy that swing-era musicians cherished and sustained. Besides excellent musicianship, this legacy entailed a preference for the blues and identification with the values of down-home people. In this latter respect, they differed somewhat from Ellington and Calloway, with their formal dress and high-toned affairs.

Often this legacy surfaced in the names of bands attempting to sustain the spirit of the Oklahoma City band. Ernest Williams and his Thirteen Original Blue Devils performed at a jamboree of music sponsored by the Musicians' Protective Union in May 1934. This probably was not Buster Smith, Lester Young, and the others whose band was destroyed by a series of disasters, but rather represented Williams's attempt to resurrect the band. Pianist and founder Willie

Lewis led Wee Willie's Memphis Blue Devils at the time he died in Bismarck, North Dakota in 1934.[1] In St. Louis, Eddie Randalls started a Blue Devils band in which the young Miles Davis played in his teens.[2] In 1935, when Basie reorganized the band at the Reno Club, he operated in the same spirit and "tried to bring some Blue Devils in there."[3]

Basie was the only Blue Devil, Moten band member, or musician from his orchestra to produce a detailed account of these years—aside from the autobiography *Night People,* by his sideman, trombonist Dicky Wells. Others' reminiscences were to be found in interviews in jazz magazines or deposited in archives, but often they were not as rich as Basie's. This pianist's evolution as a major swing bandleader, a rival of Ellington, Calloway, and Lunceford, was gradual—taking place over a period of more than a decade.

Born in Red Bank, New Jersey, in 1904, Basie lived in Harlem before he went to the Midwest, and in New York he learned from, among others, the legendary Harlem stride pianists. Fats Waller took Basie under his wing, introduced him to the organ, gave him clues on how to play for silent films, comped with him, and let his disciple sit in for him while he completed his pinochle game with Lincoln Theater stagehands.[4] Nonetheless, when he came to Tulsa, Oklahoma, as an accompanist for Gonzell White and her Jazz Band, he was not the musician he became. In fact, Rushing contended that he was an actor with the troupe, and that, at that time, "Basie couldn't play the blues."[5] He had to learn how to play the blues from Southwestern musicians.[6]

Yet Basie's ambition made up for what he lacked as a pianist in the late 1920s; by his own account, he was also quite a schemer. For example, though an unknown in Kansas City, he had the audacity to stroll into the Eblon Theatre on Vine Street (later the Cherry Blossom), wait for the organist to take her break, and then play the famous new and expensive ($15,000) Wicks organ.[7] He impressed the audience and rocked the joint, using ideas he had learned from Waller. The theater's owner, Homer Eblon, objected to his audacity, but liked his playing so much he hired him on the spot, replacing the current organist.[8] Basie did something similar when he heard about the organ at Jenkins's store in Kansas City around 1935. On learning that anyone could practice, he went over, sat down, started playing, "and that's how I met one of the VIPs at WHB radio station." This was also when he started broadcasting as a single.[9]

As he pointed out repeatedly in his autobiography, he was quite a conniver. At the Eblon and at Jenkins's, Basie hoped that his "auditions" would lead to something fruitful. When he first heard and befriended the Blue Devils in Tulsa in 1927, he sat in and impressed them with his playing, opening the door to joining up with them later. He did the same with Moten, first befriending Eddie Durham, to whom he presented himself as a budding composer and arranger, and convincing Moten to hire him even though the bandleader already had two pianists—himself and his nephew, Bus.

Basie's account of the Blue Devils in his autobiography is significant for a number of reasons. This band served as the model for his own combos, and its members predominated in the first Basie Orchestra. Unfortunately for Oklahoma City and the history of jazz, the pianist from Red Bank is invariably portrayed as a Kansas City composer and musician rather than as an Oklahoman. He starts his life story in Tulsa, where he was awakened one midsummer morning by the Blue Devils performing from a truck and advertising that night's dance. He dressed, rushed outside to hear them, and concluded "it was the greatest thing I ever heard in my life."[10] He befriended Rushing and other members of the band and learned that Rushing's father ran a restaurant in Oklahoma City, where Basie was heading with the Gonzell White show.

He maintained that the Devils' repertoire was much more than just blues. In fact, "they were not really playing that much blues that night. But they were still bluesy." What impressed him most, however, "was that they had their own special way of playing everything." They had "some kind of signal for the next number, and they would stomp off and they were gone!" When he met them the first time, Basie felt that they were simply "something else." He heard them again when they returned to Oklahoma City and, as their pianist was sick, he was asked to sit in. As a result, he was convinced that he wanted to play in this band.[11]

He joined them a year later. He related how Walter Page telegrammed him from Paris, Texas, asking him to join them when they returned to Oklahoma City. From there they headed back to Texas. On the other hand, Walter Page and Eddie Durham claimed they got Basie out of Dallas, one hot summer night around July fourth.[12] He toured with them for several months, and his account reveals that their popularity was not limited to Oklahoma. Basie also emphasized the close relations between the Blue Devils and their Lone Star State fans. "They loved the Blue Devils all through Texas."[13] Indeed, "they were really kings all down through there, and I got to play all those towns like Dallas and Ft. Worth... San Antonio and Houston; and everywhere that band went they were well loved, and you didn't have to worry about food or where you were going to stay. Because you could always stay at somebody's house. We had a whole lot of friends down there, and it was just great, and I enjoyed everything about it.... I was a Blue Devil, and that meant everything to me. Those guys were so wonderful."[14] He was particularly impressed by "the way they felt about each other." He had no expectations regarding his salary. "It was not a salaried band anyway, and you never heard anybody squawking about finances." He learned they were a commonwealth band that shared equally—"a lot of territory bands operated like that in those days." Basie concluded, "It was just like a beautiful family."[15]

He and Jimmy Rushing became very close, a friendship that marked their professional relationship; they teamed up as pianist/bandleader and featured singer for more than two decades. "Jimmy Rushing and I got to be very good friends on the road with the Blue Devils, and we used to hit those alleys and find the joints together. Me and old Rush... we were some pair." At the time, they "just wanted to have a good time. Me playing the piano and him singing. We used to do that in every town." Decades later he maintained in an interview that "Rush" was "his main man."[16]

While he was unclear on the dates, he remembered that the Eblon Theatre had obtained a new Wicks organ about the time he first came to Kansas City—before he joined the Blue Devils. Actually the theater acquired and installed the organ in November 1928, the same month the Blue Devils played several dates in Kansas City. He recalled leaving the Devils as winter approached, around 1928/1929, complaining about the cold weather and the hardships of travel. He probably confused the sequence of events, and started performing in the Eblon after he left the Blue Devils. He then joined Moten in summer or autumn of the next year.

Such was his ambition, he even schemed his way into becoming a Motenite. He did not even know Bennie was the band's pianist when he asked about joining.[17] An obstacle to his desires and ambitions was the fact that the band already had two piano players—none other than Bennie and Ira "Bus" (for Buster) Moten, the son of Bennie's sister, Lena.[18] Basie eventually realized that "Bennie was a hell of a good piano player. He could play all kinds of stuff that I wasn't even about to try to tackle." He added, "but I have always been a conniver and began saying to myself, I got to see how I can connive my way into that band. . . . I got to play with that band." He waited for his chance.[19]

He liked the Motenites because they had class. He recalled one of the first times that he saw the Kansas City bandleader in the summer of 1929:[20] "I stood there [on the corner] early that morning talking and waiting, and pretty soon the first car, carrying Bennie Moten himself, pulled in. I never will forget that. It was a Chrysler, and Bus Moten was driving."[21] The Motenites followed in their autos, and when they stopped and got out, Kansas City fans surrounded them, and Basie had a chance to meet with Bus Moten. He heard them play the next night at Paseo Hall, and "really dug them. I came away more sold on them than ever." While he did not think they "could chop the Blue Devils . . . they had a special kind of class, and they also looked like they had it made in some ways." Unlike the Devils, who were still struggling, the Motenites were "playing in a bigger league." Moten's "big-time connections and so much political pull" accounted in large part for the band's success.[22]

While he spoke with both Motens, his befriending of Eddie Durham made the difference: "That was a real piece of good luck."[23] They hung out at east side night spots like the Yellow Front and the Subway, and when he learned the trombonist/guitarist was Moten's arranger and composer, "that was when I saw my chance to make my first move." He asked Durham if he could write out whatever he played on the piano for him, and as Durham "was always on the lookout for new things to arrange" for the band, they were soon collaborating. Basie was very deliberate and calculating. He played on the piano what he wanted each section to play, and Durham wrote it down, "and we worked up a couple of arrangements." The pianist maintained, "I knew exactly how I wanted the band to sound, and Eddie picked right up on it. So I was ready for my next move."[24]

He accompanied Durham to a rehearsal, and when the band played their two new arrangements, "both of them sparked old Bennie up a bit."[25] The bandleader invited Basie to accompany them on their next trip to Wichita because he wanted him to work on some new arrangements. Basie explained, "I went along as a staff arranger, and I couldn't have written a tune on my own or worked up a chart if my life depended on it." Durham was the key to his future success in the band; "the understanding was that I was to be working with Eddie." His main objective, to play in the band, "was what I was conniving for, and I got a chance to sit in that very first trip."[26] His expectations were not far-fetched, as it was common for bandsmen to occasionally ask friends to sit in. Earlier in the year, Basie sat in from time to time for Chauncey Downs, "the orchestra leader that I got a chance to get closest to" in Kansas City while he was learning the ropes.[27]

Bennie Moten gave Basie the opportunity to show off. He often led his band for a few songs and then circulated in the audience to discuss business. As Basie recalled, "Right away he [Bennie] would just open up playing a few numbers because he knew the people wanted to see Bennie Moten in person."[28] Then, Bennie "would turn it over to me, and most of the time he would come back on the stand just before closing."[29] Bus Moten usually played accordion. Sometimes Basie played four-handed piano with either Moten. During their stint at Fairyland, the white Kansas City amusement park where they performed in the summer, "we actually used them [two pianists] on a regular basis." For them "four handed piano...was really still two-handed piano a lot of times, because one of us would just play the left hand while the other would take the treble." Basie was familiar with the practice because he used to do the same with Fats Waller on the organ in New York, just as Bus Moten grew up playing four-handed piano with his Uncle Bennie.[30]

Basie also traveled with the band to Chicago to record for Victor in autumn 1929, and Moten let him record on "Jones Law Blues," "Small Black," "Rhumba Negro," and seven other selections. "But that was just the kind of beautiful guy he was. He was always more concerned about the band as a whole than he was about featuring himself as a performer." This was just the kind of approach that appealed to a former Blue Devil. In Bennie Moten's example he found the philosophy that guided him during his five decades as a bandleader. Jo Jones agreed. The drummer explained: "Bennie was cool. He didn't browbeat his men. Whenever Bennie wanted something done, he'd call the band together, and he'd always speak softly enough so that you had to hear him. After it was all over, he'd produce a gallon of whiskey."[31]

Basie became renowned for his subtle and easy approach to bandleading.[32]

Working as a songwriter/arranger team, Basie and Durham tried to get the Motenites to swing more. Stock arrangements of popular songs were also part of their repertoire; "of course, Eddie and I did our things on a lot of pops too."[33] Basie's limited ability to read and perform the stock arrangements hampered him somewhat. "Some of them were kind of out of my reading range, but Bennie would just take over and run them down with no trouble at all."[34] The pop songs, Moten believed, permitted them to compete with other bands and secure jobs in the large and swanky hotels usually monopolized by white orchestras.

Basie and Durham conspired to have Rushing join the band in 1929 or 1930, in order to expand their popular repertoire. "Ballads were really Jimmy's thing in those days, and that fit in so beautifully with Bennie's plans." The new recruit rarely sang blues for the band. Basie recalled, "When he and I were running together he did most of his blues singing in those alley joints he and I used to go out looking for as soon as we hit another town."[35] In fall 1930, Rushing recorded with the Moten band and can be heard on "Won't You Be My Baby?" "Oh! Eddie," and "That Too, Do."[36]

Then, Maceo Birch, Kansas City pharmacist and sporting man, became the band's promoter, and he and Bennie Moten would go out and secure jobs for the band. After they headed east to Philadelphia to perform at the Pearl Theatre in late winter of 1931, Moten asked Durham and Basie to include more instrumentals, and they realized that "they had to do something a little different from what we had been doing up to then," so the two songwriters teamed up to write "Moten Swing," which became so successful it was an anthem not only for Moten, but for the swing era. They used the popular song "You're Driving Me Crazy" "to take off from." It was a common custom for musicians to use the chord structure of a well-known piece as the basis for a new melody—"I Got Rhythm" is perhaps the basis for the greatest number of jazz compositions, such as Lester Young's "Lester Leaps In." As Basie recalled, they went down to the piano in the Pearl's basement, "and I came up with a little something that Eddie liked, and while he was working on it, I slipped out and got myself a little taste and to see if I could connect with something pretty or willing."[37]

By the time he returned, Durham was ready for the channel— the alternate theme, bridge, or B section. They played what the trombonist had already written out, "and then I just went on and tried something, and he picked up on that, and I said, 'You got it,'" and then, as Durham was wont to complain, Basie "cut back out to have another little nip because I knew he knew where it went from there."[38] "Moten Swing," in fact, "turned out to be the most famous number associated with that band." In accordance with the custom of the time, the Motens copyrighted it. As Basie observed, "We didn't know anything about royalties for something you worked up like that." Bandleaders customarily copyrighted songs written by their staff arrangers. Basie noted, "If you sold somebody a piece of music, or he hired you to write something for him, he could copyright it in his name since it was his property along with the band."[39]

Though the Moten band was a life preserver for some of the Blue Devils in 1933, it, too, experienced difficulties. The bandsmen started to argue over who should lead the band. They took a vote and voted Moten out and Basie in. In an interview in the late 1970s, Eddie Durham commented on Basie's taking over the Moten band four years after joining. Durham claimed the Moten men respected Basie's intelligence and leadership abilities, and that was why he was chosen to lead the band. According to Durham, Basie "was a good thinker.... Very clever thinker. So, when Bennie died, the band said, 'Man, this guy's got all the brains.... Ed Lewis voted him to be the bandleader. That's how he got the band." He praised the pianist: "I'll tell you one thing, Basie knows tempos good. He knows how to set tempos. . . . He's a good background man." He concluded, "He plays a little bit more than people think he plays."[40]

Basie and his band are often associated with the Cherry Blossom before the Reno Club, but they were not performing there when this swanky new resort opened at 1822 Vine Street—the former Eblon Theatre—where the crowds increased every night in spring 1933. George E. Lee and his "novelty orchestra" were featured before Basie's band moved in the fall of that year. Nightclubs like the Cherry Blossom and Reno differed from other nightspots of an earlier era in that they included a floor show as part of the entertainment.[41]

The Cherry Blossom reopened in winter 1934 under the management of Mr. and Mrs. E. D. Franks, owners of the Booker T. Washington Hotel—just across the street from their new nightspot. Under their management the club employed forty workers, including a policeman stationed inside to keep order. It featured two floor shows nightly and charged an admission of only fifteen cents, except on Sundays when it was twenty-five cents; there was no cover charge unless patrons brought their own drinks. The Count Basie Cherry Blossom Orchestra was featured that winter, and its very name suggested that the band and the club were synonymous.[42]

The Cherry Blossom lasted for about two years, and many Black social clubs held their dances and benefits in this new venue. The Deluxe Girls Club of Kansas City, Kansas, was one of them. Count Basie's orchestra performed for their cabaret party late in winter 1934. "The girls have some new ideas for a floor show which will form a large [part?] of their entertainment." One of them was the famous fan dancer, Pearl Madison; she was a regular part of the show, so one must wonder if the other acts, Rajah Anderson, the fire-eater; Julia Lee, the singer and George's sister; and the Three Bad Boys, dancers, were included in the cabaret party. On Friday a week later the Loyal Knights Club sponsored a cabaret dance with four floor shows and Basie's orchestra. In June, George E. Lee's band became a permanent attraction at the club.[43]

◆ ◆ ◆

After the Blue Devils broke up, Basie was not the only former member who played a leading role in the Kansas City music scene. Oran Page also became a leader about this time, as he was featured at the Harlem Night Club, formerly the Paseo, in Kansas City in late spring 1934. He also arranged with the Lincoln Hall management to sponsor Sunday matinee dances that summer. He directed the dances and "feature[d] his 'Hot Lips' band for two shows every Sunday from 4pm until ?"[44]

James Rushing was one of the features in the show that Maceo Birch put together at the Harlem Night Club and at different venues. Working with businessman and promoter S. H. Dudley Jr., he presented Hot Pepper with the Harlem Hot Shots at the New Centre Theatre in autumn 1934. James Rushing was one of the features.[45]

The next month a new nightclub, the Sunset, opened at Twelfth and Woodland. It was newly redecorated, and its acts included Skippy, a "shake" dancer, Joe Turner, "blues singer moaning the blues throughout the night," and Pete and His Little Peters, assisted by Eddie Durham and Oran Page. Count Basie "with his Grand H.S. [*sic*] Dudley and Company," from the Harlem Night Club, welcomed patrons in the *Call* ad for the event. Moten and George Lee's band and Julia Lee, part of Birch's Harlem Nite Club show, also performed every night. The Sunset boasted female impersonators, as well, and welcomed all colors: "Come out and hear all the musicians of the city, including the Whites swing out."[46]

Former Blue Devils continued to play a prominent role in Kansas City's nightlife, as they had in previous years, and they were closely connected with community affairs. Nineteen thirty-five, however, was still a full year before the swing era was recognized as dominant by white promoters, and before they went looking for talented swing performers. In 1935 the Sunset announced a big floor show to be held in late January on Saturday and Sunday nights, "presenting the entertainers of the Coconut Grove. Formerly of the Harlem Night club." Pete and His Sunset Orchestra were guided by former Blue Devils: Hot Lips Page and "Big Page" assisted on cornet and bass violin, respectively.[47]

To survive during the Great Depression, these musicians had to remain connected to local affairs in the African-American community. Early in 1935, Basie played piano with Shaw's Melody Boys at a Grand Ball held by the National Convention of the Brotherhood of Sleeping Car Porters, the organization headed by the socialist union organizer A. Philip Randolph. The ball was the culmination of a series of meetings held by the Brotherhood in late January, including a mass meeting and open meetings held that same week. Also, former Blue Devils Basie, Rushing, and Hot Lips Page, along with Bennie Moten, played at a "Big Sunday Night Stomp" at the Labor Temple for the last weekend in January 1935. Like the Blue Devils' performance for the Communists a few years earlier in Oklahoma City, Basie's participation might have indicated his sympathies toward the Brotherhood if not his actual political stance.[48] In spring 1936, Basie's band performed for a "Monster Charity Benefit," along with the Lincoln High school chorus of 250 singers, to raise money for the Colored Rescue, Mission and Big Sisters' Home.[49]

Count Basie became the most successful bandleader of all the Blue Devils, and the Blue Devil legacy that he perpetuated was, of course, the most glorious and impressive. Moreover, in his autobiography he became the chronicler of the Devils, Bennie Moten's orchestra, and his own bands, and sometimes his recollections contrast with accepted jazz history. He was the only Blue Devil to leave a personal account of life in these bands. His retelling of the formation of the Reno Club band contradicted the widely held belief that he took over at the helm of Bennie Moten's band after Moten died; Basie denied this, and the evidence supports him.[50] In his autobiography Basie maintained "Somebody is always claiming that I took over Bennie Moten's band after he died, but that's just not what happened. Not at all." As noted above, Basie took over the band before Moten died. Then for a time Bennie Moten joined forces with George E. Lee's band. After he died on April 1, 1935, his nephew, Buster, took over the band.[51] Some sidemen went with him, but Basie, who had rejoined Moten, was then the first to leave— "I really didn't have anything definite. I just wanted to see what I could do."[52]

In Basie's reminiscences, what happened at the Reno was all very simple: Sol Steibold, who was running the Reno Club, "Gave me some money to make a few additions and changes in the group he had put me in charge of at the Reno. So I went down to Oklahoma and talked Jack Washington and Big 'Un into coming in with me, and then I went on down to Dallas and got Buster Smith and Joe Keyes to join me."[53] Prior to his actions, Basie emphasized, the Moten band had broken up and its members were scattered. "I didn't take anybody out of that band while Bus still had it."[54]

Indeed, neither Walter Page nor Lester Young was a member of the Moten band at this time, and Herschel Evans went to California. Most if not all who joined Basie at the Reno Club were not in the Moten band at the time it broke up. Early in 1935, Eddie Durham and his close colleagues, Paul Webster and Eddie Tompkins, joined Jimmy Lunceford.[55] Nor were Oran Page and Jimmy Rushing members of Basie's band at the Reno; they were singles. One M.C.'d and played trumpet, and the other sang.[56]

Basie attempted to get superior musicians for his new band, and since the Blue Devils were the best band he had ever heard, he knew whom he wanted for the Reno Club job. He fell back on the tried and true: "In a way, I guess what happened at the Reno was a little like what Eddie Durham and I did once I got settled in Bennie Moten's band. I started trying to bring some Blue Devils in there." He wanted three trumpets, three reeds, and three rhythm: "So we called it Three, Three, and Three." In reality, he had two trumpets, because actually it was only with the club's M.C., Lips Page, that they had three. In mentioning Joe Keyes and Carl "Tatti" Smith as his two trumpets, he overlooked the former Blue Devil Leonard Chadwick, who played with him at the Reno Club.

◆ ◆ ◆

In 1935, Leonard Chadwick led the Rhythmaires, a band that included Eddie and Charlie Christian and Leslie Sheffield, at the Ritz Ballroom in Oklahoma City. Basie recruited Chadwick along with Jack Washington, Willie "Mack" Washington, "Tatti" Smith, and Lester. Saxophonist Slim Freeman was already in the band. Chadwick recalled three saxes, two trumpets, and two rhythm: "That was the band in the old Reno club when Basie was broadcasting over W9XBY." They went to work at nine and played until 5:00

a.m. "Then [we'd] go over to the Crystal Bar, around on Twelfth, and play until 9, 10:00 in the morning."[57]

The Reno Club band went through a number of changes in personnel. Actually Basie and Buster Smith agreed to co-lead, and this was the band that Hammond and Goodman heard over the radio in Chicago in mid-1936. Hammond wrote about the band in *Down Beat* that summer, and before long he traveled to Kansas City, toured the local nightclubs, was enthralled by the bands, and liked Basie best. He told him he would be back to sign them to a record deal, but meanwhile, Basie was to enlarge the band from its formulaic three, three, and three. Then the entrepreneurial Dick Kapp came to town, intimated he was a friend working for Hammond, and signed the band to a record deal with no royalties.

Late that summer Buck Clayton came through from Shanghai and Los Angeles, where he led bands in the early 1930s, and stayed on to join the trumpet section. In September 1936, Lester Young traveled to the West Coast in Basie's new car, driven by Maceo Birch, to see his ailing father and to recruit new reed players—probably Caughey Roberts and Herschel Evans.[58] Hammond returned, was disappointed to learn about Kapp's venture, provided money for uniforms, and booked the band in the Grand Terrace in Chicago, where they performed after a Kansas City farewell dance opposite Ellington at the end of October. From there the Basie band went on to follow its destiny, though it was two to three years before it attained the fame usually associated with the band.

Though of course Kansas City claimed Count Basie as one of its own, so did Oklahoma City, thus complicating the heritage of his orchestra. For Basie, when his band visited Oklahoma City, it was a homecoming. Jimmy Stewart, columnist for the *Black Dispatch,* maintained in 1946: "A few of the old timers around here kinder take Oklahoma City as Count's home since he got his start with a push from Hallie Richardson and James Simpson and our 'Deep Deuce' cats." He noted they were proud of Basie and might "pull some kind of stunt for he and the other local members of his band" when they visited the city in August 1946.[59] Two years later when the orchestra played the Oklahoma capital, Stewart wrote, "The Count, and all the old-timers got real gone visiting old friends."[60] Despite these facts, it was much simpler for critics, musicians, and fans to focus solely on the Kansas City origins of the Basie band, thus separating it from its true history. Though the Kansas City music scene was indisputably rich, the origins of the Basie band were even richer and more complex than all the publicity suggested.

CHAPTER ELEVEN

Basie

The Mothership's Ascent

The Basie combo of 1935–1936 became the Basie Orchestra after they left Kansas City late in 1936, but it was two or three years before they became famous, or "hit the big time," as it was called. They performed at the Grand Terrace in Chicago,[1] and at hotels such as the ritzy William Penn in Pittsburgh,[2] at the Ritz Carlton Hotel Ballroom in Boston,[3] at the famous Roseland Ballroom in New York City —another white venue—and then at Fifty-second Street's Famous Door in the summers of 1938 and 1939. Of course, they benefited considerably from the radio hookup in the Famous Door, then they topped all this when they performed at the *Spirituals to Swing* concert in December 1938 at Carnegie Hall.[4]

Until the late 1930s they paid a price—they suffered together as they endured the hard times, the life on the road, and racial prejudice and discrimination Down South and Up South, as well. They traveled in a Greyhound bus nearly every day and many nights; in 1940 the band "was never in one place for more than two weeks and most of the time was in a different town every night." Early in 1941 they played "40 engagements in 42 days."[5] Meals were always hurried, and the food was not that good. Most of them were away from their spouses, as well. "Despite the fact that they're hardly ever at home with their families, thirteen of the seventeen musicians in the Basie outfit are married."[6] In late summer of 1939 they made the trip to California. Treasure Island is where they really hit the big time, according to Buck Clayton.

They paid another price, too, for their success, as their Midwestern and Southwestern families had to deal with an eastward migration to New York City. There was also the heartache of separation, plus the pitfalls of a celebrity's life; most of the Basie-ites wed two or three times. Indeed, Eddie Durham married four times. As he explained, the problem was *him,* that is, he was such a lone wolf that he could not settle down—not until he finally did so in New York City, as a middle-aged veteran of the music industry (and of earlier marriages). Jimmy Rushing wed at least twice, in Oklahoma City and then again on the East Coast, and the *City Directory* lists a Mabel with him during his Kansas City years.[7] He married Connie, from North Carolina, in the 1940s—this time for good. Buster Smith wed at least twice.[8] Lester Young and Beatrice broke up, then he married an Italian-American named Mary in the late 1930s and finally an African-American named Mary after World War II.

For a time these marriages saved the Basie-ites from the draft. Basie at thirty-six was one of the oldest band members and ineligible for the draft. The others were "all ineligible for draft service since every man is either married or the sole support of at least one dependent."[9] But as the need for recruits increased, eligibility rules changed, and because of the band's constant movement, some— Lester Young and Jo Jones, for example—missed their draft notices and became delinquent. After the war, the *Courier* noted how much Basie's band was depleted by the military. "No other sepia band had its ranks so heavily razed by the draft as did the Count."[10]

On the other hand, the marriages of Walter and Oran Page endured for years. Walter married Sarah in 1925[11] and does not appear to have divorced or remarried, while Oran married his high-school sweetheart in 1926 during his senior year, and then in Kansas City, he was with Myrtle, whom he took to New York and married. They had a child, Oran Jr., in 1939, and she died in childbirth in 1946. He then married Elizabeth and stayed with her until he died. Basie wed Vivian Wynn in Kansas City, and then later married his second wife.[12] Snake Whyte married only once, staying with Cecile until she died at the end of the twentieth century.

These stories of love, heartache, and breakup are interwoven with the songs as well as with the tremendous success the band finally achieved. They provided real-life experiences that gave sub-stance to some of the blues and popular songs they performed. "I'm goin' to Chicago," Rushing sang, "but I can't take you./There's noth-ing there a monkey woman like you can do." Funny to some, but sad, too. These sentiments did not always reflect the band's reality— but they knew someone who could sing this song, and truthfully, too. As Rushing, the composer, explained, "I had a little girl in St. Louis, and we fell out. That was my way of saying it."[13] The transition from Kansas City to Chicago and New York was not easy for anyone, and only the success made it worthwhile. And sometimes, as Bus-ter Smith learned (see Chapter Twelve), even this hardly made it any easier, if one valued peace of mind, friendships, lifelong rela-tionships, and fishing in the lakes and streams one had known all one's life.

The success, though, the big time, the thrill of living and playing in New York City, the pleasures of living in Harlem during the thir-ties and forties, and the security of a home in Brooklyn or Queens, were exhilarating. As singer Melvin Moore, from Oklahoma City, re-called, "To come to New York was everybody's dream then. That was it! Some of 'em made it and some of 'em didn't."[14] The Big Apple was what they had waited and worked for. This was what everyone in the sticks yearned for—success in the Big Apple, the accolades of the fans and the glare of the spotlight, the glowing warmth, deep friend-ships, and brotherhood of the band.

Just one word: Basie. That said it all—the height of ambition was to play with the Count, the epitome of swinging swing bands, the Holy Main—which became his nickname. Some band members had been bandleaders in their own right—Walter Page and Buck Clayton, for example—but nothing matched being a Basie-ite. In the histories of jazz, their names blazed like stars in a magnificent constellation—the first generation: Jimmy Rushing, Walter Page, Lester "Pres" Young, Herschel Evans, Earle Warren, Jack Washing-ton, Buddy Tate, Buck Clayton, Sweets Edison, Dicky Wells, Vic Dickenson, Jo Jones, and Freddie Green, and then the second gen-eration: Don Byas, Wardell Gray, Al Killian, Paul Quinichette, Mar-shal Royal, and others.

Perhaps Ellington's band carried more clout, but only a little

Count Basie and Jimmy Rushing at a fundraiser, circa 1940

more. Ellington was for the suave and sophisticated who liked pretty melodies and harmonies along with their swing, but Basie was for the down-to-earth swing fans and dancers who loved blues first, second, and last. Ellington's fans were society folk—doctors, lawyers, professors, fraternity and sorority members, while Basie was for the high rollers, the plumbers, maids, chauffeurs, and domestic workers as well as the professionals. Ellington appealed to longtime urbanites, Basie to the new migrants who came to the cities in the 1930s and 1940s, from places like Oklahoma, Arkansas, and Texas. Basie also won in the polls.[15]

While Kansas and Oklahoma cities hailed Basie as a native son whenever he played there, in a few years New York City—and Harlem in particular—did, too. When he was to open at the Apollo Theater for a week, "a mammoth homecoming celebration" was arranged for the "Jump King of Swing," as he became known about this time.[16] In spring 1941 he was "currently smashing all attendance marks at the Tunetown ballroom" during his one-week stand.[17] As testimony to his popularity among young fans, he and his band were slated to play at "leading spring college proms in May."[18]

Basie's band broke all kinds of attendance records during World

War II, but his phenomenal success has been overshadowed by other bands. He was crowned "Jump King of Swing" four times straight in the semiannual national poll conducted by Martin Block, a New York D.J.[19] The *Call* claimed the "indifference" of Black voters towards this poll meant that Black bands were ranked far down in the ranks behind white bands, but as usual, Basie was first among them. Jimmy Lunceford, Duke Ellington, and Erskine Hawkins were in the top thirty, in that order. Ahead of them were Glenn Miller (first), Tommy Dorsey (second), Jimmy Dorsey (third), Artie Shaw (fourth), and then Benny Goodman and others. "Colored bands have always been snowed under by inferior white bands in Block's poll due to the fact that their fans fail to rally to their support by voting." In 1941, Block maintained that Basie would have placed higher if not for "his recent inactivity due to troubles with his booking agents" and the absence of radio broadcasts.[20] Late that summer, and after his financial problems had been resolved, the *Call* maintained that Basie was "riding to glory with the greatest band of his illustrious career."[21]

In autumn 1941 the band opened at Café Society Uptown in Manhattan, and "put the New York nitery owners in a veritable uproar by playing to the greatest opening night crowd in all night life history." All the name celebrities of New York City were said to be in the audience, and these included bandleaders Ella Fitzgerald, Harry James, Benny Goodman, Vincent Lopez, and Tommy Dorsey, and celebrities such as Burgess Meredith. Indeed, "Basie gave Café Society Uptown its greatest business ever, the club taking in more cash on Basie's opening night than it did last New Year's Eve." In one week, Basie "pulled in more business than the café had done in any previous six weeks."[22]

These successes occurred the year after Basie nearly broke up his band because of his debts and problems with his management. At the end of 1940, the music world thought that Basie was through. His ascent was quick and dramatic, but as a result of "poor handling, [he] had started on the down-grade after achieving success." He was near bankruptcy, nearly $35,000 in debt. Then he acquired new management in Music Corporation of America, which was reported to have paid $20,000 to release him from his contract. A year later his new personal manager, Milt Ebbins, took over. Basie was nearly free of debt, ranked among the top Black bands, and in 1941 he grossed more than $300,000.[23]

When *Metronome* critic Barry Ulanov saw the band, he wrote, "When you haven't heard this band in a long time, say a year, you may forget just how good it is." He listened to them at the Hotel Lincoln in New York City and confessed, "I was more than merely delighted . . . I was overwhelmed." The band was happier than ever, and was "once more in a groove" that the bandleader claimed hearkened back to their Kansas City days. Because it was dinner hour in the hotel's Blue Room, with an audience of affluent diners, the Basie-ites had "to play under wraps," which the writer compared to "Marlene Dietrich in sable." The band "glitters," he observed. Basie's piano playing was "always restrained, witty, charming," and these characteristics were "picked up by the band in their quiet numbers, and the resultant music is little short of marvelous." Despite the low volume, "the beat is just as strong, the drive as great, and, therefore, the band jumps just that much more." They still opened up when they wanted to and blew "those powerhouse pieces," but because they often played more softly, the band displayed "a variety seldom encountered among the forthright jazz bands."[24]

His impact was just as dramatic and as much appreciated on the West Coast. He spent four weeks at the Club Plantation in Los Angeles and "three record-smashing weeks" at Culver City's Casa Mañana. At Los Angeles's Orpheum Theatre, "Basie rolled up a near record gross of $37,000 in a week," and had "another tremendous box-office barrage" at the Golden Gate Theatre in San Francisco.[25] In fact, the main problem his bookers faced was "how to take care of all the demands for the band's services."[26] In autumn 1945 he was booked up through the next year.[27]

In Toronto in 1946, the band was guaranteed $3,500 a week after it "rolled up record-breaking grosses" performing in Canada the year before.[28] At the Roxy in mid-1946, Basie was paid "the near record fee of $12,500 per week."[29] He drew the same sum for a week's stint at the Castle Farm, "Cincinnati's smart dine and dance rendezvous." This sum was "one of the highest figures paid any band for a location engagement."[30]

When the orchestra performed at the Municipal Auditorium's Zebra Room in Oklahoma City in winter 1948, nearly two thousand fans danced and listened to the band, and "all the old-timers got real gone visiting their old friends"—Basie, Rushing, Walter Page, and Jack Washington.[31] When he revisited Deep Deuce later that year, Rushing expressed amazement at the city's growth since he left in the 1920s.[32]

Often missed in histories of jazz are the barriers broken down by the Basie-ites. As some bandsmen claimed later, they were the first freedom riders. They also lowered some of the barriers Up South, playing in the exclusive metropolitan hotels for upper-class diners. When they were scheduled to perform in Oklahoma City's Trianon Ballroom, so many white fans called and insisted on hearing the No. 1 Swing Band that the event had to be moved to the Municipal Auditorium, which could seat thousands in its balcony. Others could sit at tables on the dance floor. In other words, both Blacks and whites were able to enjoy the occasion in the same space, though segregated by being kept distant from one another.[33]

Despite the white managers, bookers, and record company executives, the Basie band lived in an African-American world that always faced limits in the U.S. The *Black Dispatch* touted Basie in 1938 as "the first Negro orchestra leader ever to play at the William Penn Hotel, Pittsburgh." One might assume the same was true for his next engagement at the Ritz Carlton Hotel Ballroom in Boston, but this is not clear.[34] The *Dispatch* made similar claims after the band appeared at Carnegie Hall—at the concert that presented the history of the music, *From Spirituals to Swing*.[35]

Basie was clearly seen as someone paving the way for other Black bands and therefore as bettering conditions for the entire African-American populace. As late as 1946, such claims were still made. When the *Pittsburgh Courier* announced that the band was embarking upon a four-week stint at the Avodon, the weekly contended that it was "the first Negro band ever booked into the popular downtown dance rendezvous."[36] The *Courier,* one of the most race-conscious newspapers of the time, also reminded its readers that "the Count was the first Negro artist to play the Roxy stage when he made his debut there in 1944." Subsequently the band performed at this venue every year.[37]

Basie's band was advertised in the *Amsterdam News* as one of the "all-colored! Hot from Harlem!" participants in the second "Jitter, Jive and Jump" bandfest at Randall's Island in late summer 1938. The first, which was also a benefit for blind musicians, had featured white bands, but the second time around it was different, and "The crowd was much more enthusiastic than at the previous concert." Indeed, the first event "was in realty a bandfest, not a swing concert, and those who expected hot licks... were sorely disappointed."[38] As a benefit for musicians, the main gain was good publicity for their records and other engagements.[39]

In early 1941 the bandleader was hailed as the "Jump King of Swing" for perhaps the first time in print, in the Kansas City *Call*.[40] As Benny Goodman was known as the "King of Swing," Basie's title was clearly meant to designate him as a colored or African-American musician. "Jump" and "jump swing," like "Jump King," appear to have been used exclusively for Black artists, and Basie in particular, in the 1940s. In 1938, however, the *Black Dispatch* referred to him simply as "The Count of Swing"—suggesting that other possible designations simply did not take hold.[41]

Some of the ways in which Basie supported political causes are surprising, given his aversion to expressing political opinions. For example, in between shows in Philadelphia in spring 1937, Basie and the band members solicited aid for the passing of an anti-lynching bill by Congress. They collected over 200,000 signatures on a petition that Basie intended to present to his congressman when they played in Washington, D.C.[42] In another instance, he recorded "Stampede in G Minor," a composition written by Clinton P. Brewer, who served nineteen years of a life sentence in the New Jersey prison system. Like Chester Himes and other Black prison writers, Brewer discovered he had talent—enough to convince the "Jump King of Swing" not only to record his composition, but also to hire him as a staff arranger after his release.[43]

Basie's 1941 collaboration with Paul Robeson and Richard Wright for a Columbia recording was another venture that might be viewed as overtly political. Robeson, an actor, concert singer, and movie star, whose Communist sympathies made him politically controversial, was still able to express his opinions without undue criticism in 1941, and Wright, celebrated author of *Native Son* and Communist Party member from the 1930s until he renounced it near the end of the war, were leading figures in their respective fields of the stage and literature. The recording, "Joe Louis Blues" (a play on the Handy composition "St. Louis Blues"), added the heavyweight boxing champion to the mix, and the composer, the Jump King himself, was another important ingredient in this combination of internationally known artists. While Wright, a native of Mississippi, wrote about blues, this was the first occasion for Robeson to sing or record them.[44]

In 1946, Basie recorded a song, "Patience and Fortitude," that came from the local political scene: it was the radio theme song of former New York City mayor Fiorello LaGuardia. The title came from one of his "most noted sayings," and the *Courier* could not help but observe, "It is indeed an odd coincidence that Basie should be the first artist to record" the popular song. Coincidence indeed, especially since the bandleader and his family lived in the LaGuardias' former Manhattan apartment at 1275 Fifth Avenue. In a surprising instance of his new power, Basie actually turned down a script for a Palmolive show and requested a rewrite. "The re[quest?] was honored, and the result was a program of which no Negro [needs?] to bow his head in shame." The *Pittsburgh Courier* columnist contended that Basie "has never been afraid to [express?] his opinion insofar as racial practices are concerned."[45]

There were more subtle ways of alluding to the political scene and the Black world in which Basie operated. His band was all Black at a time when whites such as Goodman and Artie Shaw began hiring one or more featured Black musicians such as Teddy Wilson and Lionel Hampton, or Hot Lips Page and Roy Eldridge. As the *Courier* pointed out when it announced Basie's upcoming stint at the Strand on Broadway, "As usual he will take an all-star colored revue into the mecca vaudeville houses." The weekly could not help but observe, at the dawn of the integration struggle of the 1950s, that "His first appearance at the Strand ... will mark the first colored show to be seen on the big street [Broadway] for several months."

What headlined this particular article, however, was the news that his schedule did not permit him to hold the beauty contest that he had promised the residents of Atlantic City. Again, it goes without saying that the participants would have been all African-American in a pageant held by the "Jump King of Swing." Or as the *Courier* noted, when it first announced this contest, it "looked like the one to put beige beauty right out front" at a time when Blacks were barred from such beauty pageants in the city known for its Miss America contests.[46]

When Basie entered the music-publishing field, this, too, was heralded as a first for an African-American bandleader. The Basie Music Corporation scheduled its opening for early 1946, and the bandleader was hailed as "the first Negro bandleader to enter the music publishing field on a full scale." Milt Ebbins, his personal manager for six years, was his business partner in this endeavor. They would publish Basie material as well as popular music. In the spirit of a Blue Devil, the bandleader also sought to help his fellow Black composers: "It is Basie's idea with this new firm to give a break to deserving young Negro songwriters and to bring out their talents."[47]

There were other signs of success—the Hollywood films in which the band was featured, the jukebox sales, the number of labels trying to sign him, the shows that accompanied the band, the European tour in 1946, and celebrations of his tenth and twentieth years as a bandleader—but it was the distinctiveness of the music that stood out to astute listeners as something remarkable and new.[48] The *Black Dispatch* reporter praised the band before it became famous. The weekly noted such musicians as Jimmy Rushing, "Hot Lips" Walter Page [*sic*], Buck Clayton, and "many others" when it announced Basie's appearance in Oklahoma City in autumn 1936. The reporter was ready to be disappointed, as he had only heard the band on the radio, and was afraid he would have to retract the praises he had heaped on it, but on hearing it in person, he described it as "an experience I will never forget." After this single hearing, he "came away convinced that the band has the makings of the finest the country has ever known—it isn't so far from that state right now."[49]

Simply put, he could not believe his eyes and ears. He was "flabbergasted" when he observed that all the music he heard on the radio came from "a mere ten-piece group, three rhythm, three saxes, four brass." Also, "the voicing of the arrangements is so deft that the band had sounded at least like a five-brass, four-reed combination."

Then he praised the rhythm section, contending "the only section I have ever heard even remotely close to it is the four-piece one" of pianist Albert Ammons when he had Israel Crosby on bass. Then this was qualified: "but even Ammons doesn't begin to have the versatility that belongs to the Count's."[50] Two years later the *Black Dispatch* described the band's distinctive sound, "In a sympathetic atmosphere, the band plays with an inhuman vitality that expresses itself not in volume, but in the most subtle manner."[51]

The Kansas City *Call* also described the band's music late in 1936 as "the perfectly coordinated rhythm section and the ability to improvise collectively for indefinite periods." Basie led the band from the piano and also provided "a solid background." Just as important was the fact that "the band boasts of several soloists, notably Buck Clayton and Lester Young, who are little short of sensational." The *Call* also praised Jimmy Rushing as "one of the few singers who has something different to offer."[52]

◆ ◆ ◆

Basie described the band's goals in the columns of the *Dispatch* in 1940. First, he was introduced as a disciple of Fats Waller on piano and organ, who had attempted to put over his ideas when he was with Moten, then had formed the Reno Club combo. The writer continued, "Basie's style features coordination and smoothness rather than loudness." Though this sounded simple and easy, "actually, it's a difficult thing to accomplish, particularly with a swing band." Basie explained: "My men are learning to swing softly . . . and are not blowing the roof off. Anybody can do that but it takes real style to break it down without breaking listeners' eardrums at the same time. It's really tough getting a band to that fine stage of development, but the boys and I feel we've gotten there now."

Basie was constantly learning and developing his style. He listened to an extensive record collection—"some 2,000 in all—of hot platters" by Goodman, Ellington, Shaw, Lunceford, Dorsey, Whiteman—and, of course, Fats Waller."[53]

Though modest about his own playing and legendary for his short solos consisting of a few notes, Basie liked performing—playing piano along with showcasing the talents of a number of virtuosos: composers, arrangers, and soloists. He may very well have preferred the organ to the piano. When he played at the Roxy in spring 1946, he displayed his skill "for the first time with a special arrangement in which he shifts from his piano to the Hammond organ."[54] The next year, this devotee of the Hammond organ presented nightly recitals on it at the Club Paradise in Atlantic City, New Jersey. The bandleader was booked for the entire summer, having extended his contract by six weeks, and "he had transported to the nitery from his home at St. Albans, N.Y." his own organ. "Experts," the *Courier* noted, "rate him as one of the world's greatest technicians on that instrument."[55]

The *Courier*'s claim that this was the first time the pianist featured himself as an organ soloist was something of an exaggeration. By 1941 the band's repertoire diversified from blues and jump tunes to embrace a variety that would mollify the elite and the businesspeople who wanted to book Basie into the big hotels. That summer they performed at the swanky Ritz Carlton in Boston "before the greatest gathering since the days of the Boston Tea Party." Indeed, "Practically every famous member of Boston Back Bay Society including John Roosevelt, son of the President, and his wife, was in attendance to greet America's greatest dance orchestra." By displaying the band's versatility they staunched any criticism about the music they usually presented. The Count offered not only "his inimitable 'jump rhythms,' [but] pretty dance music, soft dinner music, waltzes, rhumbas and congas with equal ease and success." Although most regular patrons of the hotel were away for the summer, Basie's band was "doing business comparable to the best the hotel has ever seen." His attendance figures at the Ritz surpassed those attained by Paul Whiteman, Eddie Duchin, Guy Lombardo, Artie Shaw, and other bands, and he hoped to surpass even Benny Goodman's.[56]

The band was full of stars, and its singer of fifteen years was one of them. The *Black Dispatch* wrote that its homeboy, Jimmy Rushing, was without equal "in the field of swing blues singing," when it advertised the Basie Orchestra's appearance at the Trianon late one summer in Oklahoma City. The weekly referred to him as "the greatest 'swingblueser' "—one of those terms that did not catch on. It also praised tenor saxophonist Lester Young, and pointed out that he had numerous offers to join "higher paid combinations," but that the former Blue Devil stuck with Basie. Ironically, this was a few months before he left Basie and started his own combo.[57]

Rushing's movie prospects were reported to be quite good in 1941. "They want to build him up as a comedian in films," the Kansas City *Call* reported. He was supposed to take a screen test in New York City in September 1941. This was about the time the band, enjoying tremendous success, "broke Glenn Miller's all-time attendance record" at Boston's Roseland Ballroom.[58]

Metronome's description of Rushing highlighted his size, when the band played at the Strand on Broadway. After praising the band, Buddy Tate and Basie solos, and Jo Jones's drumming, the article reported, "Then came 'Peewee' Rushing. The Hep Hippo came through nobly on 'Goin' to Chicago Blues.' "[59] A few years later *Metronome* praised Rushing while criticizing his lack of opportunities: it referred to him as "surely one of the greats of jazz, [who] doesn't get enough to sing."[60]

The Blue Devil component persisted in many ways—in the Basie-Rushing duo, obviously, and also in the rhythm section, which included Walter Page, founding member and former leader of the Devils, who stayed in the orchestra until Basie broke it up in 1949—aside from a break from the band during World War II. Kansas and Oklahoma City newspapers touted him, of course, but so did East Coast journals after a few years. In spring 1946 the *Courier* observed, in an article on Basie, that Jo Jones and Walter Page were "back in the Basie fold . . . [and] the famed 'All-American Rhythm Section' is once again rocking the band's brass and reed sections."[61] This designation for the rhythm section, the only section that was awarded this honor, started around the beginning of World War II, but it was also applied to the band at least once—"The Count and His All American Music Makers."[62]

Page's influence in the rhythm section and the band is easily overlooked, but the tributes from numerous musicians illustrate his singular effect on them. Jo Jones insisted, "Walter Page had the greatest band that I ever heard in my life."[63] Furthermore, the drummer explained, "Bennie Moten played one and three. Walter Page played on two and four; but when they wedded together you had one, two, three, four. The two mediums met." The Basie band benefited considerably from this fusion.[64]

When the young Jones heard the Devils, Page was playing baritone saxophone, stringed bass, and a tuba with a light in it. "They had bottles and they did 'Little Liza Jane' and they did it on bottles. It was when they had [Reuben] Lynch and, oh my God, I never heard it better." Other bands that he heard "didn't have that kind of feeling. . . ."[65] Jones credited Page with being a kind of spiritual and musical father of numerous musicians who starred with Basie: "Without Mr. Walter Page you would never have heard of Hot Lips Page; you would never have heard of Jimmy Rushing; you would never have heard of Lester Young; you would never have heard of Jo Jones; you would have never heard of Charlie Parker because Buster Smith is there and he's still alive."

Walter Page was the force behind the Basie band, even if he was not the leader. In autumn 1936, the band refused to leave Kansas City without their bassist. According to Jones, "When we were leaving Kansas City to come to New York, his wife says, 'No, he cannot go.' We told Mr. Willard Alexander, we told John Hammond, we told the man at the Roseland Ballroom. . . . We wasn't going to leave Walter Page in Kansas City." The bandsmen begged his wife, " 'Let him come for a month and we'll send him back.' We wasn't going to leave [him]. . . . We'd stay there till we rot."[66]

Page's influence on Jones and other musicians—Freddie Green, for example—was that of a teacher who was deeply knowledgeable of music theory and who had nearly two decades' experience as a professional musician in 1936. "No, it don't go like that," Page would tell Green when he started playing with Basie as the young guitarist in 1937. Jones claimed Green had to change his playing, and he himself also had to learn because, the drummer confessed, "I didn't know how to play a major or a minor. I knew the music. I was very adept in music but I didn't know, see."[67] Page, he continued, "was my son and my father. He was the father of us all."

Jones maintained that "Count Basie's band only functioned one way and it will only function one way today [1973], because there's two ingredients that will make it function. . . . We functioned morally.... We started first spiritually. What it takes to get this spiritual ingredient, you have to live this spiritual ingredient. We lived spiritually!" Music was more than merely music for Jones, and this reflected the deep spirituality of Page's family—for example, when his aunt dreamed about the funeral of the bassist's mother, and planned it according to the dream she experienced.[68]

"When we went to work nobody spoke to us," Jones continued. "We never played with the band; we played with ourselves . . . with the four of us, if three people were down, one person was up. If two people, if three people, put one person on four cylinders, one person was up—we never heard the band. We concentrated on ourselves."[69]

The Blue Devils' influence is also evident in the rather singular influences of Buster Smith and Eddie Durham. Smith, a co-leader of the Reno Club combo, left Basie that summer in 1936 before they signed with Hammond, but Basie wanted him back. Though some band members could not forget that he left them for Claude Hopkins, he did do arrangements and compositions for the band, having learned these skills in the Blue Devils.

He co-wrote "One O'Clock Jump," and explained how this came about. Basie liked to play in different keys every night, and one night "he was playing along in F (that's his favorite key), and then he took that modulation into D♭." Then he looked up at Smith and said, "'Set something, Prof.,' so I started playing that saxophone riff. Lips (Page) set something for the brass, and pretty soon we had it going." Dan Minor contributed the trombone part. Jack Washington "had the fourth reed part and he wanted me to write his down because it was hard to hear the harmony."[70]

They performed it for thirty minutes or so and the crowd liked it, so next night they played it the same way. One night in Little Rock they were broadcasting and could not use the composition's original name ("Blue Balls") over the air because it was off-color, so, because it was about one o'clock, the announcer suggested they named it accordingly.[71]

Smith maintained, "It was my tune, but I only wrote one part of it—that was a saxophone part for Jack Washington because the fourth harmony was hard to hear." After he and Page left the band in summer of 1936, Washington taught the others their parts. Basie's name was put on it when they recorded it, and later in Chicago, Buck Clayton took the arrangement off the record. "I heard other bands playing it and tried to copyright it, but I found out it already had been. I figure I got $5.40 for it." With dry wit, the composer explained that he saw Basie one time and the pianist said, " 'I don't want you suing me so I'll give you $5, and we'll drink this fifth of gin. Next time we record I'll play any of your tunes you want me to.' He did, too." He recorded Smith's "The Blues I Like to Hear."[72]

Actually, seven musicians were involved in the creation of "One O'clock Jump," beginning with Fats Waller, "who was responsible for the original theme." When Don Redman recorded it, it was called "Six or Seven Times." Smith heard the version of McKinney's Cotton Pickers. All he remembered was the introduction.[73]

Leonard Chadwick tells the story differently; he claimed "One O'clock Jump" started with just maracas playing, "then Basie would join in, the rhythm would join in, and then Basie would come in, and that I believe is the starter for 'One O'clock Jump.' Because we would riff there, and would take solos, and riff till he got tired."

The song became synonymous with the band and was voted the "best jazz instrumental music of all time" in a poll in 1941. It took fifth place for the best stock arrangement of all time.[74]

◆ ◆ ◆

Durham's influence was deep and far-reaching, both as a composer and as an arranger. He stayed with the band for about a year, having left Lunceford in New England to join his old Moten and Blue Devil bandsmen, who were edging towards the big time in the summer of 1937.[75] Lunceford's band, he observed decades later, "wasn't too much of a swinging band," but rather "more of a novelty band."[76] Nonetheless, Lunceford's band had tremendous success, including a European tour—Durham's first— in winter 1937.[77] With Basie, he knew he could get the band to swing, and he proceeded to write a number of compositions and to arrange others. Also, Basie paid him $150 a week, while Lunceford gave him only $65 a week.[78]

His contributions are perhaps the single most important of any composer/arranger in the first Basie band, and these songs continue as a central part of not only the Count Basie legacy, but also the entire Kansas City legacy, not to mention the swing era itself. Consider the Decca recordings that he wrote and/or arranged: there were the classics—"One O'Clock Jump" (with Buster Smith), "John's Idea" (named after Hammond), "Good Morning Blues," "Time Out," the perennial "Topsy," "Out the Window," "Don't You Miss Your Baby," "Georgianna," "Every Tub," "Swingin' the Blues"—and some not so well known, such as "I Keep Remembering" and "Let Me Dream," as well as some he may deserve credit for: "Sent For You Yesterday," "Doggin' Around," and "Now Will You Be Good." No one contributed as much as Durham during these first few years of the band.

No less remarkable than the number of songs and their lasting effect is the ease with which he wrote. Like Ellington, he sometimes wrote on trains. "Topsy" was composed during a train ride to Albany to meet the Basie band. As Durham recalled, "Sat down and just thought it, wrote it up and got there, and they was already in rehearsal, out at the park." He didn't have time to prepare a score, but he dashed off something for the band members, and the song was introduced that summer in 1937.[79]

Unlike the "flag wavers" (uptempo compositions) for which Durham was known, "Topsy" has a relaxed tempo. The title came from a character in the popular vaudeville skit *Uncle Tom's Cabin,* based on Harriet Beecher Stowe's antislavery novel—one of the longest-running productions of all times. Topsy was the child with unkempt, curly hair who was very black and uneducated and who, when asked where she came from, admitted, "I spect I grow'd." Durham's song has a sprightly rhythm, more reflective of the circus than the vaudeville stage, however. The predominance of rhythm in the melody and in the featured instruments—drums—reminds one of the importance of drums in the circus, in carnivals, and in parades and military processions. At least one article in the 1930s maintained that swing started in the circus, that is, in the swinging rhythms and songs of the roustabouts who put up the tents and pounded the stakes. Also remarkable was Cozy Cole's revival of the song in 1958, and it was a bigger hit then than when it originally came out.[80]

CHAPTER TWELVE

Diaspora

Just as a number of Blue Devils went into other bands in 1928, the same process occurred with the Count's Orchestra. Buster Smith and Eddie Durham rejoined Basie in New York City in 1937 and were gone within a year to other swing bands. These outfits were often composed of former Blue Devils—Hot Lips Page and Abe Bolar, for example, and, at the end of the 1940s after Basie disbanded, Walter Page, Jimmy Rushing, and ex-Basie-ites such as Buck Clayton and Buddy Tate.[1]

Smith recorded with the Kansas City pianist Pete Johnson, worked with a few other bandleaders, and did some arranging, then abandoned the Big Apple for his hometown of Dallas during the war. He had had enough of the big lights. He led bands, composed, and arranged music for more than four decades in relative obscurity. On the other hand, Durham continued songwriting and arranging hits such as "I Don't Want to Set the World on Fire," and "In the Mood," which he did for Glenn Miller, and it became the trombonist's theme song. Then Durham became musical director of the International Sweethearts of Rhythm, a band of women, and then of other bands composed entirely of women. Leonard Chadwick led bands and played in Oklahoma City and Omaha before moving to Denver around 1950. Trumpeter-singer Oran Page led big bands and combos, made recordings and radio appearances, and even broadcast over the new medium, television, on Ed Sullivan's *Toast of the Town*.[2] He was a hit at the Paris jazz festival in 1949 and enjoyed European stints until he died in 1954.

While Basie's band enjoyed a measure of success achieved by few, the story for those who left the Holy Main was more complicated. Considering their origins in the Southwest and the limitations imposed on African-Americans by Jim Crow, most did quite well—enjoying a modicum of security, often purchasing homes and raising families in New York City. Their musical successes were even more profound, not so much in the monetary sense, but in charting major developments in music in the U.S. and in the world. Not only should they be credited with engineering the rise of swing in the mid- and late 1930s, but also with creating "jump blues," or rhythm and blues, as it was first called—the development that became rock and roll, once whites and the popular music industry caught on. Swing remained—primarily in a few big bands, such as Basie, Ellington, and Stan Kenton—but it clearly took a backseat to the music of Miles Davis, John Coltrane, and the Modern Jazz Quartet, on the one hand, and Chuck Berry, Muddy Waters, Fats Domino, and Elvis Presley, on the other.

Many former Blue Devils remained active musically in different parts of the U.S. Some, like Leonard Chadwick, never got to New York City. At the end of the 1940s he moved to Denver, remarried, and started a new career with the Denver Housing Authority, as a painter at first, while playing on weekends for another decade or so. Snake Whyte left the Devils, settled in Ohio for a time, and then received a call from Eddie Barefield to join his band around 1937 in Los Angeles. He stayed there with his wife and son until 1969, leading bands, occasionally traveling with Fletcher Henderson up and down the coast, and arranging on the side. James Simpson revived a Blue Devil band in Oklahoma City and then migrated to work in Los Angeles during the war; he went to Chicago in the late 1940s.[3]

After leaving the Blue Devils, George Hudson led a band in St. Louis and sometimes backed singer Sarah Vaughan.[4] Abe Bolar gigged in New York City, recording with Hot Lips in the 1940s and appearing with his wife, Juanita, a pianist, on a number of early rock and roll records. He gave up music to drive a taxi, however, after rock and roll prevailed as the music of the 1950s. Ernie Williams sang and fronted a band in Kansas City and went out to the West Coast in the 1950s before returning to Oklahoma City.[5] Reuben

Lynch became sick when the Blue Devils were in West Virginia, went home to Lynchburg to recuperate, and never again played professionally. He took a job in the Weirton steel mills, was active in the union, and sang in the local church choir.

These musicians continued to perpetuate, each in his own way, the unique heritage they enjoyed in their youth as Blue Devils —strict adherence to a strong sense of professionalism and brotherhood, community service, and caring for their families. They differed from the stereotypical portraits of carefree, undisciplined jazz musicians that dominate much of the popular history of jazz. Buster Smith's life was typical of a Blue Devil, in terms of his lifelong passion for playing, arranging, writing music, and leading bands.

On leaving Basie and Kansas City for Claude Hopkins late in summer of 1936, and having gone to New York City, Smith learned that "New Yorkers tended to take care of their own. The musicians' union there kept the weekend dates for home boys and gave the less lucrative week night dates to . . . the out of towners."[6] It took three months to get into the union and to become eligible for the better jobs, so he left for Omaha and played and wrote for Nat Towles.[7] He was asked by Basie to rejoin them at the end of 1936, and so he went to New York City for this reason.[8] Some band members were resentful, however: " 'Aw, don't take Buster back, he went off and left us.' So Basie said, 'Bus, some of the boys are a little hot, so just stick around a while till they cool off and then come on back.' But I never did go back as a member of the band." He arranged for Basie, and he started arranging for white swing bands, as well. "Several cats wanted me to do some arrangements for them. Out of all them great arrangers, they thought I had somethin' special—[I had] that western swing."[9] Once again he left New York for the Southwest.

In spring 1937 he performed at an Ozark tavern resort in Eldon, Arkansas, with George E. Lee, Pete Johnson on piano, Efferge Ware on guitar, and Thurber Jay on bass.[10] In early 1938, Smith played with Jesse Price, Billy Hadnott, and Prince Stewart at Kansas City's Club Continental on Twelfth Street.[11] Around this time he took Charlie Parker under his wing, and his young protégé later confessed, "Sure, I liked 'Pres,' . . . but Buster was the cat I really dug."[12]

"Charlie was just about 17 or 18 years old," Smith explained. "He thought I played a lot of alto. He stayed right on me. He was a slow reader and some fellows wouldn't play around with him. But I didn't mind. He was good and learned." Smith recalled that Parker was always talking about going home and having his mother cook some "yardbirds" [chickens] for him—thus the source of the nickname "Bird."[13]

Smith decided to try his luck in New York City again when things were slow for his band in Kansas City. He informed the sidemen, "Boys, I'm gonna try and do a little better."[14] "I thought we might get a break up there. I left Charlie [Parker] and Odel West in charge and told him I'd send for them when I found something."[15] After seven months and no word from Smith, Parker hitchhiked to New York to find him. He did, and stayed in his apartment, sleeping in his bed during the day. Smith had him leave before his wife came home from her job waiting tables at Andy Kirk's restaurant, because she didn't like him sleeping in his clothes.[16] At least one Dallas saxophonist maintained that Smith was the man behind Parker: "A lot of people attribute what Charlie Parker took and developed to the stuff Buster taught him in his early years of playing."[17]

He continued to teach others and to collaborate with former Blue Devils, particularly Hot Lips Page and Eddie Durham, as late as the 1980s, and he probably felt a special kinship with his fellows Texans. In 1939 Smith lived at 205 West 136th Street in Harlem, just a few doors down from Hot Lips at 225 West 136th Street.[18] He also tried to advise the young guitarist Charlie Christian, who had left Oklahoma City for Benny Goodman's band late in summer 1939. Smith claims he did not know that Christian was interested in music until he heard about this great guitarist with Nat Towles, then went to see him, "and there was little old Charlie playing all that guitar." When they met in New York, the elder advised the young star, "Son, you're in New York now, so take it easy. Don't stay up all night, watch yourself, and be careful." He was in the habit of advising younger musicians in this way. However, "the next thing I knew, they had Charlie out in the hospital and he died."[19]

When he tried to book his Kansas City band in New York City, Smith was unsuccessful, but spent time arranging for Eddie Durham, Ina Ray Hutton, and Joe Marsala. "I arranged a good deal but didn't do too much playing," during this stint in New York City, he recalled, except with Don Redman. He discovered that playing arrangements by one of the very first jazz arrangers presented a challenge: "It took all my time just learning to play the stuff."[20] With Redman, veteran arranger with McKinney's Cotton Pickers, he played on "Chew-Chew-Chew (Your Bubble Gum)," "Igloo," "Baby, Won't You Please Come Home," "Chant of the Weed," and others.[21] He also wrote arrangements for Benny Carter and Snub Mosely.[22]

Smith also teamed up with Hot Lips Page on "I Would Do Anything for You," "I Ain't Got Nobody," "A Porter's Love Song to A Chambermaid," "Gone with the Gin," and "Walk It to Me," early in 1940.[23] He recorded with Pete Johnson and His Boogie Woogie Boys, Hot Lips Page, Abe Bolar, and Joe Turner, and produced outstanding solos on the famous "Cherry Red" and "Baby, Look at You."[24] At the time, things were so tough that he had hocked his horn, and Johnson found him and helped him to get it out of the pawnshop.[25]

However, the Texas arranger found the pressures of deadlines to be unsettling. The pay could have been better, too. When he and Eddie Durham took a job in an expensive seaside Connecticut resort, he found that the pay was not very good, and the isolation was even worse. His doubts about the wisdom of pursuing a musician's life on the East Coast increased until he felt he had to make a decision.[26] "I stayed in New York for six years, in and out." The frugal southerner "Saved me a gang of change. Then my people started dying out." As the oldest child, he felt responsible for the family, especially for his mother, who "was going to work 'fore day in the morning, working and cleaning in a rich neighborhood till ten o'clock at night." His brother, Boston, a pianist, kept him up to date. "So I figured, music is music, no matter where you play it. I seen what it was! I seen in New York, where many of the cats that I'd idolized in my younger days—well, they was goin' 'round raggeder than a willow tree."[27]

One time he drove across the country with trumpet player Russell Smith, who complained that with all the touring he had done with Fletcher Henderson, he had spent only three days with his wife in a year. This was distinctly strange, if not bizarre, to Smith. While others in the band traveled in the bus, "I was the only one that had a car. . . . I had my wife with me, riding with me. See, I wasn't going to go for that. I just wasn't used to that life, the way them people lived up there in Harlem in New York anyhow. I didn't like that."[28]

Smith mentioned that the prevailing opinion at the time was "You had to go to New York. . . . You got to go up there to the Apple and get that stamp on you, then you come out and then you have some prestige. Yeah, you've been to New York!" This popular wisdom wasn't altogether convincing for the reedman and leading swing arranger, because he had gone "on up there . . . and I'd seen what it was all about and everything, and just seen that it wasn't nothing but just a lay-down place. Just go there and you stayed. There wasn't no work there." You had to leave New York and tour, "be gone for two-three months, and when that's over, you come back, sit down until they build up something else, and it's liable to be a half-year before they build up something else, and there you are."[29]

The Texan also criticized New Yorkers because they didn't help one another, and because of their lack of hospitality. With the Blue Devils, it was all for one and one for all, but in the Apple, "Wasn't nobody for each other. Every man will get you." He found the cliquishness of New Yorkers to be the worst part. "Even on the road, somebody invites you home for dinner," but not in the Big Apple. They were poor, too. He recalled how, when he visited musicians backstage, "they'd shut their dinners up in their dresser drawers rather than share them."[30]

Smith elaborated on how "If a guy see you comin', he's comin' down the street and it look like you want somethin', he go on the other side of the street." Even worse, "No musician there don't never invite you to his house to have no dinner." The reedman and arranger qualified this: "I had one, that was Lips. But we was already the same as brothers. We was together, come up together. But they didn['t] invite you to the house to have dinner. . . . Most of them don't even want you to know where he's staying."

People wouldn't even talk to you "until you got something that he might get off of you, and then he'll speak to you. . . . You can stay next door . . . I've seen guys stay two or three years right next door to each other, going in and out, and they never speak to each other. Never say, 'Good morning, good evening, how do you feel?' or nothing."

The Southerner confessed, "See, I wasn't used to that kind of stuff. No!" The way he was raised, "It was supposed to be all good neighborship, everybody would speak to each other."[31]

Smith was also critical of many of the arrangers as well as the much-fabled jam sessions that figure largely in the history of jazz. "Almost all of those musicians in New York, especially those arrangers, they all tried to arrange alike." Fletcher Henderson was one of the few exceptions, as the only one "that was about a little bit different, and of course, Duke, he was a little bit different, too." As for the jam session, he found nothing to it, "Just everybody for himself. Everybody... try to out-do each other and try to out-blow each other." The modest veteran of decades of touring from the 1920s complained that jam sessions were worthless. "Musicians playing music for the musicians. A musician, he don't pay to come in to hear you play, and he don't give you nothin'. So what's the use? Ain't nothin' to it. Not a thing to it." Even worse was the lack of a cooperative spirit: "He won't try to help you. No! He'll be right in there trying to get your part or trying to get something.... He ain't gonna try to show you how to go." Indeed, one "might find one out of a hundred that might show you some little points or something there. Every man for himself. Yeah."[32]

He had seen the future and rejected it outright. Smith returned to Dallas in 1940 and again in 1942.[33] But, back home, "I saw the boys were playing for peanuts and didn't have much work either. I stayed about four months and finally went back to New York the first part of 1941."[34] He played with Snub Mosley, traveling from army camp to army camp for the USO. Then he heard that his father had died, but because of his commitments he could not go back to Texas for the funeral. Smith toured with Mosley more than three months, then went back to New York City for one more year before returning permanently to Dallas.

He was relieved to be back home at the end of 1942: "It was fine to be back where you knew you were gonna sleep in the same bed every night." The veteran traveler explained, "When you're on the road, you don't know where you gonna sleep! Or when! Or when the bus gonna break down." As if he could still feel his ordeals, he observed, "I spent many, many nights in Kansas, or Nebraska, somewhere, ol' car broke down, or threw a rod, or had a flat and you didn't have no spare. Might be broke down between any town, man, nothin' out there, not even no farms! Only way to keep warm, since you didn't want to run out of gas, was to pile on out of there and make a fire. Spent many, many nights like that."[35] Smith also complained that a New York life and that of a musician on the road were too hectic and left little time for his favorite activities: "I liked to hunt and fish and relax once in a while."[36] His desire to stay at home reflected the hard-won knowledge that it was difficult to be a musician on the road and to stay married.[37] When he left New York City for Omaha, it was partly because his wife, Ruth Henrietta Jackson, was from this city, and had two children there from a previous marriage. Years later she was no longer his wife, and so one must surmise that his statements about keeping his wife with him resulted from his own direct experience as well as that of other musicians.

As his younger brothers were going into the military, Smith shouldered responsibility for looking after their mother. He started a chicken farm in her yard and opened a restaurant during the war; as late as 1956 the *Dallas City Directory* listed Smith's Restaurant at 2223 Garden Drive, the residence of "Prof" until he died late in the twentieth century. But despite these business ventures, he was not long out of the music business, and was leading bands within a year or so.

Smith arranged and wrote for his small combo, who played in Dallas at the Band Box, then he enlarged it to thirteen and performed at other venues, including the Rose Room shortly before Christmas 1944. His band accompanied a review, *Harlem's a Popping*, and before long Smith acquired the region's best musicians, such as David "Fathead" Newman.[38] He led and played with several pickup bands, backing Big Joe Turner, T-bone Walker, Peewee Crayton, Al Hibbler, Lowell Fulson, and others—rhythm and blues singers. He toured with them in nearby Louisiana, Oklahoma, and Arkansas, and led other bands as well. Some musicians criticized him for returning to the "sticks," as they referred to Texas, but Smith did not agree. He never regretted his return to the Lone Star state, because, unlike New York, it was a place "where a dollar in your pocket counts for something."[39]

Smith's departure from the Apple for Dallas was not only a rejection of all that New York stood for, for musicians and show business people, it was also a denouncement of the city of strangers and an acceptance of the traditional values of old friends, home, family, and a life of hunting and fishing. The fact that he preferred Dallas is all the more remarkable, given its harsh Jim Crow practices, racial segregation, and lynchings. Others made similar decisions, such as Snake Whyte, who decided to stay in Los Angeles with his wife and their child for three decades before returning to his hometown, Perry, Iowa, in another endorsement of home and old friends. For that matter, Reuben Lynch left the Blue Devils around 1933 and lived in Weirton, West Virginia, and Eddie Durham followed a similar route in the 1950s, although in the 1940s he had enjoyed more success than any former Blue Devil—after, of course, Basie, Rushing, and Young.

In 1938, Durham completed his year's stint with Basie and joined Cab Calloway for a week, claiming he left because of Calloway's use of profanity with the band—"I couldn't stand that at all."[40] He made classic Kansas City Six and Five recordings featuring his electric guitar with Basie sidemen—without the pianist, or any pianist, for that matter; he wrote arrangements for just about every bandleader, especially Harry James, Artie Shaw, and Glenn Miller; and he led a couple of his own bands.

Durham was evidently very much in demand as an arranger during the height of the swing era. For Glenn Miller, he arranged his theme song, "In the Mood," as well as "Sliphorn Jive," "Glen Island Special," "Tiger Rag," and "I Want to Be Happy"; for Artie Shaw, he made arrangements of "Sunny Side of the Street," "My Blue Heaven," and "I've Got the World On A String," among others. He also wrote arrangements for Jan Savitt, Ina Ray Hutton, and Jimmy Lunceford.[41]

Durham made several recordings under his own name on March 18, 1938, and then recorded again on September 27; when, in a kind of recapitulation, the Kansas City Six recorded in early spring 1944, Durham wasn't even present. Further obscuring his importance in these recordings is the fact that the ones made in late September 1938 were later attributed to Lester Young. Earlier in 1938, Leonard

Feather had featured Durham in a *Melody Maker* article in which we learn that the trombonist-guitarist had a group called Eddie Durham and His Base Four, composed of Walter Page, Freddie Green, Jo Jones, and Buck Clayton.[42] This group was the forerunner of the Kansas City Five that included Clayton, Green on acoustic guitar, Walter Page, Jo Jones, and Durham on electric guitar. The absence of a piano meant that Durham assumed the role of pianist, providing chordal backing.

The first records featuring Durham's electric guitar were paramount in the history of the instrument and in subsequent developments in music. He was still with the Basie band for the Kansas City Five records, in late winter 1938, and at the time they were installed for a week at the Savoy Ballroom in Harlem.[43] The songs recorded in March were "Laughing at Life," "Good Mornin' Blues" (the Basie-Durham-Rushing perennial), and the ballad "I Know That You Know." Walter Page, the bassist, introduced "Laughin' at Life," then the muted Clayton took up the melody, with Durham chording softly behind him, and Durham soloed for a chorus while Page and Green provided the rhythmic accompaniment.

After Durham departed from Basie at midyear, Lester Young's addition made Durham's quintet a sextet with three former Blue Devils—Young, Durham, and Page—for these pianoless recordings. Again, the format is similar to the quintet's, in that every one soloed, and Page was the only one to include his own composition —"Pagin' the Devil" (with Milt Gabler), both a pun on the bassist's name and a reference to the legendary band. Again, Green plays rhythm on acoustic guitar, while Durham accompanies and solos on electric guitar.

The orchestra was in the midst of a prolonged stay at the Famous Door[44] when they recorded some of the best examples of "cool jazz," a synthesis of New Orleans and swing idioms. "Way Down Yonder in New Orleans" reveals Young's Crescent City roots and the central role that city played in the music's origins.

Durham's writing accomplishments in 1939 outstripped anything he had done before. In the 1930s he composed eleven pieces: "Everyday Blues," "I Wish I Could Be Blue," "That Too, Do," "Oh! Eddie," "Lafayette," "Oh Boy," "Harlem Shout," "Swingin' on C,"

"Rhythm Rag," "Every Tub," and "Good Mornin' Blues." In 1939 he composed thirteen songs and the next year eight more. Some of the better-known compositions are "Sliphorn Jive," "Time Out," "Topsy," "Wham Re Bop Boom Bam," "Sent For You Yesterday and Here You Come Today," "John's Idea," "Swinging the Blues," "He Who Hesitates Is Lost," and—written together with a New Yorker from the West Indies, Bennie Benjamin—"I Don't Want to Set the World on Fire." Many of these songs were written with others, especially Basie and Moten, but this was a phenomenal output, even for a collaborator, and many became standards of the swing repertoire.[45]

After 1941 he was not so productive, as he composed and or co-composed three songs that year and only two more in the 1940s. His biggest hit of the decade, of course, was "I Don't Want to Set the World on Fire" written with the assistance of Bennie Benjamin. In the 1950s he went into real estate, having been awarded some real estate in upstate New York, along with Edgar Battle, as part of a legal settlement—but he still wrote five more songs, and in 1960 he revived his hit of the 1930s with "Topsy No. 3" and "No. 4,"[46] experiencing considerable success.

Then there was at least one song he helped out with, "Until the Real Thing Comes Along," for which he received no credit. Durham was extremely generous as well as honest when it came to helping others, and in this way he differed from many people in the music business. He assisted Pha Terrell when they were in Kansas City—probably with Moten. Terrell came to Durham's one night with his dance partner: "Man, we got a song here, listen. . . ." The arranger-composer "got up out of the bed and went down on the river bank, and didn't have any manuscript paper. So I took some plain writing paper and made some lines and went down and sat on the riverbank and let them sing it. . . . I wrote that out." He relied on his guitar in the process, at four o'clock one morning, while sitting on the bank of the Missouri River, "and I gave him that lead sheet and he tore out with it." He surmised that perhaps Kirk's pianist and arranger, Mary Lou Williams, made an arrangement out of it.[47] He received no monetary or any other kind of credit, reasoning, "I didn't see why I should go on a song just for writing some notes down for some guys. But that's the racket today. But to me, that was dishonest, in those days."[48]

In 1940 Durham organized a band including at least two colleagues from the Southwest—Buster Smith, altoist and arranger, and Joe Keyes, trumpet.[49] As *Metronome* wrote condescendingly when it announced Durham's band-leading effort, "The new outfit will be like most colored groups in that it features swing, and as such will be best suited for ballrooms and theaters." The leader intended to present "good sweet [music] also," but they would all be specials; "there will be no dull renditions of stocks."

In addition to his own arrangements, Durham was featured on electric guitar, which would be "played an octave above the sax quintet, the result being a sound somewhat similar to Glenn Miller's reed section." They performed at the Oak Grove Casino in Bridgeport, Connecticut—the spot where they later complained that the pay was not good and the isolation worse. Nor were these the worst of their problems.[50]

In the late 1930s, Durham embarked upon a dimension of his musical career that few bandleaders pursued—managing a band composed entirely of women, or "girls," in the parlance of the time. In a way he continued the Blue Devil methods of teaching young musicians, writing arrangements especially for them, and providing them with musical and professional experience by taking them on the road. His responsibilities went far beyond those of a mere manager. He started managing the Ina Ray Hutton band, led by the "Blonde Bombshell of Rhythm," who came from Chicago and grew up in show business. Her band enjoyed the support of Irving Mills, who was Duke Ellington's backer, as well. This backing gave them a decided advantage over other women's outfits, as well as men's.[51]

In an earlier version, the band was known as Hutton's Melodears. Ina Ray Hutton led the band and danced, and had some first-rate musicians—trombonist Alyse Wills and pianist Betty Roudybush, for example. Some people thought such a band should open with "A Pretty Girl Is Like A Melody," but Hutton disagreed. "I wanna sound like Benny Goodman and Basie and everybody else."[52] For this reason they sought the help of Eddie Durham.

Their new manager had nothing but praise for trombonist Wills: "She had international perfect pitch. . . . She'd go down to the dressing room and give everybody a note. They wouldn't have to tune by no piano. They'd tune by her voice. She was a great musician." Durham recalled, "She was the first trombone player, then they helped to pick the others," and helped to rehearse the section.[53]

Of Roudybush, Durham maintained, "She was about one of the best I could get at that time on the piano, who could play solid like Mary Lou Williams and those people. She was a pro." In fact, her choruses were written out in *Down Beat*. He recalled that "in those days I wasn't teaching them the get-off solo work so much as teaching them rhythm, teaching them to be an anchor personality with the instrument." He was not producing prima donnas to look good themselves, but musicians who helped others to look good. Durham's objective was achieved, as he "lined the band up to be strong."[54]

◆ ◆ ◆

Durham's All-Girl Band was so popular during the war that, after two successful days in the Paramount in Newark, promoters wanted to put them on Broadway in New York City.[55] Durham thought they were not yet ready for such a challenge, that they were being favored simply because they were women. He explained, "I didn't like that. . . . There ain't no bands can go open out of rehearsal with a new band and go to the Paramount in New York. . . . They could play. But you still needed a reputation behind you."[56]

He drew upon his show business savvy to highlight the band's talents. When they were featured with a dozen other bands at Madison Square Garden, for example, Durham asked Hutton to make sure they appeared on the program just before Basie's orchestra. They played Basie's hits, "One O'Clock Jump," "Out the Window," and "Jumpin' at the Woodside"—all of which were originally Durham arrangements—to upstage the Kansas City pianist. "The girls were wavin' their hats like [trumpet player] Harry Edison, and he ran out of the dressing room half dressed up on the stage, and they all come out and they didn't believe it." They became believers when they saw it, though. Durham recalled, "those guys, man, they felt great hearin' those girls play their solos." The veteran swing arranger explained, "That's the way that band played, just the same as the boys. They had to. I trained 'em down like that."[57]

Eddie Durham's All-Star Girl Orchestra, Howard Theater,
Washington, D.C., 1942

When he became musical director of the International Sweethearts of Rhythm, another "all-girl" band, as they were called, this
was not new terrain for him. The band started at a school in rural
Mississippi, Piney Woods, and included a variety of different ethni-
cities if not nationalities—Puerto Rican, Chinese-American, Black,
and Spanish.[58] Anna Mae Winburn—who came from a musical family in Tennessee, migrated to Indianapolis, and passed as "Spanish"
—was given the opportunity by Red Perkins to lead a men's band
in Omaha. She fronted Lloyd Hunter's Serenaders, and after the war
began and the draft took her musicians, her manager sent to Oklahoma City for several Blue Devils, one of whom was Leonard Chadwick. Charlie Christian was also a member of her Cotton Club Boys.
Then the opportunity to lead the Sweethearts presented itself
around 1941, and she sought the help of Eddie Durham.[59]

On taking the band over, Durham made a statement indicating
that he would be putting his belief in the equality of the sexes into
practice. "Women musicians can be just as good as men," he ob-

served. "All that stuff about the weaker sex not being able to blow
a horn right is the bunk!" In fact, he contended that they displayed
"better discipline, musical ability and eagerness to learn than many
of the male bands" that he worked with.[60] He intended to enlarge the
band, increasing the reed and brass sections. The Sweethearts went
on the road playing against Fletcher Henderson's band in a "battle of
the sexes" at Easter time in 1942.[61]

As Durham explained, many musicians were doubtful that he
could successfully lead such a band. Eddie Durham's actions were
quite progressive at a time when, as late as 1958, *Down Beat* ran
an article, "Women In Jazz: Do They Belong?" Durham showed that
there was indeed a place for women.[62] The veteran arranger and
composer explained, "You see, it was the gimmicks and the tricks,
and knowing how to make those girls in the tonation where they
could play. So that's how I got over that band."[63] There were practical reasons, too; the draft regularly took his male band members during the war, so he switched.[64]

After several months of traveling with them and playing USO
shows, he evidently decided that he liked the idea. He gave up the
Sweethearts and put together another band of women "to provide a
brand of music which has been the wonder of the theatrical season,"
in 1943. "I had to organize another band from the same man that
owned the Sweethearts, to make money, and use the two bands,"
Durham explained. Their backer was A. Dade, "a prominent local
businessman."[65] Ever the showman, Durham added "to his band several girl vaudeville musical acts headed by Jean Starr." He also added
the comedian-drummer Lipps Hackett. The outfit was known simply as "Eddie Durham's All-Girl Band." Starting July 9, 1943, they
played the following cities—one per night on average: Columbus,
South Carolina; Lynch, Kentucky; then a USO date; Nashville, Tennessee; Atlanta, Georgia; Macon, Georgia; Birmingham, Alabama;
USO dates for two days; New Orleans, Louisiana on the next day; and
Mobile, Alabama on July 19. They crisscrossed the United States in
their sleeper bus and traveled and performed in Canada, as well. At
least one night per week was devoted to the war effort—entertaining at military camps and USO centers, raising war bonds, and up-
lifting morale generally.[66] Reviewers such as Leonard Feather were

not always kind in their evaluations,[67] but as a measure of their success, the two bands traveled internationally—the Sweethearts to the Philippines and the Durham band across Canada.[68]

Durham explained how he "juggled" band members. "When I ran out of Black girls, I used a lot of white—I'd get them from everywhere." Down South he would "take the white girls out of the band [and] put them in this band. I kept them separated all the time."[69] He claimed that leading a band of women around the country was not a problem. "I didn't have any headaches with the girls, because they did what I said and they asked no questions." A. Dade, the backer from D.C., ensured their success, giving them a distinct advantage over most bands. "The only reason I was successful with this band is because they had unlimited money from the backer.... A Western fellow" living in the District of Columbia, who "kept a half a million standing in the banks. Money was no problem." They bought two All-American buses, sleepers, one for each orchestra, and they "had it made. That's the kind of money, man, it was." From time to time the famous husband-and-wife comedians Butterbeans and Susie and singer Ella Fitzgerald toured with them.[70]

Durham's All-Star band was made up of eighteen to twenty-two women, "musicians with reflexibility and phrasing and volume and pianissimos and everything." Durham's strategy was that he "always kept two extra trumpet players. Always had about five to six, keep trainin' em, keep 'em on hand." He maintained that his trombone section played as well as he could.[71] An incident illustrated this. When the trombones played a high note, or gliss (*glissando*) on his composition "Sliphorn Jive," he used to walk on stage and join the trombone section and make the note, too. "And they tried to write it up and say the girls wasn't makin' the note, that it was just me makin' that note. That's how close we would sound together." So to prove them wrong, he started walking out on the stage and dropping his trombone when they hit the note. "And that stopped that, 'cause every trombone player there could get that high C. Many boys' bands couldn't hit that high C. You'd find maybe one trombone player in each of them that could."[72]

Durham praised the trumpet section, as well, and at various times Dolly Jones, Edna Williams, Jean Starr, and Nova Lee McGee

passed through this section. "Those were the four best trumpet players that I knew, except for Tiny Davis. . . . Jean Starr could tear it to
pieces . . . play anything that Dizzy could play on paper, by sight, and
had the top range." He concluded, "Those girls could reach up to C.
That's why they was able to play Ella Fitzgerald's music . . . any act
you put up, that band could play."[73] In spring 1943, when his band
performed at Chicago's Regal Theatre on the South Side, the *Chicago Defender* contended that the band was "one of the hottest stage
shows that ever raised the roof of the theatre!" The weekly described
the band members as "fourteen of the swing-est chicks seen and
heard in Chicago in this or any other year." They "really swung out
on the solid standbys like 'One O'Clock Jump,' 'The St. Louis Blues,'
and the 'King Porter Stomp,'" and some of Durham's compositions.
His compositions had "a solid beat that is the envy of all the male
musicians who have heard them." A singing act, the Four Durham-
ettes, "put over a song with a sock!" The new Mrs. Durham—Earsie
Bell Hiller, his third wife, whom he married in Valparaiso, Indiana,
in spring 1939—assisted in managing this band.[74] No wonder he had
few problems. He also taught her how to copy arrangements, saving
him a lot of time.[75]

Durham claimed in one interview that this work kept him out of
the military at a time when it was depleting other bands, and some
white bandleaders, like Shaw and Miller, joined the military with
their bands. When wartime restrictions meant that other musicians
had trouble touring the nation—even bands like Basie's—Durham's
bands traveled in comfort in buses with hot and cold running water,
air conditioning, and sleeping accommodations for twenty-two people.[76] The Black educator Mary McLeod Bethune, founder of the
National Council of Negro Women and Bethune-Cook College, had
the ear of Eleanor Roosevelt, and she was successful in getting them
their busses. Besides the sleeping facilities and bathroom, there was
a private apartment and office for Durham. They had clout, and so
they also had priority; as Durham explained, they could go anywhere. "You could drive it on the Capitol grounds if you wanted to."[77]
They traveled to seventy-two army camps in Canada.[78] After VJ Day,
when they were scheduled to perform at Sweets in Oakland, California, they decided to break up the band, and Durham saw to it that

the bus took every one of them home. Back in New York City, he trained singer Jean Parks to front a band, and it became "Jean Parks' All-Girl Band," with Durham as manager. They toured with Ella Fitzgerald, Moms Mabley, and Butterbeans and Susie.[79]

◆ ◆ ◆

Another former Blue Devil arranger, Snake Whyte, also led a big band that boosted civilian and military morale. He moved to Los Angeles about the time the Basie band was playing the big hotels and traveling down South. His childhood friend, Eddie Barefield, left Calloway's band when it arrived in Los Angeles, started a band at Sebastian's Cotton Club in Culver City, and sent for Whyte to join the band. This venture did not last long, and Whyte arranged and freelanced before forming his own band in 1940. Like Durham's All-Girl band, Whyte's toured and played to maintain morale at California military bases.

In fall 1941 the *California Eagle* wrote, "Leroy Whyte and his orchestra are at the present time the most popular colored local dance band in Southern California." The band was formed in early 1940 and originally consisted of seven musicians, but Whyte expanded it. As the *Eagle* claimed, "the band has a membership of 13 cats who know the art of laying that solid jive on their instruments."

Whyte's talents and efforts at building morale in the military were praised, as well. His band was said to have "an original style of swing" due to his "fine arranging ability." He was also considered to be "one of the top trumpet players in Southern California." Evidently, New Deal programs enabled him to operate. Whyte's outfit was affiliated with the Federal Music Project of Southern California and was considered to be "the top ranking band of the large group of bands connected with this government organization." His band was touted as the only Black band on the Pacific coast "playing regular engagements at the various Army forts, Naval reservations, aircraft plants, and other national defense organizations." His concerns were not only artistic and aesthetic, but also connected with the community's needs during a time of crisis.[80]

The band received a grand ovation from the crowd that gathered

at Pershing Square on Christmas Eve 1942 to see a program sponsored by the National Defense Bonds headquarters. Whyte wrote a
new arrangement of songwriter Leon René's patriotic song "We're
In It Again and We'll Win It Again." Sung by a trio, the Three
Shades, the number brought the audience to its feet as they cheered.
Less than a month after Pearl Harbor, the crowd gave Whyte's band
"one of the greatest receptions given any of the outstanding orchestras and musical organizations which have been guest artists on this
worthy program."[81] Beginning a few months later, in winter 1942,
Whyte and his band members played dance engagements for nine
months for the soldiers of Fort MacArthur and members of the U.S.
Navy stationed in San Pedro, California. They were "the toast of the
area" and of the various military camps.[82]

Whyte collected some of the region's finer musicians and acts,
including tenor saxophonist Hubert "Bumps" Myers, who later
played with Lee and Lester Young's combo in Los Angeles. He was
said to have "a very learned musical background" and an original
style.[83] Trumpet player Monty Easter was from Los Angeles and also
possessed "a very fine musical background."[84] His vocal trio, the
Three Shades, was "no doubt the finest girl trio on the Pacific coast
and . . . one of the most versatile in the country." They were said to
have "really 'broke things up'" one Sunday night when they appeared
with Whyte's band at the New Plantation Club.[85]

A young impresario, Joe Morris, started this club, taking over Old
Jazzland, in Watts, a community several miles south of downtown
Los Angeles. He hired Whyte's band for three nights at the end of
the week, then he added a fourth (Friday). In spring 1942 he started
a collegiate night "for the various high school and college students
who will be able to 'kick their boots out.'"[86] Society people and Hollywood stars from across town were among the audience at the Plantation in summer 1942 and in subsequent years.[87]

Whyte also sat in the trumpet section of Fletcher Henderson's
orchestra when it toured the Pacific coast, but never stayed away
from home too long. In the 1940s he formed a record company and
did arrangements for a number of bands. He was able to provide for
his wife and son, Le Roy Jr., and watch the boy go to the local schools
and study music, too.

Trumpet player George Hudson made a similar decision, settling in the St. Louis metropolitan area. He led a band and was head of the musicians' union for a number of years. Hudson also taught music, training generations of students at Elijah Lovejoy High School, located just a few hundred yards from his home in East St. Louis. He helped shape the training and music careers of generations of young people in the mid- and late twentieth century.

Hudson, Whyte, and Smith's lives and careers in the 1940s represented one dimension of the Blue Devils' existence—staying in one place for the sake of home and family, only rarely touring, and then never very far away or for very long. At the other extreme, that of Durham, Oran Page, Lester Young, Basie, Rushing and others, musicians continued touring in the 1940s, only staying at home intermittently. Together, these were the architects of music in the U.S. in the 1930s and 1940s—and in subsequent decades, as well, in the guise of rock and roll. Numerous critics have pointed out that the roots of rock music can be traced to swing and the small combos of the 1930s. Protégées of these musicians (Charlie Parker is the best example) charted new directions for the music while extending the traditions established by Buster Smith, Lester Young, and Eddie Durham. John Coltrane developed the legacies of Coleman Hawkins, Lester Young, and Sidney Bechet, who inspired him to take up the soprano saxophone. The connection between the swing era and later developments is clearer, perhaps, in the music of singers Hot Lips Page and Jimmy Rushing, whose blues songs foreshadowed the popularization of blues-based music, or rock and roll, in the 1950s, and were invoked in the blues revival of the 1960s in the U.S. and England.

CHAPTER THIRTEEN

Legacy

"It's Hard to Laugh or Smile"

The Kansas City heritage was heralded in *Down Beat* by John Hammond in 1936, and, of course, when the Basie band, Joe Turner, and Pete Johnson performed at Carnegie Hall two years later, attention was directed to this Midwestern metropolis's rich musical tradition. In early 1941 in New York City, Kansas City musicians reunited for a historic recording of their music. "They had decided to make a group of phonograph records," the *Call* observed, "as a tribute to the Kansas City style of jazz pioneered here by the late Bennie Moten, George E. Lee, and others." The writer maintained that Kansas City style ranked as one of the big three styles along with the New Orleans and Chicago styles. The musicians defined their heritage as "a drive, a good beat, and a rhythmic push. It means taking a simple riff (theme) and building up to a moving mass of counterpoint against the improvisations of the soloists." It meant lots of solos, "all ad-libbed without paper" for piano, trumpet, and saxophone.[1] The event had been planned for almost six months, because it took so long to get Andy Kirk, Eddie Durham, Buster Smith, Pete Johnson, Count Basie, Joe Turner, Oran (Hot Lips) Page, and others in Manhattan at the same time. Kirk had them record "Moten Stomp" in tribute to the bandleader and "Twelfth Street Rag," an older number that celebrated this famous Kansas City street. Pianist Mary Lou Williams recorded "Paseo Strut." Formerly Kirk's pianist and arranger, she led her own band, the Fly Cats, "a term coined by Kansas City Negro musicians to describe members of their profession." Pete

Johnson and Joe Turner recorded "627 Stomp," named for the Black musicians' local, and "Piney Brown Blues." "Moten Swing," "The Count," "Lafayette," "Baby Dear," and "South" were among the other numbers that Decca recorded and issued.[2]

Basie and his men reunited a number of times in the second half of the twentieth century. The occasions were social as well as musical. The pianist looked forward to a good home-cooked meal with Leonard and Lorraine Chadwick when he came through Denver.[3] Reuben Lynch's brother explained that Reuben would sometimes drive north from Weirton, West Virginia, in the fall, if his cousin Marian Anderson "was in New York about the same time as Count Basie. 'Cause she had a partner in New York. So sometimes he would go to see Marian Anderson, and he would go by wherever Count Basie was playing." In fact, the Count gave him a key to his apartment and told him to stop in whenever he visited the Apple.

Snake Whyte left Los Angeles for his hometown, Perry, Iowa, where his wife joined him, and they started attending local churches. Few people knew about his career as a professional musician or as a Blue Devil, but eventually, word got out. On one of his birthdays in the 1970s a reunion was held for him with Earle Warren and Eddie Barefield; even Count Basie was supposed to attend but could not make it. In various ways former Moten and Basie band members, often from Oklahoma, Kansas, and Texas, preserved the legacy that was known as Kansas City jazz, but was actually much richer, drawing upon many distant spots.

These men kept alive the big band era, though for many bands it had ended, as a viable business, around 1949. Some saw the end coming as early as 1946, with the breakup of many of the large bands. Basie led a small combo after disbanding, but within a year or two reconstituted a big band. Many musicians, on the other hand, sat by idly while younger entertainers leading small combos, and blues shouters, and electric guitarists from Mississippi captivated a youthful audience—teenagers, in particular.

It was ironic in the extreme that the very architects of music known as Kansas City swing, jump swing, rhythm and blues, and then rock and roll were shoved aside while another generation was caught up in the music of youthful rebellion, as it was called.

Younger musicians played bop, cool, and progressive jazz before they—or at least some of them, like Miles Davis—eventually took up electric instruments like the rock and rollers. At midcentury, Hot Lips Page, Eddie Durham, and others played with or beside bands whose music was hardly distinguishable from rock and roll. These included the bands led or fronted by Little Richard, Wynonie Harris, and Big Maybelle.

◆ ◆ ◆

While bad management and unreliable bookers plagued many of these musicians, some, like Oran Page, persevered. He knew that, in the long run, what he was doing was for the benefit of his loved ones. His letters attest to the hardships he faced when he toured in the early 1950s, but in distinct contrast, his reception in France and Belgium was just short of tumultuous.[4]

Newspaper accounts of the reasons for his death cite strokes, heart attack, and a kidney ailment,[5] but they were questioned by his family, particularly his son, Oran Jr., who was awakened by his father early one morning in late October 1954. His father was slumped in a chair in the living room, and he was bleeding as if he had been in a fight. His trumpet was missing, but he wouldn't or couldn't talk, so his son took him to the hospital. He reasoned that his father had fought with someone and lost his trumpet, which was mysteriously returned a few weeks later by a go-between who would not tell the teenager who gave it to him. He feared that Oran Jr. would assault or kill the person, and the son admitted that this was probably true.

Ora Lee, Page's daughter, drove straight through to New York with her husband and visited her father in the hospital. He seemed to have stabilized, and she left town, driving west. Shortly afterwards she learned that he had died on the operating table, which was strange to her because she knew nothing about his need for an operation. Given his propensity for protecting people, not to mention hanging on to his horn, his getting hurt in some kind of altercation must be seen as a likely possibility. His passing cast a shadow on the celebration of Count Basie's twenty years in the "big time," held at the Waldorf.[6]

The first service for Page (one was held in Dallas as well as Manhattan) took place at St. Mark's Methodist church at 138th Street in Harlem. Leonard Feather left his recollections: "It seemed as though the whole of jazz history from 1920 on was standing there waiting to pay final homage to a loved and respected colleague." The widow, Elizabeth Page, dressed in black, sobbed quietly, and beside her sat a solemn Oran Jr. Hazel Scott sang "Abide with Me" just as she had at Fats Waller's funeral. Snub Mosley's muted trombone, with organ accompaniment, played a hymn softly.[7]

For his eulogy, the minister took his lesson from Revelation 1:10.

> *I was in the Spirit on the Lord's day,*
> *and heard behind me a great voice,*
> *as of a trumpet.*[8]

Six trumpet players were pallbearers—Roy Eldridge, Emmet Berry, Louis Metcalf, Ed Lewis, Red Allen, and Jimmy McPartland.[9] The body was shipped to Dallas for another service and burial in Lincoln Cemetery. A few years later, his mother was interred in the plot next to her oldest son.

That night a benefit was held at Stuyvesant Casino for Page's son, and the approximately $1,600 raised was given to him so he could become a doctor—as it was reported at the time. Musicians who paid their respects included Jack Teagarden, Gene Krupa, Zutty Singleton, Pops Foster, and Jimmy Rushing.[10] Because this money was needed for burial expenses, still another benefit was held at Central Plaza and produced by Jack Crystal of Commodore Record Shop. Hundreds of fans were turned away. While Benny Goodman played, the crowd was quiet and restrained, but when other bands performed Dixieland, the fans started shouting and dancing, "culminating with the playing of 'When the Saints Go Marching In.'" About three thousand dollars was raised.[11]

Then Small's Paradise, where Page had started in New York in 1937, held a benefit for the widow and teenage son. As the writer William Ewald observed, "the king of the jazz world left little material behind." Also, he added, "A man's worth is not measured by money or material things alone. It can be measured in other ways, in memories, in terms of heart and good times."

Memories were revived by Henry "Red" Allen, Sammy Price, Lucky Thompson, Louis Metcalf, and other musicians at Small's. "Everyone paid to get in—the friends, newspapermen, the musicians themselves all bought admission." Red Allen took the stand.

"No speeches. . . . The tune is a low, raucous blues. The sweetly blatant sound of Red's horn kicks off the ceiling and resounds through the room. Red plays it soulful and lush and the rhythm section catches the mood and weaves a pattern behind his horn. The piano pours in mellow chords and at the tables the couples relax and remember." Metcalf played "Lover Come Back to Me," "Summertime," and "These Foolish Things," while others performed "Stompin' at the Savoy" and "That's a Plenty." Into the night they played, and outside it rained, "but nobody is listening to the rain. Only the music. It's the music that counts. That and the good times."[12]

The story is more complicated than the press ever knew. The trumpet player told his son, but not his wife, that he had taken out a ten thousand dollar life insurance policy and designated him the beneficiary. Oran Jr. was given or located the paperwork, and as he was a savvy teenager who made money selling newspapers and other items on the streets of New York, he convinced the insurance company to issue him a check, which he deposited in a bank account. He rented his own apartment at fifteen, continued selling newspapers, completed high school, served in the military, and then used the insurance money to finance his education at Morgan State in Baltimore and then at Howard University's Law School in the late 1960s.[13]

Dan Morgenstern's comments were a fair evaluation of Page. "Some day, Oran Hot Lips Page will be accorded his rightful place in the jazz hall of fame, while many reputations now outshining his will be relegated to footnotes in the history of jazz. He was one of those happy few who seem to be the spirit of jazz incarnate. He gave freely, and the world took. Many lived longer, but few lived more."[14]

Page differed from those who worshiped at the shrine of New Orleans, as many fans did in the late 1930s. At that time, a rebirth of Dixieland or traditional jazz was sweeping the nation—supposedly in a return to the roots and a rejection of the commercialism of swing. Page's opinions of jazz's origins were expressed in a French journal in 1951, but never so sharply in any U.S. publications:

"Voyez-vous, je trouve qu'on a trop voulu compartimenter le jazz. On parle souvent de la Nouvelle-Orleans, de Chicago, de Harlem, je crois pour ma part que le jazz est né un peu partout a la fois."

("You see, I believe that people have compartmentalized jazz too much. They often speak of New Orleans, of Chicago, of Harlem, [but] I believe that jazz was born more or less everywhere at the same time."[15])

His views on the future of jazz were also noteworthy insofar as they reflected certain fundamental musical values to be found in most African-American, Afro-Caribbean, and African musics. These ideas were influenced by the music's history. After expressing the opinion that Parker's mentor, Buster Smith, "first introduced what became known as bop," he explained that, all along, he and others had played ninths and flattened fifths like the boppers. "But we never permitted them to master us. We always remained their masters." He clarified this when he spoke of the future—the next step. Jazz would not stand still, this was impossible, but no matter how it changed, it must remain jazz. The seriousness of the matter was conveyed in his summarizing statement: "The melody and the beat, must be our bible. If we lose those, then we lose our musical religion."[16]

Page's devotion to young musicians was such that even some family members, one writer maintained, thought he spent too much time counseling and advising them, but these critics did not appreciate his approach or basic values. "Although his family and friends complained frequently that he was too generous with his talents, Hot Lips remained anxious to help young musicians. He listened to their problems and gave them advice. His apartment on Edgecombe Avenue, in New York became a haven for musical tyros. 'Somebody's got to look after the future generation of musicians,' he explained."[17]

George Page Jr., the trumpet player's nephew (son of his brother, George), made clear how much Page was dedicated to his family in Dallas. While he lived in a modern apartment on Edgecombe Avenue after 1940 until he died, the space was limited—one bedroom for a married couple and Oran Jr. He could have bought a home for himself in Queens, as many musicians did, but he remained a renter. Instead, he helped his mother and family purchase property and homes, for the children as well as for her. This was no small matter for working-class African-Americans in the Deep South, especially as it was done in the late 1930s and 1940s, before the boom years of the 1950s and 1960s.

He also assisted his brother, George, in establishing his own business, a clothes-pressing establishment, and promised George Jr. that he would pay for his college education. The trumpet player helped Ora Lee, his daughter, finance her college education and planned sufficiently so that he left Oran Jr. with ten thousand dollars from a life insurance policy. This sum helped finance his undergraduate and law school education and, in fact, lasted about fifteen years, giving him a cushion of prosperity until the late 1960s. Not unlike his fellow Texans Buster Smith and Eddie Durham, Page sent his money back to Texas to his family, instead of driving a fancy new Cadillac or Lincoln every year, or wasting his money on the excesses for which show folk are renowned. In this respect he revealed remarkable discipline as well as familial devotion.[18]

His philosophy of life and basic values helped him sustain the fluctuations in his career and the hard times, and the blues ethos steeled him for the hardships he endured. At the same time, it must be recognized that his devotion was primarily to his family and to the musicians who sustained the jazz and blues traditions that his career personified.

◆ ◆ ◆

Walter Page played with ex-Basie members after his stint with the band ended in the 1940s, and occasionally with Oran Page. Both Pages and Buddy Tate performed on the records "The Egg or the Hen" and "I Got an Uncle in Harlem" in late winter 1949.[19] The songs from this session foreshadowed the rock and roll of the next decade, during which the bassist did considerable recording and studio work.[20] Two years later he recorded again with Oran Page on "Main Street" and the innovative "Sunny Jungle."[21] Ever ready for something different, he also played with the Ruby Braff sextet and octet.[22] In 1958 he was scheduled to accompany Buck Clayton's band to Europe.[23]

One day in 1957, near the beginning of winter, he headed for the CBS studio to record the music for "The Sound of Jazz" for the *Lively Arts* show. Lugging his bass, he could not find a taxi. He tried for two hours, but his efforts were in vain, and he returned home. He not only missed the session, but the telecast, too, a few days later. He had suffered from kidney ailments for a few years, and then the onset of pneumonia, probably contracted that winter day, sent him to Bellevue Hospital, where he died.

Critic Ralph Gleason's obituary was most telling. He informed readers that Basie once told him the Devils were his favorite band. Gleason contended that Walter Page "was the kingpin in Basie's band for almost a decade." None other than Jo Jones credited Page with teaching him drums. Besides his huge fat tone, he swung the band with a power that was impressive, and the stacks of Basie hits were testimony to his abilities.[24]

Lester Young was the next Blue Devil to pass. His tremendous success with the Basie band and remarkable accomplishments as a combo leader after the war are often overshadowed by his last few years, when he was sick. Nearly two decades of alcoholism took its toll on his body. From the mid 1950s he was chronically ill and was hospitalized more than once. He continued to play, however, touring with the Birdland All-Stars and Jazz at the Philharmonic, even though he was in pain. Late in 1956 he went to Paris with the Birdland contingent. Around 1958 he moved out of his home in Queens, where he was living with his wife and two children, to reside in the Alvin Hotel across the street from Birdland and near Fifty-second Street.

His family and friends looked in on him, and after Marshall Stearns introduced him to Dr. Luther Cloud, who treated him, he appeared to get better. He played at the event celebrating his thirty years in show business late in summer 1958, and a few months later traveled to Paris again. He became sick there, however, and began drinking again. He recorded, nonetheless, and did the famous François Postif interview, but in March 1959 he flew back to New York City and died at the Alvin Hotel shortly afterwards. It was many years before his accomplishments as a creative artist were appreciated in circles outside his devoted fans.

After Basie, Jimmy Rushing had one of the most successful careers of any of the band members, and darkly tragic aspects did not accompany his accomplishments. For a few years he led his own combo, and then at some point he considered retiring and went to North Carolina to live and venture into business with his brother-in-law, but he loved the nightlife and singing too much to retire. In 1958, 1959, and 1960, he won first place as the best blues singer in *Down Beat's* critics' poll.[25]

He was usually presented as a genuine blues shouter with a voice like a horn and as an expert witness on this genre. As mentioned in Chapter Five, he maintained that blues came from slavery days, "from the time when those people weren't treated right."[26] "Blues," he explained, "is a moody feeling that the individual has at different

Jimmy Rushing and unidentified friend,
circa 1925

times in his life. Different feelings for different times"—a paraphrase of what Abe Bolar said about bands and the feeling changing. Rushing emphasized the permanence of blues: "The blues is the way an individual feels. And there will always be the blues, because there will always be moody people." He also maintained that he could not really record a blues until he felt it. As far as the music was concerned, however, blues were contagious. "Usually, in a session, if the other fellows on the date feel the blues, and then put that feeling into their horns, I get it, too, after a while, even if maybe I didn't start the date with that feeling."

Rushing wrote blues, as well, explaining, "One way I write ... is I sit down and play the piano. Different things come to me." "Goin' to Chicago" came this way after he broke up with his St. Louis love. "It's not always a particular event," he added. At times, "it's a feeling, a mood you get into ... that produces a blues." This music was complex: "And there can be a blues from when you're happy, too."[27]

In 1961, Rushing publicized the urban blues of the 1920s when he issued an album on Columbia that featured songs of Mamie Smith, credited with recording the first blues. The album, "Jimmy Rushing and the Smith Girls," with Clara, Bessie, and Trixie Smith, included "Trouble in Mind," "Gulf Coast Blues," and "Arkansas Blues."[28] He gave the material his own interpretations, however. His backing included Coleman Hawkins, Buck Clayton, and Buster Bailey.[29]

But as critics observed, he was also a jazz singer,[30] something that he thought had to come instinctively—it could not be taught. "My idea of a jazz singer is a person who sings rhythm tunes. Everybody can't sing rhythm because they don't all have a conception of a beat. Anybody can come along and sing a ballad, because it's so much easier than a rhythm tune, but to be a jazz singer, you have to know chords."[31] Rushing's early musical training in the Oklahoma schools gave him this advantage.

Rushing was ranked among the greatest singers in popular music in the 1960s. One critic wrote that only recently had the public discovered that Rushing was far more than "the world's best blues singer. ... The truth of the matter is that little Jimmy Rushing is a jazz singer first and a blues shouter, second, and along with Louis

Armstrong, Henry (Red) Allen, Jack Teagarden, Oran "Hot Lips" Page . . . and the young Bing Crosby, one of the few truly memorable singers in the history of the form."[32]

He had trouble with musicians who tried to change the blues. After hearing Jimmy Yancey, Rushing pointed out that "Too many blues players today try to add to the blues." He was of the opinion "that's wrong—it isn't necessary. . . . If you try and augment the blues, then they become something else. I have sung with people who try and add to the blues and it all comes to nothing, when they try and add to those basic chords."[33]

The veteran singer mixed ballads, standards, and blues during a typical set. At Boston's famous Storyville in early 1958, he shared the bandstand with the Lambert-Hendricks-Ross Modern Jazz Singers. Backed by the Lou Carter Trio, Rushing opened with "Sunny Side of the Street" and "If I Could Be With You One Hour Tonight," then he sang "Good Mornin' Blues," "See See Rider," and "Sent for You Yesterday, Here You Come Today." Then the Modern Jazz Singers, who sang lyrics to instrumental jazz arrangements, joined him on some old Basie blues standards. The next week he had Buck Clayton, Pee Wee Russell, Vic Dickenson, and Bud Freeman backing him.[34] He continued to sing the blues, at the Newport Jazz Festival and other venues, and in reunions with Basie. He sang with different groups, even Dave Brubeck's Quartet,[35] and went to Canada,[36] Europe, and Japan, enjoying the life of a blues legend. He worked on his memoirs as early as 1947, and he titled it *Singin' the Blues*. Several years later he collaborated with Helen McNamara Dance on his autobiography, *Raise Your Window High*.[37]

His popularity was such that Harvard University, the subject of Rushing and Basie's recording "Harvard Blues," took an interest in him after the singer's death. In 1979, *Harvard Magazine* announced it "had made arrangements with Columbia Records to reissue 'Harvard Blues' in a specially re-engineered and re-mastered 45-rpm version, pressed exclusively for readers of Harvard Magazine and available nowhere else." Readers' interest in the song played a part in their decision, but so did the need to "help meet the cost of publishing" the periodical.[38]

Rock and roll did not displace him as it did many other musicians.

He had "nothing against it," maintaining that without the "twanging guitars . . . it is simple rhythm and blues." Nobody, Rushing pointed out in an interview in Canada, could define rock and roll. The singer maintained, "When you get right down to it, it's nothing but a beat. There's nothing new here. It's the way I've been singing all my life." If the rock and roll was bad, it was the singer's fault.[39]

Rushing's family and friends were another source of satisfaction during these years. After weeks on the road, he anticipated returning to the companionship of his wife, Connie, to home-cooked meals, and to visiting with their sons and grandchildren and friends. William Staton, Rushing's older stepson, spent quite a bit of time with him after leaving the military. He recalled the good times at Croton-on-Hudson in the late 1940s. When William was a band boy, the Basie-ites would travel up the Hudson River to their favorite picnic spot, prepare feasts, and play softball and poker. "Count Basie's wife, and some of the fellows [who] had girlfriends . . . they cooked everything. We had bacon, eggs, grits, and ham in the morning, and we had barbecue ribs, barbecue steak, we had chicken, we had greens, we had macaroni and cheese. . . . apple pie, potato pie . . . watermelon, all types of fruit—they had some of everything you could think of."[40]

And on weekends at their home, whether it was in Jamaica, East Elmhurst, or Corona, they would cook, drink, play cards, eat, laugh, joke, and play piano and sing. "My mother was master chef," her son recalled. "We entertained all the time." Rushing, Rudy Powell, and another partner played pinochle with William, and he remembered "we would play cutthroat pinochle, for a dollar, or five dollars, or whatever it was. And he hated to lose. (laughs) I was young and fast and could think. And I used to beat him . . . all the time (laughs) at pinochle." On weekends they played all day and all night, and "three or four o'clock in the morning, we would have to bring one of the fellows back, or two of the people back to New York." They got the car, and "I'd ride with my father, and we'd drop 'em off, or either we'd go to a place called the Turk club . . . at Broadway . . . and they would get a cup of coffee or a sandwich." After dropping their friends off, they returned to Queens and slept.

William recalled his stepfather reading the Bible all the time,

Jimmy and Connie Rushing and grandchildren, circa 1965

and he blessed the food at mealtime. Rushing "was very sincere, and very honest . . . and we went to church once in a while, as a group." They spent considerable time together, and William Staton concluded, "He was my stepfather, but he was the greatest father a son could have and was a tremendous influence in my life. . . . He would always try to give me information about the streets, and life as a whole, and how you treat your fellow man. My father kept me on the straight and narrow." They did "so many things together . . . I'd take him downtown, to take care of his business, to go to an office, and I would drive the car and would sit in the car and wait for him, or . . . we'd go to the lawyer's office . . . or someone's office." Staton concluded, "It was a beautiful life. It was a beautiful life, and I still miss him very, very much."

Rushing's reputation grew through the years. Ralph Ellison reminisced in "Remembering Jimmy," "Rushing is one of the first singers to sing the blues before a big band, and even today he seldom comes across as a blues 'shouter,' but maintains the lyricism which has always been his way with the blues." Ellison maintained that the more closely we listen, the more "we become aware of the quality which makes for the mysteriousness of the blues: their ability to imply far more than they state outright, and their capacity to make the details of sex convey meanings which touch upon the metaphysical." He also observed that because of his "middle class background," Rushing was very much concerned with proper diction when he sang even the blues. Ellison wrote, "Out of the tension between the traditional folk pronunciation and his training in school, he has worked out a flexibility of enunciation and a rhythmical agility with words which make us constantly aware of the meanings which shimmer just beyond the limits of the lyrics."[41] Ellison credited Rushing with preserving the blues tradition before it became popular on college campuses and in concerts. The author wrote that Rushing was quite popular in Europe, "And I think we need him more here at home." The new Rushing issues "will make us aware that there is emotional continuity in American life, and that the abiding moods expressed in our most vital popular art-form are not simply a matter of entertainment; they also tell us who and where we are."

Rushing died in a Manhattan hospital in spring 1972. The funeral was held at Convent Avenue Baptist Church, and then more than three hundred mourners attended the memorial service at St. Peter's Lutheran Church on June 12. The Reverend John Garcia Gensel, the "jazz minister," gave a tribute. Musical tributes included Joe Newman's trumpet solo on "Sometimes I Feel Like a Motherless Child," and Louis Metcalf's rendition of "My Buddy," with Junior Mance on piano on both selections. When Rushing's grandchild saw Count Basie and all the celebrities in attendance, she was able to appreciate his rather singular importance, and understand that he had an impact not only on entertainers, but also on the world.[42]

◆ ◆ ◆

Eddie Durham traveled with Oran Page and Jack Teagarden in the Jazz Cavalcade after the war's end, and then played opposite small rhythm and blues combos. He and his orchestra engaged in a "Battle of Blues" at the Municipal Auditorium, Oklahoma City, in spring 1952. Wynonie Harris and Larry Darnell also performed with their respective bands.[43] A few years later he traveled and played opposite two other bands, one led by Little Richard shortly before he recorded his rock and roll hits. Durham wrote most of the music program.[44] First one band would play, then the other, and then Durham and a few band members played together.

He wrote few songs after World War II. In 1945 he composed "Four Letters," then "My Whole Life Thru" six years later. Eight more appeared during the 1950s, including "Big Foot Blues" and "Blow, Boy Blue," and "Topsy" No. 3 and No. 4 came out in 1960. Often he teamed with co-composers such as Edgar Battle and Sarah McLawler.[45]

As a result of a court settlement, he and Edgar Battle were awarded some property in Oswego, in upstate New York, and for several years Durham went into real estate and was not a visible performer on the music scene. There is reason to believe he may have withdrawn altogether in the late 1950s and early 1960s. About this time he met his fourth wife, Lillian, who came into the marriage with two children, and within a few years, they had three more. Besides the property in upstate New York, he owned a three-story building in Brooklyn where he settled in with his new family and his older brother around 1960. It was bought with money from "I Don't Want to Set the World on Fire," according to his daughter Lesa.

Durham enjoyed his newfound role as husband and father, and stayed with his family in Brooklyn for about fifteen years. "He didn't travel anywhere," Lesa affirmed. Durham admitted he loved children, and his daughter Marsha recalled that he was always at home and taking care of their needs while their mother worked. If he played late-night gigs, the children did not seem to know much about it. He oversaw his children's music instruction, not in any obvious way, but more in the way of encouraging their efforts. He was very handy around the house and could repair anything—including doing plumbing, wiring, and carpentry. He installed a small pool in the backyard and a music studio in the basement with a recessed ceiling, electrical outlets, and colored lights to give the proper atmosphere. His children practiced here, and his son Eric was active in the group Cameo in the 1980s.

In summers they piled into the car or cars with the neighbors' children and headed for the upstate resorts, or west to Pennsylvania, or even beyond, where they camped and fished. His wife recalled that he was always ready to go somewhere with the children. In this way he was spontaneous, and also flexible, as only someone who spent a lifetime on the road can be.

He was always working on something on the organ, an arrangement or composition, and he supposedly played weekends at a club on Long Island called Moby Dick's, but it is not clear which years these were. Lesa Durham maintained, "Just about every night he would be up with the music," and "he was always at the [organ]." One of his friends said that Durham was outstanding on piano and excelled at playing the blues very soulfully when he was at home.

He was active in the community, as well. "We always had bands in the house, in the basement. . . . He always had the young ones coming." He seemed to surface again on the club music scene in the late 1960s when he teamed up with some old-timers and one former Blue Devil. The Kansas City All-Stars, who included Durham with Eddie Barefield, Snub Mosley, Ed Lewis, and Abe and Juanita Bolar, performed in Orange, Connecticut and New York City. The old-timers performed "South" and "When the Saints Go Marchin' In," "One O'Clock Jump," and Ellington compositions in spring 1969.[46] Durham was given considerable praise: "Here was yet another example of a great jazz musician who had been allowed to pass from sight, not so much because of public apathy, nor because of the booking network's callous disregard, but because of neglect by the critical fraternity." Stanley Dance, the reviewer, contended that "millions" of words had been written about musicians "who haven't, and never will have, a tenth of Durham's talent." Dance considered this fact "a monumental scandal."

Durham's experiments with guitars continued for years. For example, at Orange, Connecticut, when Abe Bolar, the bassist, was late, Durham's National guitar "was moaning out of the box with an arresting sound that seemed to compound those of jug and tuba." In other words, he provided the bass part, and "it was noticeable during the evening that he had a liking for this instrument's lower register." Durham's solos on "South" and "St. Louis Blues" were "full of surprises, tonally and conceptually." Then he and Snub Mosley went into a routine, a "battle of the blues, with solo choruses, dialogues and unisons."[47]

Early the next year, Durham and guitarist Lawrence Lucie and a combo performed at Town Hall in Manhattan. On "Satin Doll," the opening, Durham "used baritone guitar for rumbling chords and riffs that suggested nothing so much as a trombone section." Susan King, Lucie's wife, sang three songs, and then Durham was featured on "Moonlight in Vermont." He used first plunger and then straight mute on different choruses. Stanley Dance thought his playing reflected the influences of Tricky Sam Nanton, with his "upper-register keening," and Mosley, with his sudden jumps and "audacious use of the slide." On "Topsy," the composer delighted in playing "low, jungly sounds of a kind that are quite unique."[48]

In 1977, Valerie Wilmer noted that the swing innovator, when not playing trombone at the West End, switched "between two amazing guitars." One was a custom-made twelve-string, and the other was a six-string bass guitar that could be converted to a baritone guitar with a switch. Durham explained, "That's an octave lower than the regular guitar and an octave higher than the bass." Only six such guitars had been made, and when programmed, it sounded "not unlike a baritone saxophone," according to Wilmer. Durham could use it to imitate several different instruments, in fact.[49]

Around 1973 he and his wife broke up, and he moved with three of their children to stay at the Orange Inn in Goshen, New York, near where he played. Then, during a performance, his wife came and took the two youngest children and went to England with them for two years. Durham went to court to try to regain custody of them, and he maintained that he asked the FBI for assistance, but there was little anyone could do, even though his custody rights had been violated. His friends Earle Warren and Buddy Tate reported on his children from Europe, and then the children returned and stayed with him for three more years. Lesa thought that this was a time of heartbreak for her father, because of the acrimonious contention over the children and the end of the marriage, and that he poured himself into his music as a result.

He was a very loving and attentive father. Whenever he fixed something around the house, he made sure one of the children learned how it was done. "My most memorable times are with my father," Lesa reminisced. She and her youngest brother, Edward, trav-

The Harlem Blues and Jazz Band, circa 1980 (front row: Eddie Durham, Al Casey, Bobby Williams, George Kelly, and Johnny Williams; back row: Al Vollmer, Charlie Bateman, Ronnie Cole)

eled with him on the road. "Wherever he went, we went." He made sure they were registered in school, picked out the school clothes they wanted, and "if it was a little bit too big or whatever, then he himself would tailor it for me." He did this by hand.

In the late 1970s he resumed touring again, played on a number of cruise ships, and received a warm reception in Europe. He often toured with the Harlem Blues and Jazz Band, which included Al Casey, guitar, Tommy Benford, drums, Johnny Williams, bass, George James, alto saxophonist, and Gene Rodgers, piano—veterans of Jelly Roll Morton, King Oliver, and Louis Armstrong bands. Despite their name, they played more in Europe than in Harlem. Dr. Albert Vollmer, a jazz fan and orthodontist, put the band together for parties at his house and then decided to go to Europe with them. In spring 1983 the band performed at five different events in Germany in five days.[50] Sometimes they performed in New York clubs as well.[51]

Together with David Lahm, the son of songwriter Dorothy Fields, Durham and four other entertainers participated in the Veterans Bedside Network (VBN) program. Hospital Show Tour #5, *I Can't Give You Anything But,* consisted of these volunteers, who went around to hospitals to entertain veterans, and the show featured many of Fields's songs. In addition, the program announced, "as a special added treasure, Eddie Durham will perform some of the numbers he wrote for Count Basie" and other bands. Significantly, the VBN produced musical variety hours and dramas "in which the patients become the actors and singers." "Participation Therapy," as it was known, was the central purpose of VBN.[52]

Durham's honors included seventieth as well as eightieth birthday celebrations, the latter at St. Peter's church.[53] He was honored again at the Institute of Jazz Studies, along with Sonny Greer and Snub Mosley, when it was announced that the Smithsonian's Jazz Oral History Program would be housed at Rutgers University, Newark, New Jersey.[54]

Other honors included an invitation from Algeria's permanent U.N. representative to a reception to commemorate the "27th anniversary of the launching of the Algerian revolution" at the Waldorf-Astoria late in 1981.[55] In 1983, Durham was inducted into the National Association of Recording Arts and Sciences Hall of Fame for his arrangement of Glen Miller's "In the Mood."[56] He was inducted into the American Jazz Hall of Fame in spring 1989.[57]

Eddie Durham died suddenly of a heart attack at his daughter's house, while preparing for the funeral of guitarist Freddie Green in late winter 1987. He was honored at the tenth annual Salute to Women in Jazz, which was dedicated to his memory. Sarah McLawler, pianist, organist, and singer, led the Big Apple Jazz Women, who performed many of Durham's compositions at this event.[58]

Buster Smith managed quite well after returning to Dallas. In summer 1944 his arrangement of the Nat King Cole hit "Straighten Up and Fly Right" won praise as "groovy and packed with jive."[59] His talents as a bandleader won recognition a few months later: "Buster has the most surprising band of the year." Though his band did not have many veterans, "yet the maestro has put together some arrangements that won't puzzle his musicians and are most enjoyable from a listener's point of view." Smith was, in fact, "tops among arrangers," because "his efforts show harmony, originality and good taste."[60]

Late in the war and after, he traveled about the region with his combo. In 1944 he played in Greenville and Little Rock, Arkansas, as well as Dallas.[61] In 1951 he returned to Oklahoma City with his band "Heat Wave of Swing," because of popular demand. They performed at the Up-to-Daters' Club in spring 1951 and had a singer and child dancer accompanying them.[62]

In 1959 Gunther Schuller succeeded in getting Smith to record his only album as leader and instrumentalist; his brother, Josea Smith, on piano, and Leroy Cooper on baritone sax were among the musicians in this combo. Smith recorded his compositions "Buster's Tune," "E Flat Boogie," "King Alcohol," "Kansas City Riffs," and "Late, Late," as well as two standards. One of them, "September Song," displayed his expressiveness and virtuosity on a ballad.[63] Shortly afterwards, problems with his teeth caused him to give up the saxophone, but he still played piano and guitar on gigs.

In 1979 the Sixth Annual Tribute to Charlie Parker honored Buster Smith at the Recovery Room in Dallas. "Several noted jazz musicians" were expected to sit in with the band that was featured, the Marchel Ivery Quartet.[64] Smith was honored on numerous other occasions in Dallas but always chose to remain in the background rather than let himself take the limelight.

In the 1980s he often played in North Texas clubs. Early in 1981 he was on electric guitar, with his brother Boston on piano, tenor saxophonist Adolphus Sneed, and Leslie Finney-Mo on drums, in a small Denton, Texas, club. Described as "slow moving old men in black suits," the musicians arrived at the gig in twos and set up. When they hit the first notes, a noticeable change took place:

> Nimble fingers cover the strings and keys as adroitly as they have for scores of years. And the sound, if not youthful, is warm, rich and smooth. Rather than bubbling along, the music flows with a sense of dignity and just a touch of majesty. It speaks of decades of complete immersion in jazz and the excitement of its beginnings. It encourages the listener to hum under his breath and tap his foot.... Music pours from the

Adolphus Sneed Combo like warm molasses from a jar, easing troubled minds and beguiling tired feet onto the dance floor. With 172 years shared experience among them, it's no wonder they sound so smooth.

These veterans knew how to please their audiences. "The band puts its individual stamp on everything from New Orleans style jazz to rock and roll and even country music." They performed "Alley Cat," "Blue Moon," "Your Cheating Heart," "Up Above My Head," and "Shake, Rattle, and Roll." As Sneed explained, "You have to play what the audience responds to...the mood changes several times during the evening with people coming and going, and you just have to pay attention and change with it."[65]

During intermission, Smith played around on piano and reminisced for the interviewer about Kansas City, and how he used to dine with Tom Pendergast, who gave him wine-soaked cigars. He told the story about Basie and "One O'clock Jump." "Basie couldn't read a note back then, and he probably cant read one now," Smith informed the reporter. These men had no plans for retirement. "Playing music—that's your life," Smith said. "You don't quit that."[66]

The author met Smith twice in the 1980s. On the first occasion, the arranger, who was seventy-seven at the time, explained why he had not been home to answer the telephone during the day. He worked as a roofer, helping a friend, he explained. That day the temperature in Dallas was the usual ninety-plus degrees. On the second occasion, a few years later, Smith and Herb Cowens, a drummer with Fletcher Henderson who had returned to his hometown, were found working on the rear differential of Smith's truck, which sat on the lawn. Outside of music, working on cars and fishing were his two favorite pastimes. The two consented to be interviewed that afternoon and temporarily halted their work.

A few years later Smith suffered a stroke, and a few weeks before his eighty-seventh birthday, in summer 1991, a Dallas reporter noted that the past weekend Buster Smith had died "much the way he lived. Quietly." He passed either in his home in South Dallas or at Southeastern Methodist Hospital. The journalist wrote, "his was a star that sparkled among peers and devotees, but his acclaim never matched his contributions as a jazz musician who benefited many a swing band and played a significant part in shaping be-bop."

Allison Tucker, a longtime friend of Smith's, declared that he was "a musician's musician . . . a guy who loved to play music and write music. It meant something to him that everyone else got something from what he was doing. His love of the music was unconditional." Ft. Worth educator and jazz historian Marjorie Crenshaw maintained that "people in New York, Kansas City, Los Angeles, all over the country, knew who he was—everyone except Dallas, his hometown. Whenever I travel, people always ask me, 'How's Buster Smith?' It's incredible that a musician of his stature never really got the recognition he deserved at home."[67]

When Tucker was asked what he remembered most about Smith, he responded: "When I watched him take a series of arrangements and write it at one time. The way he'd pick up and learn something in no time. The way he loved music unconditionally. The way he had those moments when everything would just pour out of him at once. That's what I remember."[68]

◆ ◆ ◆

Leonard Chadwick worked a day job and performed on weekends during the 1950s. He attended church regularly and served as a trustee, was quite active in his college fraternity, and was given increasing responsibility at his job. After all, he was college-educated, having taken a pre-dental program at Fisk in the late 1920s. Upon moving to Denver, he played around town with Sticks McVey, then he started working for the Denver Housing Authority as a painter and handyman. His subsequent career was a classic rags-to-riches tale, as he started at the bottom, worked his way up through the ranks, and eventually became executive director of the Denver Housing Authority. He developed close ties with Denver's African-American community—initially as a musician, but also through his church, his fraternity, and in other ways, as well. He was awarded a number of civic and fraternal honors in the 1970s and 1980s. It was very clear that the welfare of the community was foremost in his mind.

During his leadership in the Housing Authority, Chadwick worked with his church and fraternity and the federal government to fund low-cost housing and a large multistory apartment complex for the elderly residents of Denver, among other projects. He also teamed up with his son, Leonard Jr., to form a consulting firm and organized an international jazz festival in Aruba, a quiet location in the Caribbean. The event was so successful it was repeated the next year, and then the government of Aruba, convinced of the current success and the future viability of this new venture, took it over.[69] Though he had given up playing at some point, his wife always carried his mouthpiece in her purse just in case he was invited to sit in.

Eventually, Chadwick was "discovered" as a former Blue Devil in the 1970s. Writers called him from afar, asking for information and photographs, and he was written up in the local newspapers as part of a legendary band. He was not featured, however, in the 1979 film *Last of the Blue Devils*, which was situated in the 627 Musicians' Union building in, of all places, Kansas City—thereby obfuscating the band's true roots and, also, the history of the Basie legacy. Leonard Chadwick died in 1991.

◆ ◆ ◆

Snake Whyte stayed in music, writing arrangements for Los Angeles bands and occasionally playing after World War II. He started an independent record label, Supreme, which had a hit with Paula Watson's "Little Bird." He continued arranging, often staying in the background, but sometimes his contributions were surprising testimony to his modernity. For example, he wrote the arrangement for the young Ray Charles's "Someday" in 1950.[70] He also worked and hung out with bandleader Desi Arnaz, but much of his work was probably unaccredited. Then his son died under tragic circumstances, and shortly afterwards Whyte became ill. His doctor could not diagnose the malaise, but advised him to return to Perry, Iowa, his hometown. Whyte went back and stayed for thirty years until he passed.

When the Perry townspeople discovered his past profession and link with the Blue Devils, a number of them approached him about starting an orchestra for their sake. These were bankers and other professionals who played some music, but never got a chance to play professionally. So Whyte organized a big band that played religious music, and they were quite popular in central Iowa. They also issued a record.[71]

◆ ◆ ◆

In 1990 the Blue Devils and Jimmy Rushing were inducted into the Oklahoma Jazz Hall of Fame.[72] The next year Buster Smith and Leonard Chadwick died. Snake Whyte passed away in his hometown shortly after 2000. He was perhaps the last surviving Blue Devil at the time. This is not altogether clear, however, for after Juanita Bolar passed, her husband, Abe, went to live with family in Los Angeles.[73]

The story of the Blue Devils reveals that the origins of their music are complex, and that designations such as Kansas City jazz do not explain a great deal. Oklahoma City's contributions can be dated from the early 1920s, which suggests, as Oran Page believed, that the music emerged simultaneously in many cities in the 1920s. As evidence of this, the founding Blue Devils came from such distant points as Indiana and Illinois, as well as Missouri. Unlike other bands that have been favored in the chronicles of jazz, the Oklahoma City Blue Devils stand out as a symbol of the longevity, the vitality, and the legitimacy of the early swing tradition. The fact that the band is remembered by so many, although so little has been written about it, indicates the degree to which its successes were firmly etched in the memory and oral traditions of a people.

ACKNOWLEDGMENTS

The research that produced *Lester Leaps In: The Life and Times of Lester "Pres" Young* (Beacon, 2002) led me to the Blue Devils, because musicians often mentioned, "You know, Lester was a Blue Devil," as if it were a degree certifying his authenticity. Eddie Durham was the first Blue Devil that I interviewed, in New York City. Then in Dallas I met and interviewed Buster Smith, and he told me where the others lived, but at the time I did not realize the significance of this information. Two years later I drove to Oklahoma City to meet and interview Abe Bolar. I was also able to research the band and the city's history in the Oklahoma State Museum.

Oklahoma City public librarians directed me to Leroy Parks, and to Henry Butler, who gave me a number of his photographs; both of them helped me to understand the local music scene. While waiting for a connection at the Denver airport, I located Leonard Chadwick in the telephone directory, called him, spoke with him briefly, and arranged my interview. Earle Warren informed me of Snake Whyte in Perry, Iowa. Ray Marcks, Mr. Whyte's friend, led me to George Hudson in East St. Louis, and in the 1980s and early 1990s I visited with some of these gentlemen on several occasions to interview them and go through their photograph collections.

While working on the Pres biography, I realized that the Blue Devils tale was a story waiting to be told. In short, these men mesmerized me. Though a few were at first reluctant to delve back into the early 1930s, I noted that they all spoke of the band, their colleagues, and their experiences with great conviction, as if that time had molded them into what they became. Their eyes occasionally gleamed with a faraway look, and they might stop in mid-sentence and pause, but they always took the time to explain to me what that band meant to them and what it was like barnstorming through the Southwest and Midwest.

I even had the good fortune to hear two of the legends play— Durham with Al Grey and Joe Bushkin, in the dining room of an expensive midtown Manhattan hotel, and Buster Smith with his combo in North Texas. I now realize what a privilege that was. Whatever in-

225

formation I obtained made me want to dig deeper into the archives, and I began to collect marriage licenses, death certificates, and, under the Freedom of Information Act, Social Security application forms; find their families in the Manuscript Census; and photograph their homes and the clubs where they performed. As they died in the late 1980s and 1990s, I began to interview some of their family members and trace the relatives of other Blue Devils.

Thanks to the suggestion of my colleague Professor Earl Stewart, I wrote ASCAP to locate the descendants of Durham, Smith, Rushing, Oran, and Walter Page. ASCAP advised me to send them letters, which they would forward to the descendants, and within a few weeks I heard from Eddie Durham's daughter, Marsha, and Jimmy Rushing's granddaughter, Lynn M. Staton. They both had extensive photo collections and some documents, and permitted me to interview them and one or more family members. To them I am especially grateful. Marsha also enabled me to interview Rudine Battle. I also want to thank Ines Wagner of the Genealogy Section of the Corsicana Public Library for helping me to find Oran Page's daughter, the late Ora Lee, who very kindly allowed me to interview her, and also put me in touch with her brother, Oran Jr., and with George Jr. and Tracy Page Willis.

I wish to express my utmost gratitude to these family members: to Lorraine Chadwick, Leonard Chadwick Jr., and Janiss Watkins; to Marsha, Lesa, Eric, and Edward Durham Jr.; to George Hudson and his wife; to Ray Marcks in Perry, Iowa; to Phil Schaap, who introduced me to Earle Warren, who informed me of Leroy Whyte and gave me his phone number. I want to thank Dorothy Lynch, Reuben Lynch's daughter, who consented to be interviewed, and former student James Lesniak, who helped to locate James Rudolph Lynch, Reuben's youngest brother, who then put me in touch with his sister, Annis. The family helped me to contact Mrs. Essie Mae Lynch, Reuben's second wife. Edith Hamilton, one of Durham's bassists in one of his women's bands, gladly consented to sharing her photographs and memories with me, and for this I am extremely grateful.

In Oklahoma City, Bervis McBride was extremely helpful, informing me of people whom I should interview and providing his gracious hospitality. I would also like to thank Pat Kemp, who introduced me to him. Eddie Durham's cousin, the late Jeri Wilson, informed me of her family's history in Texas. In West Virginia, Joe Bundy and his parents, Sam and Julia, musicians Fred Dodson and E. G. Watkins, and the journalist Bill Archer enabled me to recreate the Bluefield years of the Devils.

Of course I believe that the public libraries are one of the greatest of resources for my research, and I would like to thank these institutions and their staffs in locations from Queens Borough to Los Angeles for assisting me. Numerous other public libraries in the heartland were of value, including those in Indianapolis, Minneapolis, Peoria, Sioux City, Oklahoma City, Kansas City, and Tulsa, Oklahoma; Dallas, Houston, San Marcos, Terrell, and Corsicana, Texas; Weirton and Bluefield, West Virginia; and Lynchburg and Martinsville, Virginia. The Oklahoma State Museum's newspapers and City Directories were invaluable, and I would also like to thank the Chicago Historical Society, archivist Jacqueline Brown of Wilberforce, and Jay Glatz, director of alumni relations at Bradley University, Offices of Vital Statistics, county property records, and clerks of the courts in Minneapolis, Los Angeles, Queens Borough in New York City, Kansas City and Oklahoma City, Dallas, Waxahachie, Corsicana, San Marcos, and Gonzalez, Texas, and Valparaiso, Indiana, were quite helpful in providing documentation. National Archives at San Bruno and Laguna Nigel, California, and Ft. Worth, Texas, yielded census data. The online search engines of ancestry .com and the New York Genealogical and Biographical Society, in particular, provided information in seconds or minutes, cutting down on the time spent driving to these archives, and allowing me to view the blocks and neighborhoods where Blue Devils grew up and resided.

Jimmy Stewart, NAACP leader and columnist in the *Black Dispatch* for a number of years, consented to speak with me at length about some of Oklahoma City's residents and the community. Chuck Haddix, scholar and archivist at the University of Missouri, Kansas City, helped me with the Frank Driggs interviews with Blue Devils and Kansas City musicians, and also in mastering some of the details of the music scene in this city. There have been many others who assisted me, and I apologize if I overlooked any of these people.

My gratitude, as well, to the students and research assistants, particularly Helen Kim and Mark Berman, who found valuable material and sharpened my insights.

Members of my family helped, too, including my brother, Dennis, and the three children to whom the book is dedicated. My wife, Claudine, has patiently watched this book grow from the inspiration that these men gave me.

AJ   Archives of Jazz label
AN   *Amsterdam News*
CL   Classics label
ED   Enumeration District (part of USMC)
DCD   *Dallas City Directory*
IJS   Institute of Jazz Studies, Rutgers University, Newark, New Jersey
JOHP IJS Jazz Oral History Project
OCBD *Oklahoma City Black Dispatch*
OCCD *Oklahoma City City Directory*
USMC U.S. Manuscript Census

A Note to the Reader Concerning USMC and IJS Entries

Census officials began taking the census in 1790, and by 1860 it was sufficiently detailed to constitute a gold mine for social historians. It permits the tracing of families and individuals from decade to decade—though not always successfully. For one thing, there are the problems of recording people who did not wish to be recorded, either because they distrusted whites or because they distrusted the authorities. For different reasons, one might encounter inaccuracies, but following individuals through the censuses of, for example, 1910–1940 gives a very good idea of their social origins, housing conditions, family structure, neighbors and neighborhoods, occupations, military service, literacy, and whether their children attended school. The census for 1930 is the latest one available at this time. The Internet permits almost immediate access to this information via various search engines.

The tape-recorded interviews at IJS were the result of a Smithsonian initiative and National Endowment for the Arts funding, and they were deposited at Rutgers University, Newark, New Jersey, where they were transcribed and are currently housed. Other interviews resulted from the research of individuals such as Frank Driggs, Nathan W. Pearson Jr. and Howard Litwak, Phil Schaap, and the author.

It is important to understand that the quoted statements from tape-recorded interviews often read somewhat differently than they sound. As with any interview, the speaker did not always answer questions directly, clearly, or in complete sentences; these typed transcriptions preserve the speakers' exact words. Understandably, under such circumstances, people will sometimes sound incoherent—stopping in mid-sentence, losing their train of thought, suddenly changing the subject, or leaving things unsaid ("You know what I mean . . ."). When you are there at the interview, observing gestures along with spoken words, it is all comprehensible, but it can be less clear on the printed page. This is a different issue than interpreting the speaker's meaning, which can depend on understanding his or her history. For example, the statement one musician made after a trip into the South, that no one would ever have any trouble getting him to go down South again, can convey different meanings to different people. Some will take it literally, meaning that he wants to go again, while others—familiar with the experiences of Northern Blacks in the Deep South—will interpret it differently: He will not ask about wages, length of time, or the ultimate destination of the proposed trip, because he will not go under any circumstances.

For the IJS interview, "Reel 1" or "Reel 2" refers to the actual tape-recorded interview. When it was transcribed, the reel number was kept and printed at the beginning of each new section of the interview. In other words, in the transcribed interview the reel number corresponds to the chapter and the subsequent pages are numbered. "Reel 2, page 3" means page 3 of the second part of the interview.

NOTES

Please note: "c" means "colored" (African American); "r" means "residence"; and "mus" means "musician."

Chapter 1

1. USMC, 1930, Oklahoma City, ED 55, sheet 2A.
2. USMC, 1910, Fannin County, Bonham, TX, ED 36, sheet 3A. The Christians lived at 600 Johnson Street (*OCBD*, October 16, 1948, 1–2).
3. "Edward Christian Dies," *OCBD*, October 16, 1948, 1–2; Harold S. Kaye, "Francis 'Doc' Whitby," *Storyville* 110 (December 1983–January 1984), 50–64.
4. See her obituary, "Pioneer Music Teacher Dead," *OCBD*, November 2, 1956, 1–2.
5. USMC, 1930, Oklahoma City, ED 55, sheet 7A.
6. Jimmie Lewis Franklin, *Journey Toward Hope: A History of Blacks in Oklahoma* (Norman, OK: University of Oklahoma Press, 1982).

Chapter 2

1. Most focus on Kansas City, of course, and Texas cities receive little attention. See Frank Driggs and H. Lewine, *Black Beauty, White Heat: A Pictorial History of Classic Jazz 1920–1950* (New York: DaCapo Press, 1996); Ross Russell, *Jazz Style in Kansas City and the Southwest* (Berkeley: University of California Press, 1982) and *Bird Lives!: The High Life and Hard Times of Charlie (Yardbird) Parker* (New York: Charterhouse, 1973); Nathan W. Pearson Jr., *Goin' to Kansas City* (Urbana: University of Illinois, 1987).
2. Jimmie Lewis Franklin, *Journey Toward Hope: A History of Blacks in Oklahoma* (Norman, OK: University of Oklahoma Press, 1982), 3–33; John Hope Franklin and John Whittington Franklin (eds.), *My Life and an Era: The Autobiography of Buck Colbert Franklin* (Baton Rouge, LA: LSU Press, 1997).
3. U.S. Bureau of the Census, *Fifteenth Census of the United States, 1930, Population,* Vol. 1 (Washington, DC: Bureau of the Census), 27, 71.
4. Ibid., 22–23.
5. Introduction, *OCCD*, 1920, page 7; *OCCD*, 1927, page 7.
6. Introduction, *OCCD*, 1920, page 7; *OCCD*, 1927, page 7.
7. Ibid., 1920, p. 7; ibid., 1927, p. 7. The school system is detailed in "The Social Whirl," *OCBD*, May 19, 1927, 5.
8. Jimmie Lewis Franklin, 27–28.
9. Ibid., 108–127 and 43–52.
10. Ibid., 21. See ad in *OCBD*, Dec. 2, 1926, p. 7. The work, with "facts drawn only from authentic sources . . . revealing an ancient black race that ruled in far distant ages over three continents for three thousand years," was published by Ethiopian Press, Oklahoma City.
11. Harriet P. Jacobson, "Oklahoma City Mourns Death of Very Prominent Pioneer Citizen," *OCBD*, February 13, 1928, 1, 6.
12. "Pioneer Passes," in "Social Whirl," *OCBD*, January 16, 1930, 5; on J. D. Randolph, see "Pioneer Dies," *OCBD*, July 15, 1939, 1–2.
13. "Pioneer Passes," in "Social Whirl," *OCBD*, January 16, 1930, 5.
14. *OCCD*, 1922, 1927, and 1934.
15. "Pioneer Passes," in "Social Whirl," *OCBD*, July 28, 1927, 5; *OCCD*, 1927. According to the *OCCD*, 1920: "Rushing, Andrew (c: Cora) porter Oakland Motor Car Co. r 307 E 7th."

    The 1920 USMC, Oklahoma City, Vol. 49, ED 153, sheet 19, lines 75ff., listed "Andrew Rushing, 44 years old, born in Alabama, his wife, Cora, 37, born in Tennessee, James, their son, 19, an Oklahoman, a second son, Evoid, 16, also born in Oklahoma, a niece, Gertrude Goodman, 16, of Oklahoma, and Bettie Mason, mother-in-law of Andrew, 67, from Mississippi."

16. "Dr. Whitby's Mother Dies at Wewoka," *OCBD,* January 9, 1930. Ad for Dr. A. Baxter Whitby, "expert in plate, crown, and bridges, 630 1/2 East Fourth Street," *OCBD,* April 29, 1926, p. 5. On Francis Whitby, who played with Joe "King" Oliver and others, see Frank Büchmann-Møller, *You Just Fight for Your Life: The Story of Lester Young* (New York: Praeger, 1990), 38–39.

17. "Pioneer Passes," in "Social Whirl," *OCBD,* January 16, 1930, 5; "Slaughter Building Oklahoma City," *OCBD,* January 4, 1923, 1; "Doings of the New Era A.C.," in "Social Whirl," *OCBD,* June 10, 1926, 5; "Dreamland Billiard Parlor Opens," in "Social Whirl," *OCBD,* January 4, 1923, 1.

18. "Slaughter Building Oklahoma City," *OCBD,* January 4, 1923, 1.

19. "Dr. W. H. Slaughter," *OCBD,* December 22, 1927, 1; *OCCD, 1920*; USMC, 1920, Vol. 47, ED 137, sheets 9B–10A, lines 1–3 on 10A; "Saretta Slaughter Wins Prize with 'The Negro's Possibilities,'" *OCBD,* January 5, 1928, 1.

20. "The Hall Building, Oklahoma City," *OCBD,* February 1, 1923, 1.

21. "Wealthy City Couple Takes Vacation," in "Social Whirl," *OCBD,* July 8, 1926, 5.

22. "Buys $3,500 Piano," in "Social Whirl," *OCBD,* July 27, 1922, 5; "Gone on Vacation," in "Social Whirl," *OCBD,* September 15, 1927, 5.

23. "Proprietor of 'Men's Rest Billiard Parlor' Buys Lincoln Sport Roadster," in "Social Whirl," *OCBD,* May 12, 1927, 5.

24. "Social Whirl," *OCBD,* April 1, 1926, 5.

25. Jimmie Lewis Franklin, 21, 29, 54–57, 102–103, 118–119, 163, 198–199. USMC, 1930, Oklahoma City, ED 139, sheet 5B.

26. Ibid., 162; "Its 'Colonel' Roscoe Dunjee Now," *OCBD,* April 5, 1923, 5.

27. "Pythians Lay Cornerstone" *OCBD,* April 1, 1926, 5. The church was estimated to cost $25,000, measured 48 by 73 feet, and included the main auditorium, an upper floor "so that accommodations will be given to the choir, trustee boards and pastor's study," and a basement with a kitchen, dining room, and bathrooms.

28. "Social Whirl," *OCBD,* April 1, 1926, 5.

29. "When Bill Took Guthrie," *OCBD,* June 7, 1923, 1; "Special Interurban to Guthrie With 'Bills,' Band and Bunch," *OCBD,* May 24, 1923, 1; "City Ready for Songs Of Damon and Pythias," *OCBD,* July 16, 1925, 1.

Chapter 3

1. In *Kansas City Jazz: From Ragtime to Bebop* (NY: Oxford UP, 2005), Frank Driggs and Chuck Haddix maintain that the Blue Devils played with Billy King's show in Kansas City in Nov. 1922 (p. 76); this information was not available at the time of researching *One O'clock Jump.* Count Basie, *Good Morning Blues: The Autobiography of Count Basie,* as told to Albert Murray (NY: Random House, 1985), 5; Jo Jones concurred: "The greatest band I've heard was Mr. Walter Page's Blue Devils," Stanley Dance, *The World of Count Basie* (NY: Scribner's, 1980), 53–54; Gonzell White's troupe performed in St. Louis in June 1927. The "Theatres" column "Gonzell White and Her 'Big Jamboree' Score Hit at Booker Washington" in the *St. Louis Argus,* June 24, 1927, p. 4, described the musical comedy and mentioned trumpet player Harry Smith as well as pianist William Basie, who appeared in a comedy skit.

2. Author's interview with Abe Bolar.

3. Ibid.

4. On Moten, see Marc Rice's Ph.D. dissertation, *The Bennie Moten Orchestra, 1918–1935: A Kansas City Jazz Ensemble and Its African American Audience* (Louisville: University of Kentucky, 1998).

5. Ross Russell, *Jazz Style in Kansas City and the Southwest* (Berkeley: University of Cali-

fornia Press, 1971); Nathan W. Pearson Jr., *Goin' to Kansas City* (Urbana: University of Illinois, 1987).

6. Rice, 168–185. I would like to thank Professor James Campbell for this information on commonwealth bands; Jimmie Lewis Franklin, 127.

7. Author's interview with Cornelius Pittman.

8. Author's interview with Henry "Buster" Smith. Professor James Campbell, of Marquette University, informed me of the fact that at one time commonwealth bands were quite common in this region.

9. U.S. Bureau of the Census, *Fifteenth Census of the United States, 1930, Population*, Vol. 1 (Washington, DC: Bureau of the Census), 27, 71.

10. See Russell, 84, on these recordings. The Blue Devils can be heard on Territory Bands, Historical HLP-26.

11. Don Gazzaway, "Conversations with Buster Smith, Part 1," *The Jazz Review* II (December 1959), 21–22, 18, "Conversations with Buster Smith, Part 2" (January 1960), 11–13, "Buster and Bird: Conversations with Buster Smith, Part 3" (February 1960); author's interview with Buster Smith.

12. Driggs and Lewine, *Black Beauty, White Heat* is an example of the traditional approach to the history of jazz. See R. Russell, N. Pearson Jr., and interviews in the Kansas City Jazz Oral History Collection, Western Historical Manuscript Collection, KC-12, University of Missouri, Kansas City, MO.

13. "'Moonshine' Is Coming," *OCBD*, January 25, 1923, 5. See Ted Vincent, *Keep Cool: The Black Activists Who Built the Jazz Age* (Boulder, CO: Pluto Press, 1995), 43, 59–60, 88 on the creation of TOBA. The famous singer Ethel Waters and her husband, Earl Dancer, appeared in *Moonshine* when King presented it in St. Louis the next year: "Theatres" column, "'Moonshine' Is Very Good Show at the Palace," *St. Louis Argus*, May 9, 1924, 4. He presented it the week before without these famous stage personalities: "Theatres" column, "Billy King Forced to Leave Chorus Girls in Chicago," *St. Louis Argus*, May 2, 1924, 4. No mention was made of the Blue Devils or any other band.

14. "'Moonshine' Is Coming," 5.

15. Ibid.

16. Walter Page, "About My Life in Music," as told to Frank Driggs, *The Jazz Review* 1 (November 1958), 13.

17. "Seven Bands, Floor Show at Annual Jamboree of Music," *Kansas City Call*, May 12, 1933, 7B. The bands of Bennie Moten, Andy Kirk, Clarence Love, George E. Lee, Paul Banks, and Thamon Hayes also performed: "Slaughter's Hall," "Amusement Reporter," *OCBD*, July 29, 1937, 8.

18. Page, "About My Life in Music," 13–14. Author's interview with Henry "Buster" Smith. A copy of the photograph of Eddie Christian with Leroy Parks and five other musicians at the 330 Club, Oklahoma City, appeared in Anita G. Arnold, *Legendary Times and Tales of Second Street*, (Oklahoma City: Black Liberated Arts Center, Inc, 1995 limited edition); I wish to thank Mr. Bervis McBride and Ms. Anita G. Arnold for providing me with a copy of this publication and two others: Anita G. Arnold, *Charlie Christian Photo Collection* (Oklahoma City: Black Liberated Arts Center, Inc, 1995 limited edition) and Anita G. Arnold, *Charlie and the Deuce* (Oklahoma City: Black Liberated Arts Center, Inc, 1994 limited edition). Eddie Randall's Seven Blue Devils was another outfit that took on the name; see ad in *St. Louis Argus*, October 20, 1933, 3.

19. "Special Interurban to Guthrie With 'Bills,' Band and Bunch," *OCBD*, May 24, 1923, 1; "Dance All Christmas Tide," *OCBD*, January 3, 1924, 5.

20. "Coleridge Taylor Club to Have Christmas Program," *OCBD*, December 20, 1923, 5.

21. Page, 13. *The Ten Commandments* played in the Aldridge Theatre in late summer of 1925; see ad in *OCBD*, September 3, 1925, 5.

22. "Parade Is Feature of Thursday's Session . . . ," *OCBD*, July 16, 1925, 1.

23. "Alegria Heurreux Hold Annual Affair," *OCBD*, December 17, 1925, 5.

24. "First Annual Charity Ball," *OCBD*, December 17, 1925, 5.

25. "The Social Whirl," *OCBD*, March 11, 1926, 5.

26. *OCBD*, January 4, 1923, 7. The East Side Cafe was located at 310 East Second Street, next door to the East Second Street Shining Parlor, which was at 308, and across from the Aldridge Theatre at 303–05; the cafe's proprietors were Washington and Woody. "Moonshine Co. Celebrates Billy King's 54th Anniversary," *OCBD*, February 8, 1923, 5. Howard Metropolitan C.M.E. was probably the church to which he referred; Reverend E. F. B. Amos was pastor late in 1923. "Howard Metropolitan C. M. E. church," in "Churches," *OCBD*, December 27, 1923, 5.

27. " 'Moonshine' Is Coming," 5; Sylvester Russell, "Chicago Weekly Review," *Indianapolis Freeman*, July 31, 1915, 5.

28. "Chicago Theatrical News," *Chicago Defender*, June 30, 1928, Part 1, 6; "Dramatic Criticism," *Indianapolis Freeman*, January 22, 1916, 3.

29. Earl J. Morris, "Grand Town Day and Night," *California Eagle*, February 15, 1942, 2B. Rogers became known as "Garbage" Rogers and he was a well-known M.C. and comedian at Chicago's Regal. He came from St. Louis. Evangeline Roberts, "Garbage Goes Over Big This Week at Regal," *Chicago Defender*, August 10, 1929, Part 1, 9; "Garbage," in "dance gossip by e. w. w.," *Kansas City Call*, March 13, 1931, 7; The Rambler, "3 Leading Comedians Neither Sing Nor Dance; but Are Hits," Baltimore *Afro-American*, October 17, 1931, 9.

30. "Moonshine Co. Celebrates Billy King's 54th Birthday," *OCBD*, February 8, 1923, 5. While later Blue Devils provided no information about Billy King, they gave some details about the first members of the band. Ernest Williams claimed the original members were Harry Youngblood, trumpet; Edward McNeil, drums; A. K. Godley, trombone; Ermal "Bucket" Coleman, trombone; Blue, clarinet; and Jimmy Rushing, singer. Yet Williams was not on the scene in 1923; he was either in China, where he voyaged while working on a ship, or in Harlem (Kansas City Jazz Oral History Collection, Western Historical Manuscript Collection, KC-12, Kansas City, MO). Also, Godley was a drummer, not a trombonist. Very little is known about Lawrence "Inky" Williams except that he conducted the Douglass High School band around the time of the Blue Devils' founding. William Thornton Blue was from St. Louis, and around 1924 he went to New York City. On June 17, 1928, he and his band sailed for Paris, where he had a contract at the Ambassador Club (Frank Mitchell, "William Thornton Blue and Gang Arrive in Paris," in "The Musician's Chatter Box," *St. Louis Argus*, July 20, 1928, 5). Lewis was said to be the "Brains behind the operation" (author's interview with Cornelius Pittman). Abe Bolar, an Oklahoman who joined the band late in 1929—replacing Walter Page—corroborated Page, naming Edward McNeil and Ermal Coleman as founding members, and adding Little Willie Lewis (author's interview with Abe Bolar). Buster Smith was recruited by the band in 1925 in Dallas, and he also recalled Coleman as the leader of the original band. He was "a fine trombone player and everybody called him 'Bucket.' " Coleman hailed from Indianapolis. He also named Harry Youngblood and several who later joined as early members (Gazzaway, "Conversations with Buster Smith, Part 1," 21).

31. Lewis Porter, ed., *A Lester Young Reader* (Washington, DC: Smithsonian Institution Press, 1991), 134. This article originally appeared as "You Got to Be Original, Man" *Jazz Record* (July 1946).

32. Jack McDaniels, "Buster Smith," *Down Beat* 23 (July 11, 1956), 13; Gazzaway, "Conversations with Buster Smith, Part 1," 21–22; ibid., "Part 2," 11–13; Gazzaway, "Buster and Bird, Part 3," 13–16.

33. "Pneumonia Victim," *OCBD*, November 22, 1934, 5. Marriage License, Marriage Records, page 300, number 600, Peoria County, Illinois. Lewis died in Bismarck, North Dakota, in 1934; a copy of his death certificate was obtained from Vital Records, State

Department of Health, Burleigh County, North Dakota, and the *Peoria City Directory, 1925.* See Page, "About My Life in Music," 13.

34. "Pneumonia Victim," 5. I want to express my gratitude to Elaine Pichaske Sokolowski and the reference staff at the Peoria Public Library and to Pat Hickman, Deputy Clerk, County Clerk's Office, Peoria, Illinois. According to Robert Case, Alumni Affairs, Boston Conservatory, their institution's records before 1930 were destroyed by fire; personal communication.

35. "Coupon Dance," *OCBD,* January 21, 1926, 4. Mr. Alphonso Hall was described by the *Dispatch* as "one of the substantial property holders of the race [Blacks]" in the capital. Hall's hall was located on the northwest corner of Second and Central. Stores and apartments occupied the first floor, while the Elks had their offices on the second; Victory Lodge No. 248, I.B.P.O.E.M. was on the third floor. "The Hall Building, Oklahoma City," *OCBD,* February 1, 1923, 1.

36. "New Orchestra Makes Hit," *OCBD,* September 20, 1928, 5.

37. "Pneumonia Victim," *OCBD,* November 22, 1934, 5.

38. This was the daughter of Abner Burnett, (Inez) grocer, 309 East First Street, residence 838 East Seventh Street; *OCCD, 1930.* I wish to express my gratitude to Mr. Burnett's daughter and Mr. Cornelius Pittman for this information.

39. Susan Curtis, *Dancing to A Black Man's Tune: A Life of Scott Joplin* (Columbia, MO: University of Missouri Press, 1994). "Will Offer New Sonata At Grand Lodge," *OCBD,* July 13, 1928, 5.

40. "City Ready for Songs Of Damon and Pythias," *Black Dispatch,* July 16, 1925, 1.

41. I would like to thank Benjamin Cohen for this information on *Kol Nidrei.* Eddie South recorded it around 1944; "Eddie South: the Dark Angel of the Fiddle" Soundies (SCD 4128).

42. "Will Offer New Sonata At Grand Lodge," *OCBD,* July 13, 1928, 5.

43. Page, "About My Life in Music," 13. See "Jazz Encyclopedia," Questionnaire of Leonard Feather, in Walter Page Vertical File, IJS. The *St. Louis City Directory, 1924,* page 538, listed William Blue, musician; his father was also a musician, ibid., 1920, page 715. His full name was William Thornton Blue; Frank Mitchell, "William Thornton Blue and His Gang Arrive in Paris," in "The Musician's Chatter Box," *St. Louis Argus,* July 20, 1928, 5.

44. USMC, 1900, Davies County, Union Township, ED 61, sheets 4B and 5A. "Funeral Services for Mrs. Blanche Page Sunday Night," *Kansas City Call,* May 25, 1934, 11, and "Funeral Services Held for Mrs. Blanche Page," 15. Nearly nine hundred mourners attended her funeral service, evidence of the regard with which she was held in the community; evidently her leadership abilities were passed on to her son. Interestingly, "the services were carried out as revealed in a dream" to Blanche Page's sister, evidence of a powerful religious heritage and, possibly, African cultural heritage, in which dreams play an important role in religion and in family matters ("'Funeral Services Held," 15). This obituary also informed readers that her husband, Edward, died eight years earlier.

45. Walter Page, "About My Life in Music," 12.

46. "Symphony Orchestra Plays Composition of Major N. Clark Smith, *Kansas City Call,* January 20, 1933, 3B; his *Negro Folk Suite* was composed of three parts, "Airs from British Guinea," "Martinique Melody," and "St. Helena Island Melodies," and was performed by the St. Louis Symphony. It won the Wanamaker award in 1930. It is noteworthy that the song titles, if not the compositions, in this suite were all West Indian; the form presages Duke Ellington's "tone poems" and other extended compositions. On Smith, see "Major N. Clark Smith Is Buried," *St. Louis Argus,* October 11, 1935, 1, 5. Born in 1874, in Leavenworth, Kansas, where his father was a soldier, he graduated from the University of Kansas and the Chicago Music College and traveled extensively in Europe and also in Africa, where he studied local musics. When Smith went to the Columbian Exposition in Chicago, Frederick Douglass took an interest in him, tuning

and playing Smith's violin as well as the organ, and encouraging him to take an interest in spirituals: "Major N. Clark Smith Has An Interesting Career," *St. Louis Argus*, July 1, 1932. Smith wrote the *Frederick Douglass Funeral March* in the abolitionist's honor.

47. Page, "About My Life In Music," 12–13.
48. "Funeral Services for Mrs. Blanche Page Sunday Night," *Call*, May 25, 1934, 11 and "Funeral Services Held for Mrs. Blanche Page," 15.
49. Page, "About My Life in Music," 12–15.
50. For Kirk, see Dave Peyton, "The Musical Bunch," *Chicago Defender*, June 16, 1928, Part 1, 8.
51. "Heart Attack Is Cause of Death of City Musician," *OCBD*, April 27, 1935, 1. *OCCD, 1926, 1928, 1931*. He was an assembler in the Alligator Manufacturing Company and resided at 615 East Second Street.
52. "Heart Attack Is Cause of Death of City Musician," *OCBD*, April 27, 1935, 1–2. See also the photograph and poem in ibid., 5.
53. Edward Christian, "Musical Low-Down," *OCBD*, April 25, 1938, 8.
54. USMC, 1910, Indianapolis, Marion County, ED 109 (ward 6), sheet 1B, lines 65–66; USMC, 1920, Indianapolis, Marion County, ED 145 (ward 8), sheet 3B, lines 65–66. The *Indianapolis City Directory, 1922*, listed Ermel Coleman at 610 North West. I would like to thank the Indianapolis Public Library for this directory information.
55. *OCCD, 1930, 1931–32, 1933, 1935*. According to the death certificate, he went for treatment to a veterans hospital, where he died (Certificate of Death number 002315, Vol. 38, page 297, Marion County Health Department, Indianapolis, IN). The date of death was January 17, 1937. Coleman's hospitalization in the Richard L. Roudebush V.A. Medical Center suggests that he may have served in the U.S. military.
56. See Edward Christian's column, "Musical Low-Down," *OCBD*, April 20, 1935, 8. See E. Christian and F. Pennington, ibid., April 4, 1935, 8; June 20, 1935, 8; and June 27, 1935, 8.
57. "Bozo, Drummer Who Took 'Bucket' Coleman Home To Die, Returns," *OCBD*, December 20, 1941, 5. This article reveals more about Bowler than about Coleman; it relates how after his good friend's death, he walked for three days to Cincinnati to work with bandleader Andy Kirk, then went to Cuba before returning to join Silas Green Minstrels. He finally returned "home" to Oklahoma City on the eve of World War II.
58. Dave Peyton, "The Musical Bunch," *Chicago Defender*, September 15, 1928, Part 1, 6; Frank Mitchell, "William Thornton Blue and Gang Arrive in Paris," 5; USMC 1920, St. Louis, MO, ED 329, sheet 5B; Driggs and Lewine, *Black Beauty, White Heat*, 130, 214.
59. Author's interview with Henry "Buster" Smith; Gazzaway, "Conversations with Buster Smith, Part 1," 18, and McDaniels, "Buster Smith," p. 13. See Ross Russell, *Bird Lives!: The High Life and Hard Times of Charlie (Yardbird) Parker*. "The Famous Blue Devil Orchestra of Oklahoma City Booked at Chester Park," *Dallas Express*, July 16, 1926, 3; this article gave a bit of history of the band, maintaining it was six years old (instead of three), played for a year at Oklahoma City's Huckins Hotel, and was composed of nine members—eight instrumentalists and one "entertainer." The article also claimed out that "each and every member... is a college graduate of music and have degrees from various Colleges." The band's "exclusive agent" was Mr. A. L. Jaffee, 3128 San Jacinto.
60. "At the Mardi Gras Ball," *OCBD*, February 18, 1926, 5.
61. Basie, *Good Morning Blues*, 21–22.
62. "At the Aldridge This Week," *OCBD*, May 20, 1926, 5.
63. Author's interviews with Henry "Buster" Smith and Le Roy "Snake" Whyte.
64. "Coleridge Taylor Club to Give Initial Recital," *OCBD*, November 22, 1923, 5. Needless to say, seven hundred dollars represented quite an investment in an instrument at this time, as well as approximately a year's salary for a working man. These must have indeed been good years for the bassist.

65. "The Coleridge Taylor School of Music," *OCBD*, September 3, 1925, 5.

66. "The Social Whirl," *OCBD*, August 13, 1925, 5. Williams appeared in a photograph of the first Douglass High School band along with twenty other musicians and a drum major. Edward Christian, brother of Charlie Christian, Wyatt H. Slaughter Jr., son of the doctor, and Henry P. Butler also appeared in the photo, which was published in the *Oklahoma City Black Dispatch* in January 21, 1971; I wish to thank Mr. Henry P. Butler for a copy of this photo. Mrs. Zelia N. Breaux was the band's first director.

67. The USMC, 1920, Oklahoma City, Vol. 47, ED 137, sheet 10, line 34, listed the thirty-eight-year-old music teacher. Born in Missouri and daughter of the educator and Brown University graduate Inman Page, she resided at 303 East Second Street with her son, Inman Junior, who was eleven years old. Fred Whitlow was her business associate in the Aldridge. Mrs. Breaux was also supervisor of music instruction at Douglass High School (*OCCD, 1920*). Her contributions are legendary; see Edison H. Anderson Sr.'s Ph.D. dissertation, *The Historical Development of Music in the Negro Secondary Schools of Oklahoma and at Langston University* (Iowa City: Graduate College of the State University of Iowa, 1957), 29, 106–109, 165, 273.

68. Page, "About My Life in Music," 13.

69. Ibid.

70. In a letter, the bassist reported the band's itinerary and listed its members in spring of 1931; Walter Page, Letter to Editor, dated May 16, 1931, Sioux City, IA, in "Editor's Mail Bag," *OCBD*, May 21, 1931, 4.

71. Author's interviews with Leonard Chadwick, Le Roy "Snake" Whyte, and Henry "Buster" Smith.

72. USMC, 1930, Oklahoma City, ED 58, sheet 2A.

73. *OCCD, 1930, 1931*, and *1934*. Edward Christian, "Musical Lowdown," *OCBD*, April 25, 1935, 8.

74. "Social Whirl," *OCBD*, December 16, 1926, 5; "'Simp' Makes Good," *OCBD*, January 20, 1927, 5.

75. *OCBD*, January 29, 1931, 1; Walter Page, Letter to Editor, refers to the band as Page's and lists Simpson as a member; "Back Home Again," *OCBD*, February 6, 1932, 5. In the *Chicago Defender*, April 9, 1932, 5, the band is referred to as "the Original '13 Blue Devils.'" E. Christian and F. Pennington, "Musical Lowdown," *OCBD*, April 4, 1935, 8; Edward Christian, "Musical Low-Down," *OCBD*, April 25, 1935, 8.

76. Ad in *OCBD*, October 12, 1933, 3.

77. Page, "About My Life in Music," 13. See "The Social Whirl," *OCBD*, February 12, 1931, 5, on the Elks engagement. The band was particularly special for African-Americans in Oklahoma and in the territories generally. Their very name was understood by this ethnic group as a color reference, according to Eddie Durham (author's interview). Also, as "blue devils" are the sharp barbs on barbed wire, the band's name carried the implication that they looked and played sharp enough to cut. I wish to thank Professor James Campbell for the suggestion about the connection between the band's name and that of barbed wire. T. Terence Holder's Dark Clouds of Joy and Gene Coy's Black Aces also communicated their ethnicity to Blacks with their very names; this was an expression of pride in color or race; Ron Welburn, "Ralph Ellison's Territorial Advantage," *The Grackle: Improvised Music in Transition*, 4 (1977–78), 8. I would like to express my gratitude to Professor Ron Welburn for providing me with a copy of this issue. Ellison suggested: "the term 'Blue Devils' is English and referred to a state of psychic depression, but during the range wars in cattle country those who were given to cutting barbed wire fences were called 'Blue Devils.' Perhaps Walter Page chose the name because of its outlaw connotations." Eugene Clark's Black Devil's Minstrel, a troupe that traveled with the John Robinson Circus, may have initiated the tradition; *Indianapolis Freeman*, August 16, 1919, 6. Druie Bess mentioned Grant Moore's Black Devils and Eddie Randall's Blue

Devils in his University of Missouri interview, pages 70–71 (Kansas City Jazz Oral History Collection, Western Historical Manuscript Collection, KC-12, University of Missouri, Kansas City, MO). In baseball, there were the Memphis Black Devils; see Margaret McKee and Fred Chisenhall, *Beale Black and Blue: Life and Music on Black America's Main Street* (Baton Rouge, LA: Louisiana State University Press, 1981), 63.

78. Ron Welburn, "Ralph Ellison's Territorial Advantage," 8. See "Where to Go and What to See: Slaughter's Hall," *OCBD*, January 5, 1933, 5, for an occasion when Oran Page tried out his new English horn, suggesting the ways in which Blue Devils experimented with new sounds in Oklahoma City; also, "His Symphony On Air," *OCBD,* November 22, 1934, 8, on Ralph Ellison's trumpet playing in Oklahoma City.

79. "Oran 'Hot Lips' Page, Famed Trumpeter, Dead," Kansas City *Call,* November 19, 1954, 8.

Chapter 4

1. Social Security application gives birth date as August 26, but the death certificate gives August 24. According to a November 6, 2003, e-mail from Gerri L. Brannan, Genealogical Room, Dallas Public Library, Dallas, Texas, "Alsdorf is on a spur of State Highway 34 five miles northeast of Ennis, Texas in east central Ellis County. The population never got above 100 and the post office closed in 1920. The last population count was in 1949 at which time there were 50 people."

2. Author's interview.

3. Alsdorf, Texas in Driggs interview, University of Missouri at Kansas City; Don Gazzaway, "Conversations with Buster Smith, Part 1," *The Jazz Review* II (December 1959), 18.

4. USMC, 1920, ED 49, Justice Precinct 2, Delta County, sheet 13B; USMC, 1930, Dallas County, Dallas, ED 44, sheet 58A.

5. Curiously, two neighbors, both "general farmers," are also surnamed Smith, and because they are white, one wonders if all these Smiths are related or if the census taker made a mistake with the racial identity of the "general farmers." USMC, 1920, ED 49, Roll 625–1795, Justice Precinct 2, Delta County, sheet 13B, lines 37–47. Author's interview: father played guitar and mother piano.

6. USMC, 1930, Dallas County, Dallas, ED 44, sheet 58A, lines 40–47.

7. Alan Govenar, *Meeting the Blues* (Dallas: Taylor Publishing Co., 1988), 40.

8. Ibid.

9. Gazzaway, Part 1, 18.

10. Author's interview with Henry "Buster" Smith; Gazzaway, "Conversations with Buster Smith, Part 1, 18.

11. Author's interview with Henry "Buster" Smith. Smith may have been the banjoist and saxophonist identified as Henry Emith [*sic*] in the Ideal Orchestra, an early jazz band linked to Oklahoma City; "Ideal Still Favorites with Dance Fans," *OCBD*, December 27, 1923, 5.

12. Tim Schuller, "The Buster Smith Story," *Coda Magazine* 217 (December 1987), 2, 8; Gazzaway, "Conversations with Buster Smith, Part 1," 18. On the Ella B. Moore revue, see D. Thomas Ireland, "Motion Picture News," *Chicago Defender,* November 22, 1924, Part 1, page 8.

13. Smith interview, IJS, KC-12, 2, 8–9.

14. Ibid.

15. Smith interview, IJS, KC-12, 148; *DCD, 1922:* "Hooker Jesse (c) musician rms 2821 Commercial Al." Gazzaway, Part 1, 20, names Hummingbird on Hall Street and I. B. Mose theatre downtown as important venues.

16. Smith interview, IJS, KC-12, 148. Page 149 says if he had stayed with this profession he would have been much better off, not running all up and down the road. *DCD, 1924,* lists three African-Americans named Henry Smith; two are waiters, and one works in a clean-

ing establishment. The latter might have been Buster, because his wife's name was Ethel, and this was the name of the cleaning establishment worker's wife. *DCD, 1924:* "Henry (c: Ethel) prop Peoples Tailoring & Press Club r 1810 Allen"; *DCD, 1927:* "Henry F. [Franklin] & Ethel Smith retd 2223 Garden."

17. Smith interview, IJS, KC-12, 2, mentions Bechet's "Kansas City Blues."
18. Smith interview, IJS, KC-12, 1.
19. Scott Ellsworth, *Death in a Promised Land: The Tulsa Race Riot of 1921* (Baton Rouge: Louisiana State University Press, 1992); *Tulsa City Directory, 1923,* 568. Ibid., 204: "Henry Smith (c) musician, Dreamland Theater Dreamland Theater (c) Mrs. Lula Williams propr 127 N. Greenwood Ave."
20. Smith interview, IJS, KC-12, 5
21. Ibid., 4–5.
22. Ibid., 7–9.
23. Ibid., 21. The Driggs interview (Marr Sound Archives, Miller Nichols Library, University of Missouri at Kansas City) claims that things were decidedly better in Oklahoma City.
24. Smith interview, IJS, KC-12, 21.
25. Gazzaway, "Conversations with Buster Smith, Part 1," 21, names Reuben Roddy, James Simpson, Harry Youngblood, Willie Lewis, Walter Page, and later Reuben Lynch.
26. Jack McDaniels, "Buster Smith," *Down Beat* 23 (July 11, 1956), 13.
27. Smith interview, IJS, KC-12, 12.
28. Ibid., 8.
29. Ken Parish Perkins (staff writer, *Dallas Morning News*), "Fame Was a Melody Lost on Buster Smith," *Dallas Morning News,* August 18, 1991, 3C.
30. Smith interview, IJS, KC-12, 202.
31. Smith interview, Reel 3, page 2: IJS, 111.
32. Smith interview, IJS, KC-12, 151; DCD, 24: "John (c: Annie) lab Vilbig Bros; John Clark, porter The Ritz, rms 300 San Jacinto; John Clark (Annie), r 109 Chestnut; Johnnie (c) porter Cluett Peabody & Co rms 3003 San Jacinto."
33. Smith interview, IJS, KC-12, 111–112.
34. Schuller, 4.
35. Ibid., 21. Basie is on the Chicago, October 23, 1929, Moten recording; Rushing and allegedly Oran Page are on the October 24, 1929, date, but as Page does not solo, this is unlikely; *Bennie Moten's Kansas City Orchestra, 1929–1930,* Classics 578.
36. Schuller, 21.
37. Schuller, 22.
38. Smith interview, IJS, KC-12, 53, 50–51.
39. Ibid., 56–57; see a similar incident on page 54.
40. Ibid., 57.
41. Ibid., 60.
42. Ibid., 61–62.
43. "The Social Whirl," *OCBD,* December 16, 1926, 5.
44. "They Saw the Panthers and Wild Cats Fight," *OCBD,* October 24, 1929, 8.
45. Ibid.

Chapter 5

1. One of the first articles on Rushing stated that he would be forty-four on his next birthday. As it was published in 1946, this suggests he was born in 1902, but on nearly every other occasion he gave 1903 as his year of birth. An Institute of Jazz Studies ad in the Rushing Vertical File, "City Blues and Country Blues"(1955), the former featuring Rushing, also gives his year of birth as 1902. "Daddy of the Blues," *Hollywood Note* (April 1946), 8, article in Rushing Vertical File, IJS. See also USMC, 1920, Oklahoma

City, Vol. 49, ED 153, sheet 19, line 75, in which James Rushing is listed as nineteen years old. See the following note, which indicates that he was born in 1899. See Nat Hentoff, "Jimmy Rushing," *Down Beat* 24 (March 6, 1957), 20, for information on his father.

2. The USMC for 1900, Oklahoma City, ED 171, sheet 5B, line 99, lists James A. Rushing, son of Andrew and Cora, born June 1899 and ten months old the day the census was taken—June 9th, 1900. The USMC for 1920, Oklahoma City, ED 153, sheet 19B, line 77, also gives 1899 as his year of birth. Rushing may have changed his month of birth from June to August to have an interval of nine months between his parents' wedding and his birth, but we do not know.

3. Nat Hentoff, "Jimmy Rushing," *Down Beat* 24 (March 6, 1957), 20.

4. "Daddy of the Blues," *Hollywood Note* (April 1946), 20.

5. In the USMC for 1900, Oklahoma City, ED 171, sheet 7, line 73, Wesley J. Manning is listed as the son of John Manning, who worked for the water company, and Mattie, who does not appear to have been his mother, given that her state of birth is listed as Arkansas, and his mother's is given as Tennessee. Mattie may have been the sister of Cora, James Rushing's mother; the Mannings lived at 203 East First Street.

6. Hentoff, "Jimmy Rushing," 20.

7. Ibid. He also mentioned Ethel Waters as having "a real fine voice" in "Doug Hague Interviews Rudy Powell and Jimmy Rushing," *Jazz Journal* 10 (July 1957), 3.

8. Frank Driggs, "Jimmy Rushing's Story," April 1966. Clipping in Rushing Vertical File, IJS.

9. Ibid.

10. Chris Albertson, "Jimmy Rushing: A Sturdy Branch of the Learning Tree," *Down Beat* 36 (November 13, 1969), 17.

11. S. Trail, "Jimmy Rushing—In My Opinion," *Jazz Journal* 17 (January 1964), 14.

12. Ibid., 15.

13. Douglas Hague, "Jimmy Rushing Tells His Story to Douglas Hague," *Jazz Journal* 10 (September 1957), 1.

14. Driggs, "Jimmy Rushing's Story."

15. Dave Caplan, "Man About Jazz: 'Gotta Feel Blue to Sing the Blues,'" *Toronto Daily Star*, November 18, 1961, Rushing Vertical File, IJS.

16. "Daddy of the Blues," 8.

17. On his maternal grandmother, see her obituary, "Pioneer Citizen Passes," "Social Whirl," *OCBD*, July 28, 1927, 5.

18. Hentoff, "Jimmy Rushing," 20.

19. Death certificate of John Wesley Manning, number 42,513, Oklahoma State Board of Health, Vital Statistics, Oklahoma City, Oklahoma, dated April 13, 1935. Like guitarist Charlie Christian, his brother, Eddie, and bassist Jimmy Blanton, Manning died of tuberculosis, probably the leading cause of death for African-Americans at that time.

20. See the USMC for 1900, Oklahoma City, ED 171, sheet 5B, lines 96–100 and sheet 6A, lines 1–3; the USMC for 1920, Oklahoma City, Vol. 49, ED 153, sheet 19, line 75, gives Cora Rushing's place of birth as Tennessee; USMC, 1930, Oklahoma City, ED 55, sheet 7A, lines 21–23.

21. USMC, 1900, Oklahoma City, ED 171, sheet 5B, line 100. *OCCD*, 1920. They lived at 307½ East Second Street, next door to the Aldridge Theatre. Walter Page and his family boarded with them that year. Jimmy Stewart, "Jimmy Stewart Says," *OCBD*, January 11, 1947, 12. "City Boy with Basie," *OCBD*, September 14, 1940, 8. *OCCD*, *1927*, *1930*. Ibid., *1927*, *1930*.

22. See the USMC for 1900, Oklahoma City, ED 171, sheet 5B, lines 96–100 and sheet 6A, lines 1–3; USMC, 1930, ED 55, sheet 7A, lines 21–23.

23. "Norman Wilner Interviews," clipping in Rushing Vertical File, IJS. USMC, 1900, Oklahoma County, ED 171, sheet 5B; USMC, 1920, Oklahoma County, ED 153, sheet

19B, line 75; *Wilberforce Bulletin Wilberforce University Catalogue, 1918–1919*, Series 4, No. 4 (Wilberforce, OH: Combined Normal and Industrial Department at Wilberforce, June 1919), 181. I would like to thank Jacqueline Y. Brown, librarian, Rembert E. Stokes Learning Resources Center Library, Wilberforce University, for verifying that Rushing attended Wilberforce 1918–1919. On Evoid's attendance, see "Social Whirl," *OCBD*, September 24, 1920, 5.

24. "Social Whirl," *OCBD*, September 24, 1920, 5, reported that Evoid Rushing was "making high marks in his school classes" and returned to Wilberforce in autumn 1920. Yet Wilberforce had no record of his having attended this institution; I would like to thank Jacqueline Y. Brown, librarian, Rembert E. Stokes Learning Resources Center Library, Wilberforce University, for this information. Evoid Rushing worked as a clerk in 1930, and as a store porter during the Depression; *OCCD, 1930, 1935*.

25. Helen McNamara, "Pack My Bags and Make My Getaway: The Odyssey of Jimmy Rushing," *Down Beat* 32 (April 8, 1965), 22.

26. Driggs, "Jimmy Rushing's Story," April 1966, 64–65. See Helen McNamara, "Pack My Bags and Make My Getaway," 24. In Stanley Dance, *The World of Count Basie*, 18, Rushing claimed he went to California first in 1921, where he sang in a club where Buddy Petit, Buster Wilson, and other New Orleans musicians performed. In an interview with Frank Driggs, he stated he went to California in 1923: Frank Driggs interview with Jimmy Rushing, Frank Driggs Collection, Disc 25 (April 2, 1957), Marr Sound Archives, Miller Nichols Library, University of Missouri, Kansas City, Missouri.

27. The *Los Angeles City Directory* for 1923 lists James Rushing, bootblack, living in South Central. Aside from this year, he was not listed between 1921 and 1925.

28. *Jazz Casual—Jimmy Witherspoon/Jimmy Rushing*, Koch Jazz (KOC CD-8561), band 13. His grandmother's obituary also mentioned a wife: "Card of Thanks," in "Social Whirl," *OCBD*, July 28, 1927, 5.

29. Driggs, "Jimmy Rushing's Story," 64–65.

30. McNamara, "Pack My Bags."

31. Hague, "Jimmy Rushing Tells His Story to Douglas Hague," 1.

32. Phil Pastras, *Dead Man Blues: Jelly Roll Morton Way Out West* (Berkeley: University of California Press, 2001). On early West Coast jazz, see Tom Stoddard, *Jazz on the Barbary Coast* (Berkeley: Heyday Books, 1998).

33. Hague, 1.

34. Ibid.

35. Driggs, "Jimmy Rushing's Story," 65. Besides Stoddard and Pastras, see Floyd Levin, *Classic Jazz: A Personal View of the Music and the Musicians* (Berkeley: University of California Press, 2000), 9–63, 230–267. Pastras, 91, referring to Professor Larry Gushee's research, noted that Buddy Petit "returned to Los Angeles from New Orleans in 1922," so it is probable that Rushing heard him shortly thereafter.

36. Albert "Budd" Johnson interview, IJS, Reel 1, 31.

37. Driggs, "Jimmy Rushing's Story," 65; Hague, 1. Rushing is mentioned in *OCBD* as a champion dancer at the Mardi Gras Ball: "The Social Whirl," *OCBD*, (February 18, 1926), 5.

38. In the interview with Helen McNamara, page 22, Rushing gave 1928 as the date of this historic recording, which is interesting, because most sources give 1929. Significantly, the Blue Devils were in Kansas City in November. Nonetheless, Chuck Haddix of the Marr Sound Archives at the University of Missouri, Kansas City, has verified that the actual date of the recording was 1929.

39. Hague, 1. Rushing (or the reporter) erred when he gave Moten's death as occurring in 1934; it was spring 1935. Actually, the story of the succession from the Blue Devils to Moten to Basie is more complicated.

40. Driggs, "Jimmy Rushing's Story," 65. While he usually referred to Manning as his uncle,

in McNamara, "The Odyssey of Jimmy Rushing," 22, he explained: "He was a honky tonk pianist, the son of my aunt, who owned the Dixie Theatre." This would make him a cousin. While the author has not been able to find a Dixie Theatre in Oklahoma City, there was one at 120 Greenwood in Tulsa in the 1920s; see the *Tulsa City Directory* for 1921, page 659, and for 1923, page 744.

41. S. Trail, "Jimmy Rushing—In My Opinion," *Jazz Journal* 17 (January 1964), 15.
42. Ibid., 14.
43. Ibid. Singer Jessie Derrick was featured at the Entertainers' Café, a new resort that opened downtown on January 15, 1924; "Ragtime" Billy Tucker, "Coast Dope," *Chicago Defender*, January 28, 1924, 8. A week later at the Entertainers' Café, Dink Johnson, who was Jelly Roll Morton's brother-in-law, led a six-piece combo that included one of the other New Orleans musicians Rushing identified as present in Los Angeles during his stay—the famous cornetist Buddy Petit; "Ragtime" Billy Tucker, "Coast Dope," *Chicago Defender*, February 2, 1924, 6.
44. Ralph Ellison, "Remembering Jimmy," in *Shadow and Act* (New York: Signet Books, 1966), 237.
45. Florrie D. Pugh, "Sunshine Club Holds Frolic," in "The Week's Doings," *OCBD*, January 30, 1920, 5.
46. "The Social Whirl," *OCBD*, February 18, 1926, 5. He was first mentioned in the *OCCD* in 1927.
47. "Back in the City from Tulsa," in "The Social Whirl," *OCBD*, December 22, 1921, 5.
48. "Ideal Jazz Grab Biggest Crowd," in "The Social Whirl," *OCBD*, December 29, 1921, 5.
49. "The Social Whirl," *OCBD*, January 5, 1922, 5.
50. Basie, *Good Morning Blues*, 21–22.
51. "Elks Hold Services for Departed," *OCBD*, April 13, 1922, 1. The *OCCD* for 1930 listed the Bethel Hotel, where Oran Page lived in 1929; significantly, Walter Page resided in the Tucker Building at this time, underlining the close ties between local businessmen and the Blue Devils.
52. Ibid. Rushing was also secretary of the entertainment committee when the Grand Exalted Ruler visited the capital city: "Grand Exalted Ruler Coming—Greatest Affair of the Capital," *OCBD*, May 24, 1922, 1.
53. Driggs, "Jimmy Rushing's Story," 65. "Singer Brothers" may have been the typical mistake made by reporters not familiar with names of musicians and bands. Singie Smith's Orchestra was from Fort Worth, Texas; see "Norman Mob After Singie Smith Jazz," *OCBD*, February 9, 1922, 1, in which a lynch mob in Norman, Oklahoma, ran the band out of town because of the racism of the townsfolk. The local sheriff deputized Oklahoma University students "in order to protect the musicians" when they were escorted to the interurban station.
54. "The Social Whirl," *OCBD*, May 6, 1926, 5; ibid., November 18, 1926, 5, and December 12, 1926, 5.
55. "Aldridge Dancing Academy," *OCBD*, September 1, 1921, 5.
56. "Wedding Bells," in "The Social Whirl," *OCBD*, October 13, 1921, 5. Whether this James Simpson attending the wedding is the bandleader is unclear; he would have been about ten years old in 1921.
57. Scott Ellsworth, *Death in a Promised Land*; "Norman Mob After Singie Smith Jazz," *OCBD*, February 9, 1922, 1.
58. Los Angeles County Recorder, Real Estate Book number 1754, page 368, document number 436, filed February 15, 1923, indicated that William R. and Saloma L. Rushing, the singer's uncle and aunt, mortgaged their home for the sum of nine hundred dollars; thanks to Naima Daniels for uncovering this information. See "Pioneer Citizen Passes," in "Social Whirl," *OCBD*, July 28, 1927, 5.
59. *Los Angeles City Directory, 1923*, page 2663. In 1922, William, possibly James's uncle,

and Olin W. Rushing, who was probably his cousin, resided at 1038 East Twenty-eighth Street. William Rushing sold cigars at 1105 South Central Avenue. Another, or perhaps the same, William Rushing was engaged in car repair in 1923.

60. *Los Angeles City Directory, 1925,* page 1678; she was identified as "Genie" Rushing, and we assume it was his wife, but it may have been someone else.
61. Driggs, "Jimmy Rushing's Story," 65.
62. Ibid.
63. Trail, "Jimmy Rushing—In My Opinion," *Jazz Journal* 17 (January 1964), 15.
64. Driggs, "Jimmy Rushing's Story," 65; McNamara, "Pack My Bags," 23. See also Basie's autobiography, *Good Morning Blues,* pages 17–18, where he claims that he got a telegram sent from Paris, Texas, asking him to take over on piano for the band, but that he became a Blue Devil when he joined them in Oklahoma City.
65. Driggs, "Jimmy Rushing's Story," 65.
66. Chris Albertson, "Jimmy Rushing: A Sturdy Branch of the Learning Tree," 17.
67. Ibid.; McNamara, "Odyssey of Jimmy Rushing," 22.
68. Albertson, 17; Trail, 14.
69. Driggs, "Jimmy Rushing's Story," 67.
70. Hague, 1.
71. "Coupon Dance," in "The Social Whirl," *OCBD,* January 21, 1926, 4; "At the Mardi Gras Ball," *OCBD,* February 18, 1926, 5; "The Social Whirl," *OCBD,* March 4, 1926, 5; "Dances for This Week," in "The Social Whirl," *OCBD,* April 8, 1926, 5; "Dances for This Week & Next," in "The Social Whirl," *OCBD,* April 14, 1926, 5; ibid., April 22, 1926, 5; "The Season's Dances," in "The Social Whirl," *OCBD,* May 6, 1926, 5. "The Blue Devils at Forest Park," in "The Social Whirl," August 19, 1926, page 5, reported that the Blue Devils were playing at Forest Park "and they are hot!" They had recently returned from Dallas, and coming home "seems to have added zeal and pep to the orchestra." This article also referred to the "Mighty Blue Devil Band."
72. "What's This," in "The Social Whirl," *OCBD,* January 20, 1927, 5.
73. "'Twenty Club' Stages Most Delightful Affair of the Season," in "The Social Whirl," *OCBD,* June 9, 1927, 5.
74. "The Social Whirl," *OCBD,* October 13, 1926, 5.
75. "New Orchestra Makes Hit," in "The Social Whirl," *OCBD,* September 20, 1928, 5; Alvin "Fats" Walls organized this new orchestra in late summer: Walls, manager and reeds; Theo Ross, reeds; Charley Lewis, reeds and violin; Harry Youngblood, brass; Hiram Harding, brass; "Flip" Benson, brass; Grant Williams, banjo and guitar; Willie Lewis, piano and arranger; Eugene Hill, drums; Albert Morgan, tuba and bass violin; Bar Birt, entertainer and director. Youngblood and Ross later played with the Blue Devils
76. "New! Hot!" Blue Devil advertisement, Kansas City *Call,* October 26, 1928, 9; "Blue Devil Orchestra at Paseo Hall," ibid., Part 2, 13.
77. Photograph in Kansas City *Call,* October 26, 1928, 12. In the photo, the image appears to have been reversed, because the print does not match the order of the musicians, except for Walter Page, who is in the center.
78. "Walter Page and His Blue Devil Orchestra" advertisement, Kansas City *Call,* November 2, 1928, 10. Some think Basie was on piano, or T. B. Thomas, or Charlie Washington, but another possibility is that it is Willie Lewis.
79. "Dance War Sunday at Paseo Hall," Kansas City *Call,* November 23, 1928, 10.
80. "Musicians 1st Annual Ball" advertisement, Kansas City *Call,* November 29, 1929, 2.
81. Basie, *Good Morning Blues,* 113; Basie also quoted Walter Page on the matter: "I wanted to battle with Bennie Moten in the worst way because I knew I could beat him. He never would give me one, and we never did get the chance." (See Walter Page, "About My Life in Music," *The Jazz Review* 1, November 1958, page 14.)
82. "Musicians 1st Annual Ball" *Call* advertisement.

83. Ralph Ellison, "Remembering Jimmy," *Shadow and Act* (New York: Signet Books, 1966), 238. Basie emphasized this point, as well: Rushing "wasn't really a blues singer in those days. He was really a ballad singer. But there was a blues flavor about the way he was singing," Basie, *Good Morning Blues*, 6.

84. Ellison, "Remembering Jimmy," 235. Ellison lived with his younger brother, mother, and stepfather at 812 Stonewall in 1935 (*OCCD, 1935*).

85. "Elks in Big Smokey," *California Eagle*, November 30, 1923, 2.

86. Basie, *Good Morning Blues*, 7–8.

87. Dan Burley, "Fame and Fortune for Fat Folks!" *AN*, November 30, 1940, 21.

Chapter 6

1. Valerie Wilmer, "Eddie Durham," *Coda* 158 (November–December 1977), 6.

2. Phil Schaap, tape-recorded interview with Eddie Durham, February 2, 1977, Eddie Durham Papers (privately held by the Durham family). I wish to thank Marcia Durham, the musician's daughter, for providing me with copies of this and other tape-recorded interviews with her father. Eddie Durham's parents lived in adjacent Gonzales County as early as 1900, but were back in Hays County in 1910 (USMC for 1900, Vol. 47, ED 53, Gonzales County, Justice Precinct 3, sheet 26B, and USMC for 1910, Hays County, ED 39, sheet 11B). See also Eddie Durham, JOHP, IJS, Reel 1, page 1. The JOHP interviewer reports that Durham's brother added a few extra years to his age "with the idea that it was going to help [Eddie] in not having to go off into the Army," page 61. According to his death certificate, Roosevelt, Durham's brother, was born May 22 that year, making it most unlikely that the same mother would bear a second child in August— assuming that this date is correct (death certificate of Roosevelt Durham, Eddie Durham Papers). In one of the first articles on Durham, "He started in the [music] game in 1918," and claimed that he was thirty-one years old, suggesting that he was born in 1906 (Leonard Feather, "32-Year-Old Trombone Veteran," *Melody Maker*, May 21, 1938; Durham Vertical File, IJS). On his marriage license application in 1939, he claimed that he was born in 1909. His Social Security application also had the same birth year. In a 1962 interview, he claimed to be "pushing 53," which corresponds with the 1909 birth date (George Hoefer, "Held Notes: Eddie Durham," *Down Beat* 29, July 19, 1962, 57).

3. Eddie Durham IJS interview, Reel 1, pages 2–4, 59. The father was also a jockey, ibid, page 82, and a sharecropper, page 84. See also the USMC for 1900, indicating that Joseph Durham, born in 1875, was a farm renter and literate; his wife, Luella, also literate, was born in 1877 (according to her age; the year of birth must be incorrect at 1886). They had been married seven years and had two sons, Joseph, five years old, and Early, one year old.

4. Eddie Durham IJS interview, Reel 1, page 4; Joel A. Siegel and James Obrecht, "Eddie Durham: Charlie Christian's Mentor, Pioneer of the Amplified Guitar," *Guitar Player* 13 (August 1979), 56.

5. USMC, 1900, Gonzales County, ED 53, sheet 26B, line 8; Ibid., sheets 62–66. In an interview with the author, Lesa, Durham's daughter, reported that her father spoke Spanish as a youngster, possibly as his first language.

6. USMC, 1870, Hays County, Texas, Precinct 2, sheet 19, September 1, 1870; USMC, 1880, ED 76, Hays County, Precinct 1, June 22, 1880.

7. Ibid., sheet 67.

8. Joel A. Siegel and James Obrecht, "Eddie Durham: Charlie Christian's Mentor, Pioneer of the Amplified Guitar," 55–56.

9. Eddie Durham interview, IJS, Reel 1, pages 68–72.

10. Ibid., pages 3–5. According to the USMC for 1920, Freestone County, Texas, ED 16, sheet 7A, lines 19–23, Roosevelt Durham, aged sixteen and a driver for a grocery, lived with Step, a farm laborer, and Millie Moses, his wife; he was listed as stepson. Eddie sug-

gested he was older than Roosevelt (IJS, Reel 1, page 6), but the census and his Army records indicate otherwise.

11. Eddie Durham IJS interview, Reel 1, page 87. Edgar Battle was born in Atlanta, Georgia, October 3, 1907, and died in February 1977 in New York City; according to the USMC for 1920, Fulton County, Atlanta, Georgia, ED 72, sheet 6B, Battle lived with his mother and grandmother in an extended family.

12. Author's interview with Rudine Battle, the daughter.

13. Phil Schaap interview with Eddie Durham, February 25, 1977.

14. Paul Meskil, "Maestro Still Jazzing It Up at 80," Durham Vertical File, IJS.

15. Eddie Durham IJS interview, Reel 1, pages 7, 59. He had a banjo as late as 1927. In Moten's band he sometimes played violin; Charles I. Brown, "On the Air," OCBD, October 19, 1933, p. 5. Two other Motenites also doubled on violin. In 1988 he said that his brother bought him his first guitar (Alan Govenar, "Eddie Durham: Interview," *Living Blues Magazine* 83, November–December 1988, 35). In the Siegel and Obrecht interview, page 56, he explained that his brother bought him a four-string guitar, and then later Morgan purchased a six-string Stella guitar for him.

16. Eddie Durham IJS interview, Reel 1, page 88.

17. Ibid., Reel 1, page 6. Govenar, "Eddie Durham: Interview," 35.

18. Eddie Durham IJS interview, Reel 1, pages 8–9.

19. Ibid., page 9.

20. Phil Schaap interview with Eddie Durham, February 25, 1977.

21. Eddie Durham IJS, Reel 1, page 42.

22. Ibid., Reel 1, page 43; see Phil Schaap interview, February 25, 1977, on Terrell, Texas.

23. Quotes from document on Burnett from Terrell Public Library, which cites G. T. Overstreet, "A Late Educator, William H. Burnett The Shadow of Burnett High School," Dallas *Star Post*, October 1, 1955, and E. P. Shaw, "Burnett High: Long Time Since Yesterday," Terrell *Tribune*, July 27, 1990; Durham quotes are from IJS interview Reel 1, page 43.

24. Phil Schaap interviews with Eddie Durham, November 7, 1988 and February 25, 1977.

25. Eddie Durham IJS interview, Reel 1, pages 9–10.

26. Ibid., Reel 1, page 10. Amon Carter Museum of Western Art, *The Wild West or, A History of the Wild West Shows* (Ft. Worth: Amon Carter Museum, 1970), 6, 9, 73, 76, 77, 80ff.; Paul Reddin, *Wild West Shows* (Urbana: University of Illinois Press, 1999).

27. Eddie Durham IJS interview, Reel 1, page 12.

28. Eric Lott, *Love and Theft: Blackface Minstrelsy and the American Working Class* (New York: Oxford University Press, 1993).

29. Eddie Durham IJS interview, Reel 1, page 12.

30. Ibid.

31. Ibid.

32. Ibid., page 13.

33. Ibid., page 25.

34. Durham was also with Battle's Dixie Ramblers ca. 1926; Siegel and Obrecht, 56.

35. Govenar, "Eddie Durham: Interview," 35. Wilmer, "Eddie Durham," *Coda*, 7. In the Phil Schaap interview, Durham says he was in short pants, suggesting that he was probably less than nineteen or twenty.

36. Durham IJS interview, Reel 1, page 19.

37. Ibid.

38. Ibid., page 20.

39. Ibid., page 28.

40. Ibid., page 18. I wish to thank Dennis G. Daniels for this information on the American Music Company.

41. Ibid., pages 18, 29–30.

42. *Chicago City Directory, 1923*, Vol. 2, pages 2853 and 2542; thanks to Dennis G. Daniels for assistance in this research.
43. Durham IJS interview, Reel 1, page 29.
44. Michael W. Harris, *The Rise of Gospel Blues: The Music of Thomas Andrew Dorsey in the Urban Church* (New York: Oxford University Press, 1992).
45. Ibid., 79.
46. "Come Along Mandy at the Grand; Bessie Smith & Co. at the Avenue," *Chicago Defender*, May 10, 1924, 6.
47. Durham IJS interview, Reel 1, page 34.
48. Ibid., pages 32–33.
49. Phil Schaap interview with Eddie Durham, February 25, 1977, and author's interview with Rudine Battle.
50. Durham IJS interview, 35.
51. Ibid., page 36.
52. On Tompkins family (Professor and Mrs. M. H. Tompkins, 2229 Tracy), Eddie as Lincoln High alumnus, Eddie's first job with Moten at Lincoln theater, and Eddie's three years at the University of Iowa, see L. Herbert Henegan, "Lunceford's Ambition Is to Be Best Orchestra Leader," Kansas City *Call*, March 2, 1934, 11.
53. Durham IJS interview, Reel 1, pages 38–39.
54. Ibid., pages 40–41.
55. Ibid., pages 42–43.
56. Ibid., page 44.
57. Ibid., pages 52–53.
58. Ibid., pages 52, 58.
59. Ibid., page 58.
60. Dave Peyton, "The Musical Bunch," *Chicago Defender*, August 17, 1929, Part 1, page 8.
61. Walter Barnes Jr., "The Musical Bunch, "*Chicago Defender*, November 2, 1929, 13; "New Cabaret Jammed With Enthusiastic Crowds for Opening on Last Saturday," Kansas City *Call*, January 23, 1931, 7.
62. Ed Lewis corroborated this: "Ed Lewis' Story" (as told to Frank Driggs), *The Jazz Review* II (October 1959), 64. See also "Kansas City Brass: Ed Lewis' Story as Told to Frank Driggs," *The Jazz Review* II (May 1959), 64.
63. George Hoefer, "Held Notes: Eddie Durham," *Down Beat* 29 (July 19, 1962), 54.
64. Marc Rice, *The Bennie Moten Orchestra;* see also Gunther Schuller, *Early Jazz: Its Roots and Musical Development* (New York: Oxford University Press, 1986), 312: These recordings "inaugurated a conception of orchestral jazz distinct from that of Henderson and the eastern axis, a conception moreover which was to bypass the inherent stylistic hazards of the Swing Era and provide at least one of the routes leading to modern jazz and bop." On Barefield, Bob Queen, "Eddie Barefield Rated Top Musician-Arranger," Baltimore *Afro American*, February 15, 1947, 3.
65. Eddie Durham IJS interview, Reel 1, pages 58–59.
66. Ibid, page 59.
67. Ibid.
68. Ibid., page 60.
69. Ibid.
70. *Bennie Moten's Kansas City Orchestra, 1929–1930*, Classics 578.
71. Durham IJS interview, Reel 1, page 65.
72. Ibid., pages 68, 70–71.
73. *Bennie Moten's Kansas City Orchestra, 1929–1930*.
74. Eddie Durham IJS interview, Reel 1, page 73.
75. "'A Night in Harlem' Is Offering of Bennie Moten Monday, Nov. 17," Kansas City *Call*, November 14, 1930, 9, credited Basie with composing "The Count."

76. Eddie Durham IJS interview, Reel 1, page 69.
77. Ibid., page 66.
78. Valerie Wilmer, "Eddie Durham," 7.
79. Val Wilmer, "Durham: The First Man to Plug-In," *Melody Maker* 50 (December 13, 1975), 7; Schaap interview with Durham, February 25, 1977.
80. Schaap interview with Durham, February 25, 1977.
81. Govenar, 35. Wilmer, "Eddie Durham," 7. On Stuff Smith's experiments with electrifying the violin, see Stanley Dance, "Stuff Swings On," *Down Beat* 32 (December 16, 1965), 24.
82. Wilmer, "Eddie Durham," 7.
83. Wilmer, "Durham: The First Man to Plug-In," 7.
84. Ibid.
85. Govenar, 35. Wilmer.
86. Ibid.
87. Siegel and Obrecht, 58. Peter Broadbent makes this point in *Charlie Christian: Solo Flight — The Seminal Electric Guitarist* (U.K.: Ashley Mark Publishing Co., 2003).
88. George Hoefer, "Held Notes: Eddie Durham," *Down Beat* 29 (July 19, 1962), 54.
89. Ibid.
90. Siegel and Obrecht, 55.
91. Ibid.
92. Ibid.
93. Ibid.
94. "Count Basie and Orchestra Featuring James Rushing," *OCBD*, April 9, 1938, 8.
95. Broadbent, 59.

Chapter 7

1. License of Alfred Page and Maggie Veal, Dallas County, Texas, January 20, 1907; Marriage Records, Vol. 001, page 427. Actually several infants, born before and after Oran, died in infancy. In an interview with the author, George Page Jr., Oran's cousin, maintained that his uncle was born in Cuervo, Texas, Maggie Page's home town; Dan Morgenstern, "Oran Hot Lips Page: A Trumpet King in Harlem," *Village Voice*, August 1990, 73.
2. *Corsicana City Directory, 1926,* 8: Corsicana had a population of 20,000 and was located in "black belt land," an area of particularly rich soil. In the *DCD* for 1908–1909, Alfred Page was listed as a teamster rooming at 309 San Jacinto. It is noteworthy that despite this and subsequent listings of Alfred, Maggie is not listed until 1918, after Alfred's death (women were often listed with their husbands). She lived in Cuervo, her hometown, and Palestine, Texas, her new husband's home, when the children were very young.
3. Author's interview with George Page, the trumpet player's nephew. In the USMC for 1910, Dallas County, Vol. 35, ED 43, sheet 8, lines 21–26 (taken on April 15, 1910), Oran was listed with Alfred, thirty-two years old and from Louisiana, Maggie, his wife, who was twenty-eight, Oran A., two years old, Eunice Veal, a ten-year-old sister of Maggie, and a possible lodger. See also *DCD, 1914,* page 718. In 1910, the *DCD* lists the Pages as living at 258 Eakins (page 680). Alfred Page was not in the 1908 or 1915 directories. I wish to thank Allison Baker, archivist, Dallas Public Library, for the directory information on the family.
4. Alan B. Govenar and Jay F. Brakefield, *Deep Ellum and Central Track: Where the Black and White Worlds of Dallas Converge* (Denton, TX: University of North Texas Press, 1998); Charles Wolfe and Kip Lornell, *The Life and Legend of Leadbelly* (New York: HarperCollins Publishers, 1992), 42–48; USMC, 1910, Dallas, ED 43, sheet 8, and Dallas County, Vol. 35, sheet 1A (this census was taken on April 5, 1910). It appears his par-

ents were also listed in the census in the USMC for 1900, Dallas, Vol. 55, ED 39, sheet 25. Dan Morgenstern, "Oran Hot Lips Page: A Trumpet King in Harlem," *Village Voice* (August 1990), 73, in Oran Page Vertical File, IJS.

5. "Moanin' Dan" is mentioned in Morgenstern, "Oran Hot Lips Page: A Trumpet King in Harlem," 73. It can be heard on *Jammin' at Rudi's* (Jazzology JCD-262). See Charles Wolfe and Kip Lornell, *The Life and Legend of Leadbelly* (New York: HarperCollins Publishers, 1992), 42–48.

6. Dan Morgenstern, "Oran Hot Lips Page: A Trumpet King in Harlem," 73. For one of the most famous children's bands, see John Chilton, *A Jazz Nursery: The Story of the Jenkins' Orphanage Bands* (London: Bloomsbury Book Shop, 1980).

7. Dan Morgenstern, "Hot Lips Page, Part 1," *Jazz Journal* 15 (July 1962), 2, 5; Hot Lips Page (as told to Kay C. Thompson), "Kansas City Man: Hot Lips Page" *The Record Changer* 8 (December 1949), 9; "Harrington's Pot-Pourri," *The Record Changer* 7 (November 1954) in IJS Vertical File on Oran Page. Page maintained he attended Texas College for a time (Dan Morgenstern, "Hot Lips Page, Part 1," 5).

8. "Reminiscing with 'Hot Lips' Page," *Jazz Hot* 58 (September 1951), 10. This appears to be the only time he mentioned this "New Orleans" outfit or Goog and His Jazz Babies.

9. Jimmy Dee Powell and Wyvonne Yaws Putman, "Fred Douglass-G. W. Jackson School," *Navarro County History, Volume Five: Public Buildings, Historical Events, and Early Businesses* (Corsicana: Navarro County Historical Society, 1985), 175. The *Corsicana City Directory, 1924*, page 17, listed "G. W. Jackson School, 1012 E. 5th Ave., Prin. G. W. Jackson."

10. Page (as told to Kay C. Thompson), "Kansas City Man: Hot Lips Page," 9.

11. "Oran 'Hot Lips' Page Est Déc'd," *Jazz Hot* 94 (December 1954), 21.

12. *Corsicana City Directory* for 1924 and 1926.

13. Ibid., 1926. According to the author's interview with Ora Lee Page, her grandfather worked at a crematory, and another probable relative, Fronsell, a clerk in the Economy Drug Store, lived at the same address.

14. His address was 326½ East Second in *OCCD, 1930*. In 1931 and 1932, the *City Directory* listed him as residing with Theresa, presumably his wife, at 715 East Second and 714 NE Third, respectively. Oran did not appear in the 1933 directory, but Theresa did that year and the two years following.

15. Morgenstern, "Oran Hot Lips Page," *Village Voice*, 73. Max Jones, "Hot Lips Page Dies in New York," *Melody Maker* 30 (November 13, 1954), 1, 7. Page, "Kansas City Man: Hot Lips Page," 9, 18. He played with Sugar Lou and Eddie at the Hotel Tyler in Tyler, Texas, according to a George Hoefer article ("Oran 'Hot Lips' Page") printed in *Down Beat* 21 (December 15, 1954); ms. in Oran Page Vertical File, IJS. Hoefer also claimed Page played with Troy Floyd's band around San Antonio. See also Daphne Duval Harrison, *Black Pearls: Blues Queens of the 1920s* (New Brunswick, NJ: Rutgers University, 1988), 98–99, 232–233. James Lincoln Collier, *Louis Armstrong: An American Genius* (New York: Oxford University Press, 1983), 177, informs us that Hill toured with Ma Rainey and recorded with Armstrong late in 1925 in Chicago.

16. Collier, 151.

17. Harrison, *Black Pearls*, 232.

18. *Chicago Defender,* April 10, 1926, 6, May 22, 1926, 6, and May 15, 1926, 6.

19. See *Chicago Defender,* October 9, 1926, 6; Collier, 162; "Dave Peyton's Cabaret Revue," *Chicago Defender,* April 24, 1926, 6. This reasoning is corroborated by the 1926 date given by Page in Michel Boujut, "Jazz Dans Le Monde: L'Homme aux Levres Chaudes," *Jazz Magazine* 131, June 1966, 142: "En 1926, il débarque a Chicago. . . . Louis Armstrong officie au Sunset Café. . . . 'C'est Louis,' devait-il confier plus tard, 'qui a eu le plus d'influence non seulement sur ma musique, mais sur ma vie.'" ("In 1926, he arrived in Chicago. . . . Louis Armstrong was the bandleader at the Sunset. . . . It was Louis, he

admitted later, who had the greatest influence—not only on my music, but on my life.")

20. "Oran 'Hot Lips' Page Est Déc'd," 21.

21. "Cabaret and Style Show," *Chicago Defender,* May 29, 1926, 6; "Okeh Cabaret and Style Show Sure to Be Success," *Chicago Defender,* June 5, 1926, 6; "Twenty Thousand Expected At Mammoth Musicians' Ball," *Chicago Defender,* June 5, 1926, 6; Mildred Ann Henson, "Coliseum Will Resemble A Scene from 'Arabian Nights,'" ibid., Music Edition Extra, 1.

22. Ross Russell, *Jazz Style in Kansas City and the Southwest* (Berkeley: University of California Press, 1971), 80–85. Walter Page, "About My Life in Music," 13. In Thompson, 18, Oran Page claims he joined the Blue Devils in 1928, and refers to Walter Page as his older half-brother.

23. Ross Russell, 88–109.

24. Budd Johnson, IJS, Reel 1, page 31; he may have confused the Serenaders with the Blue Devils.

25. "Bennie Moten's Farewell A Real Send-Off," in "The Social Whirl," *OCBD,* January 19, 1933, 5. The arrangements of Basie and Durham, the bass playing of Walter Page, and the accordion and singing of Bus Moten were also singled out for praise.

26. Phil Schaap interview with Eddie Durham, February 25, 1977; "Bennie Moten's Farewell," *OCBD,* January 19, 1933, 5.

27. Advertisement, Kansas City *Call,* November 19, 1934, 13; ibid., November 23, 1934, 11.

28. "Rhythm Rendezvous, New Night Club Here, Opens," Kansas City *Call,* December 6, 1935, 8.

29. Card advertising Small Paradise date, in Oran Page Vertical File, IJS. John Hammond, *John Hammond On Record: An Autobiography with Irving Townsend* (London: Penguin Books, 1981), 170–171.

30. "Oran 'Hot Lips' Page Makes New York Debut," Kansas City *Call,* August 20, 1937, 3; "Sunday Matinee dances," ibid., June 1, 1934, 11.

31. Michel Boujut, "Jazz Dans Le Monde: L'Homme Aux Levres Chaudes," 43. "A Band for 'Hot Lips' Page" in "Out of Harlem: Billy Rowe's Notebook," *Pittsburgh Courier,* January 23, 1937, Part 2, page 6; "'Hot Lips' Page to Assemble A New Orchestra," *Chicago Defender,* January 25, 1937, 13.

32. Michel Boujut, "Jazz Dans Le Monde," p. 43. "Limehouse Blues" can be heard on *Hot Lips Page Story,* Jazz Archives No. 105.

33. "'Hot Lips' Page to Open at Small's," *AN,* August 14, 1937, 16. "'Hot Lips' New Band to Make N.Y. Debut," *Pittsburgh Courier,* August 14, 1937, 21.

34. "Archie Seale Around Harlem," *AN,* August 28, 1937, 16; on Ed Small, see "Around Harlem with Archie Seale," *AN,* April 17, 1937, 17.

35. "Archie Seale Around Town," *AN,* September 4, 1937, 20; in the article "Night Clubs Debut New B'way Revues," *AN,* September 18, 1937, page 20, the trumpet player's name is spelled Paige, though in previous issues it was Page. It was frequently spelled both ways in newspapers.

36. St. Clair Bourne, "Smalls' Offers Speed, Rhythm In New Show," *AN,* October 2, 1937, 18.

37. "Around Harlem with Archie Seale," *AN,* November 20, 1937, 18.

38. "Small's Big Jam Torrid," *AN,* January 28, 1938, 19.

39. Allan McMillan, "I Cover New York...," *AN,* March 24, 1938, 16.

40. "Louis 'Satchmo' Armstrong" advertisement, *AN,* April 9, 1938, 21.

41. Allan McMillan, "I Cover New York...," *AN,* April 9, 1938, 20.

42. "Satchmo and Ork at Rockland Soon," ibid.

43. Allan McMillan, "I Cover New York...," *AN,* May 21, 1938, 16; ibid., June 25, 1938, 8.

44. Apollo ad, *AN,* August 20, 1938, Section 2, page 6; "'Hot Lips' Page's Band Plays Apollo Next Week," ibid.

45. Charles W. Edgar, "Jitterbugs At Randall's Are Sent by Bands," *AN*, September 17, 1938, Section 2, page 9.

46. "Bandfest Music to Feature Hot Harlem Outfits," *AN*, September 3, 1938, Section 2, page 7.

47. See photo in *Metronome* (March 1939), 17, in which the trumpet player performed "at a benefit for the poorer Chicago-styled musicians."

48. "Around Town with Archie Seale," *AN*, November 22, 1938, 16.

49. Michel Boujut, 43 (author's translation).

50. *From Spirituals to Swing*, Vanguard VCD2-47/48.

51. "Hot Lips and 6 Spirits Hit," *AN*, May 20, 1939, 20.

52. "Musician Blames Local for Not Having a Job," *AN*, August 13, 1938, Section 2, page 6.

53. Frank M. Davis, "Bands Are Worrying," *AN*, September 10, 1938, Section 2, page 6.

54. "Joe Glaser Goes for Self Now," *AN*, May 21, 1938, 16.

55. Bill Chase, "All Ears," *AN*, October 28, 1939, 21.

56. "Hot Lips Paige, Honi Coles, Dynamite Hooker at West End," *AN*, November 2, 1940, 21. Romayne Jackson spent time in California before joining Page and was in the 1933 production of *Change Your Luck*; Harry Levette, "Coast Codgings," *Chicago Defender*, February 18, 1933, 8.

57. Advertisement, "3rd Annual Bar-Grill Popularity Contest," ibid., November 30, 1940, 20; "Basie, Bostic, Page Bands to Play at Xmas Basket Affair," ibid., 21; "Bar and Grill Popularity Contest Looms as Best," ibid., December 7, 1940, 20; "Count Basie Aids Xmas Basket Fund Bar-Grill," advertisement, ibid., 21.

58. *Hot Lips Page and His Band, 1938–1940*, Classics 561; on the first group of selections, the sidemen were Ben Smith, clarinet and alto saxophone; Sam Simmons on tenor saxophone; Jimmy Reynolds on piano; Connie Wainwright on guitar; Wellman Braud on string bass; and Alfred Taylor on drums. There was a larger band on the summer 1938 recordings.

59. Frank M. Davis, "Rating the Records," *Chicago Defender*, March 22, 1941, 9.

60. Manhattan Telephone Directory, 1940; according to the *Kansas City Directory, 1935*, the couple lived at 1227 Garfield with the William M. Young family.

61. "Big Brooklyn Benefit to Star Jazz Greats," *Metronome* (June 1941), 33.

62. Dan Burley "Back Door Stuff," *AN*, June 7, 1941, 13.

63. "'Harlem Jive' Solid; Burley Loaded," *Pittsburgh Courier*, December 2, 1944, 13; see "Dan Burley Appears on Variety Show at Rockefeller Center," Kansas City *Call*, October 10, 1941, 14.

64. "Swingin' At Kelly's," *AN*, June 7, 1941, Part 2, page 21; Alvin Moss, "Footlite Flickers," *OCBD*, June 14, 1941, 8.

65. Dan Burley, "Back Door Stuff," *AN*, October 7, 1939, 16.

66. "'Sneak Thief' Steals Musician's Trumpet; Finds It's 'Too Hot,'" November 24 clipping in Oran Page Vertical File, IJS.

67. Max Kaminsky, *My Life in Jazz* (New York: Harper and Row, Publishers, 1963), 124–125.

68. Ibid., 126.

69. "Many Refugees Flock Back to Artie Shaw's New Band, *Metronome* (September 1941), 11.

70. "Artie Shaw Plans Concerts with Fifty-two Pieces," *Metronome* (August 1941), 1.

71. "Shaw Band Moves in Caravan," *Metronome* (November 1941), 10.

72. Jimmy Stewart, "Jimmy Says," *OCBD*, August 30, 1941, 8.

73. "'Hot Lips' Page Here Saturday," *OCBD*, October 18, 1941, 9.

74. Ibid.; "Shaw Cancels Dance Dates in Deference to 'Hot Lips,'" Kansas City *Call*, October 3, 1941, 12.

75. Jimmy Stewart, "Jimmy Says," *OCBD*, October 25, 1941, 9.

76. Ibid.

77. Schaap interview with Eddie Durham, February 25, 1977.

78. *Artie Shaw and His Orchestra: Hollywood Palladium 1941* (Hep CD 19); "Record Reviews: Benny, Artie Again Lead Waxworks," *Metronome* (January 1942), 12.

79. "Record Reviews: Benny, Artie," *Metronome* (January 1942), 12.

80. Kaminsky, 129.

81. "Artie Shaw Sick; Out for Six Weeks; Dates Cancelled," *Metronome* (February 1942), 1.

82. Russell, 139. Card advertising Small Paradise date, in Oran Page Vertical File, IJS.

83. "Four New Faces in All-Stars," *Metronome* (January 1942), 22; "Goodman, Miller Win Down Beat's Poll," *Down Beat* 16 (January 1, 1942), 21.

84. Morgenstern, "Hot Lips Page, Part 1," 6.

85. *Hot Lips Page and His Band, 1938–1940* (CL 561); Don Gazzaway, "Before Bird—Buster," *Jazz Monthly* 7 (January 1962), 6–7; Buster Smith interview, IJS, 26–28.

86. Scott DeVeaux, *The Birth of Bebop* (Berkeley: University of California Press, 1999). DeVeaux gives the date of the live session as May 12, 1941; quite often Joe Guy is credited with the trumpet on "Topsy" and "Savoy."

87. Barry Ulanov, "Count Basie (A-1)," *Metronome* 57 (October 1941), 13, 31; author's conversation with bassist Red Callender, ca. 1985.

88. "Oran 'Hot Lips' Page, Famed Trumpeter Dead," Kansas City *Call,* November 19, 1954, 8.

89. At the Reno, "I had been acting as MC when we put on shows, helping with radio announcements during broadcasts, and handling various promotional activities," Page, with Kay C. Thompson, "Kansas City Man," 18.

90. Ted Yates, "'Hot Lips' Page, Dallasite Dies in New York Hospital," *Dallas Express,* November 13, 1954, 1, 10; "Oran 'Hot Lips' Page, Famed Trumpeter, Dead" Kansas City *Call,* November 19, 1954, 8.

91. "Heads Travalcade," *Philadelphia Afro-American,* December 21, 1946, 18.

92. "'Hot Lips' Page to Head Revue," *California Eagle,* February 20, 1947, 18; "All Star Jazz Unit Readies Concert Tour," *Down Beat* 14 (March 28, 1947), 15.

93. "Rosedale Beach" ad, *Pittsburgh Courier,* November 1, 1947, 3.

94. "Shoutin' the Blues: Hot Lips Page with Big Maybelle, Wynonie Harris, and Marion Abernathy," Blue Boar label, CDBB 1010.

95. "Old Paree," Oran Page, Foxy 9006/B; "U.S. Jazzmen to Play Paris Festival," *Down Beat* 16 (April 22, 1949), 3.

96. Ibid.

97. Boujut, 43.

98. "Billy Rowe's Notebook," *Pittsburgh Courier,* May 28, 1949, 18.

99. Author's interview with Oran Page Jr.

100. "Hot Lips Page Snags a New Kind of Job," *Pittsburgh Courier,* August 27, 1949, 18.

101. "Watch Accent, Hot Lips!" *Pittsburgh Courier,* November 29, 1949, 18.

102. Blake Green, "Loesser's Great American Songbooks Get A New Read," *Los Angeles Times,* December 26, 2003, E46; Loesser got credit for the lyrics and the music and won an Oscar in 1949 for best new song of the year. Bertrand Deneusy, Otto Flückiger, Jorgen Grunnet Jepsen, and Kurt Mohn, compilers, *Hot Lips Page* (Basel, Switzerland: Jazz-Publications, November 1961), 13.

103. "With Pearl?" *Pittsburgh Courier,* August 20, 1949, 19; "Pearl, Page Pair Up," *Down Beat* 16 (September 23, 1949), 7. The author recalls "the Hucklebuck" from his childhood as one of the first songs and dances he learned.

104. "Page Swings Hot at Ryan's," *Pittsburgh Courier,* September 24, 1949, 19.

105. "Strictly Ad Lib," *Down Beat* 16 (October 7, 1949), 5.

106. "Hot Lips in TV Talk," *Pittsburgh Courier,* November 12, 1949, 19.

107. *OCBD,* February 26, 1944, 6.

108. Author's interview with Hank Jones.
109. " 'Hot Lips' Page Is Rated Favorite of New Yorkers," *Pittsburgh Courier*, November 25, 1944, 13.
110. Morgenstern, "Hot Lips Page, Part 1," 6.
111. Author's interviews with Ora and Oran C. Page Jr., the daughter and son of the trumpet player. A wedding reception invitation in the Page IJS Vertical File indicates that his third wife, Elizabeth, was from Salem, Virginia.
112. Author's interview with Oran C. Page Jr.
113. Morgenstern, "Hot Lips Page, Part 1" 6.
114. Kaminsky, 125–126.
115. Ibid.
116. "Billy Rowe's Note Book," *Pittsburgh Courier*, June 12, 1943, 20.
117. Ibid., June 5, 1943, 20.
118. *Chicago Defender*, May 15, 1943, 13.
119. Author's interview with Oran C. Page Jr.; Miles Davis and Quincy Troupe, *Miles: The Autobiography* (New York: Simon and Schuster, 1990), 238–239.
120. Oran Page, letter of March 31, 1949, from 105 Edgecombe Ave. to Jose and Jerry; courtesy of Val Wilmer.
121. Author's interview with Oran C. Page Jr.
122. *Hot Lips Page and His Band, 1938–1940*, Classics 561.
123. *Hot Lips Page, 1940–1944*, Classics 809.
124. Ibid.; *Hot Lips Page 1944–1946*, Classics 950; *Hot Lips Page 1946–1950*, Classics 1199. Boujut, page 42, mentions Chester Himes's *La Reine de Pommes (For Love of Imabelle)*.
125. See " 'Hot Lips' Page to Hit Road," *Pittsburgh Courier*, November 11, 1944, Section 2, page 13, which mentions his "Pagin' Mr. Page" and "Uncle Sam Blues" as songs that "have really caught on."
126. *Hot Lips Page 1938–1940*, Classics 561. Recorded late in 1940, "Rhumbain' the Blues" foreshadows Afro-Latin influences that became especially popular during the bebop era, as in "Cu-bop" after World War II.
127. *Jammin' at Rudi's*, Jazzology, JCD 262.
128. *Hot Lips Page with George Wettling's Stuyvesant Stompers*, "Dr. Jazz Series," Vol. 6, STCD 6046; *"Hot Lips" Page Play the Blues in "B,"* Archives of Jazz 3801172.
129. *Hot Lips Page, 1944–1946*, Classics 950.
130. *Hot Lips Page with George Wettling's Stuyvesant Stompers*, "Dr. Jazz Series," Vol. 6, STCD 6046; *"Hot Lips" Page Play the Blues in "B,"* Archives of Jazz 3801172.
131. Page (as told to Kay C. Thompson), "Kansas City Man: Hot Lips Page," *The Record Changer* 8 (December 1949), 9.
132. Dan Morgenstern, "Hot Lips Page, Part 1," 5.
133. "Capsule Comments," *Down Beat* 16 (December 2, 1949), 13.
134. Page (as told to Paul Eduard Miller), "Forget High Ones and Stick to Melody, Advice Of Lips to Trumpeters," *Down Beat* 10 (July 1, 1943), 15.
135. "It Was Fats Who First Cried: 'Stop That Bopping!' " *Melody Maker* 25 (August 6, 1949), 9.
136. Ibid. See also "wil," "Hot Lips Page Bop 'The Weirdest Yet,' " *Down Beat* 16 (October 21, 1949), 5. Edison often expressed this idea in conversation with the author.

Chapter 8
1. *OCCD, 1930*: "Ermal (Maude) Coleman, shoeshiner Hallie Richardson r 331 E 5th." Ibid., 1927: "Lawrence (Mary) Williams, musician r 221 E 2d."
2. "Hayes to Make Bow," in "Dance Gossip," Kansas City *Call*, March 4, 1932, 7b, announced the takeover by James Simpson.

3. USMC, 1930, Oklahoma City, ED 55, sheet 16 B: Webster roomed at 422 East First Street. He was probably with Gene Coy's Black Aces at the time.
4. Author's interviews, with Henry "Buster" Smith, LeRoy "Snake" Whyte, Abe Bolar, and Leonard Chadwick; USMC, 1930, Oklahoma City, ED 35, sheet 10B: Reuben Roddy was born in Arkansas in 1906 or 1907 and died in New Orleans in 1959. In 1930 he lived in Oklahoma City with his wife at 508 East Second. Thanks to Dick Allen for information on him in New Orleans. What were very likely his forebears can be found in the USMC of 1870 in Big Bottom Township and in 1880 in Batesville, Arkansas.
5. Author's interview with Buster Smith; "Hits and Bits," *Chicago Defender,* July 12, 1930, 3.
6. Walter Barnes Jr., "The Musical Bunch," *Chicago Defender,* October 12, 1929, Part 1, page 10.
7. Ibid.
8. "They Saw the Panthers and Wild Cats Fight," *OCBD,* October 24, 1929, 8.
9. "Billy King to Open in Detroit Nov. 18," *Chicago Defender,* November 16, 1929, 10.
10. "Orchestral Doings," *Chicago Defender,* December 6, 1930, 9; W. Page gave this address the next year, *OCCD,* 1931: "Walter F. (Sarah) Page, musician, Ritz Brm r 311 1/2 E 2d."
11. "Hits and Bits," *Chicago Defender,* July 12, 1930, 3.
12. Author's interview with Abe Bolar; Walter Barnes Jr., in "The Musical Bunch," *Chicago Defender,* November 19, 1929, page 11, places them at the Winter Garden Amusement Hall in Seminole, Oklahoma, and lists Chadwick, Ermal Colman, and Abe Bolden [*sic*] with Bill Lewis and his orchestra; author's Chadwick interview, 1990.
13. Author's interview with Leonard Chadwick.
14. Ibid.
15. Ibid.
16. "Local Musicians' Ball Monday at Paseo Hall," Kansas City *Call,* May 1, 1931, 9.
17. e.w.w., "Musicians' Ball," in "dance gossip," Kansas City *Call,* May 8, 1931, ; e. w. w., "Artists Ball," in "dance gossip," ibid.
18. *Sioux City Directory, 1931,* page 359: "Rigadon Ball Room (Thos H. Archer) 712 Pierce"; *Sioux City Journal,* Wednesday, May 20, 1931. Thanks to the Sioux City Public Library.
19. "Editor's Mail Bag," *OCBD,* May 21, 1931, 9.
20. Advertisement, *Sioux City Journal,* May 16, 1931: "Saturday George E. Lee Coming Wed., May 27, One Night Only—Ben Bernie and His Orchestra Advance ticket sale now on. prices $2.50 per couple—after 5/25, $3.00 per couple."
21. Advertisement, *Sioux City Journal,* Sunday, May 17, 1931: "Rigadon Tonight—Big Music Battle Walter Page and His 13 Blue Devils vs. Geo. E. Lee and His Orchestra."
22. "Workers, Clubs Offer Plays, Dances," Kansas City *Call,* October 23, 1931, 9.
23. "Musicians Ball On Monday," Kansas City *Call,* September 4, 1931, 10.
24. "Walter Page at Paseo Hall Monday," Kansas City *Call,* October 23, 1931, 9.
25. "Blue Devils Orchestra Is Here 2 Days," Kansas City *Call,* November 20, 1931, 6B.
26. Ibid.
27. "Eight Bands Are Ready for Musicians' Ball Monday," Kansas City *Call,* December 4, 1931, 7B.
28. e.w.w., "dance gossip," Kansas City *Call,* December 11, 1931, 6B.
29. "Blue Devils Orchestra To Entertain Boys at Jackson County Home," Kansas City *Call,* December 18, 1931, 6B.
30. *OCBD,* January 23, 1932, 8.
31. "Back Home Again," *OCBD,* February 6, 1932, 8.
32. "Blue Devils Hold Big Cabaret Fete," *Chicago Defender,* April 9, 1932, 5.
33. "The Band that Never Lost a Battle," *OCBD,* April 9, 1932, 5.
34. "Eight Bands to Play at Musicians' Ball Monday Night," Kansas City *Call,* April 19, 1932, 7A.

35. "Yo-yo Ball," *OCBD*, May 12, 1932, 8.
36. "Whites and Negroes Dance at Forest Park," *OCBD*, May 26, 1932, 5.
37. "New Head of Blue Devils" (with picture of Bill Little), Kansas City *Call*, July 22, 1932, 5B; e.w.w., "Band Contest Tonight," in "Dance Gossip," Kansas City *Call*, April 11, 1930, 10; Bill Little was reported to be the promoter of the Moten dance: "Moten's Band Draws Crowd at Paseo Hall," Kansas City *Call*, September 14, 1928, 4.
38. "Bill Little and Band to Feature Monarchs Victory Dance, August 7," Kansas City *Call*, August 5, 1932, 5B.
39. "13 Original Blue Devils Under New Management," Kansas City *Call*, September 9, 1932, 3B; author's interview with Leroy Whyte; USMC, 1920, Spring Valley, Dallas, Iowa, ED 16, sheet 2A.
40. In an interview with the author, Chadwick mentioned Whyte's filing his mouthpiece to obtain the high notes.
41. Author's interview with Snake Whyte. He performed "Blue Devil Blues" with the band, but as the record was a head arrangement, a written score had to be made; the same happened with Basie arrangements years later—the recording became the written arrangement, instead of the opposite.
42. Ibid.
43. Ibid.
44. "Fourteen Original Blue Devils of Oklahoma City," *St. Louis Argus*, November 4, 1932, 3; "Sun. Nov. 20 14 Blue Devils," *ibid.*, November 18, 1932, 3.
45. Ibid.
46. Author's interviews with Dorothy, Essie Mae, James Rudolph, and Annis Lynch, the musician's daughter, wife, brother, and sister.
47. Don Gazzaway, "Conversations with Buster Smith, Part 1," *The Jazz Review* II (December 1959), 22.
48. Author's interview with Abe Bolar.
49. Gazzaway, Part 1, 22; thanks to John D. Harris files, Bassett Historical Center, Bassett, Virginia, for information on Dr. Baldwin.
50. Gazzaway, Part 1, 22.
51. *Bluefield City Directory, 1934:* "hotel at 602 Raleigh"; thanks to Joseph Bundy, who suggested that the Travelers Hotel was where they probably stayed.
52. Author's interview with Abe Bolar for the Easter date of departure.
53. Gazzaway, Part 1, 22; author's interviews with Abe Bolar and Buster Smith; Lewis Porter, ed., *A Lester Young Reader* (Washington, DC: Smithsonian Press, 1991), 143.
54. "First Anniversary Dance of Eddie Randle's [sic] Seven Blue Devils," *St. Louis Argus*, October 20, 1933, 3.
55. Arnita G. Arnold, *Legendary Times and Tales of Second Street* (Oklahoma City: Black Liberated Arts Center, Inc., 1995), 30; "Slaughter's Hall," in "Amusement Reporter," *OCBD*, August 29, 1937, 8.
56. Author's interview with Abe Bolar.
57. Ibid.

Chapter 9

1. "Dance Gossip," Kansas City *Call*, March 25, 1932, p. 7B, Moten band in Ft. Smith and Shreveport. See Frank Driggs, "Eddie Barefield's Many Worlds," *Jazz Review* 3 (July 1960), 21: "We didn't make any money; got stranded in Columbus, Ohio, got stranded some more here and there, and finally we got our break to open the Pearl Theatre in Philadelphia."
2. On Ross's first mention, see: "Hits and Bits," *Chicago Defender*, July 12, 1930, 9; "The Orchestras," *Chicago Defender*, October 28, 1933, page 9, lists the musicians as "Bill Pugh,

ldr & drms, Harry Pittiford, tenor, crooner, arranger, Rook Ganz, trumpet; Harold Booker, pno, Walter Rouse, gtr."

3. Jack Ellis, "The Orchestras," *Chicago Defender*, October 6, 1934, 7.
4. Basie, *Good Morning Blues*, 149.
5. Jack Ellis, "The Orchestras," *Chicago Defender*, November 17, 1934, 6.
6. Phil Schaap, November 7, 1988 interview with Eddie Durham; Jo Jones, IJS, page 32.
7. Page, "Kansas City Man: Hot Lips Page," 18.
8. "Moten at Mainstreet," "dance gossip by e. w. w.," Kansas City *Call*, January 16, 1931, 7. E[arl] W. Wilkins, or "e. w. w.," the "dance gossip" reporter for the *Call*, was the younger brother of Roy Wilkins, who left the *Call* for an NAACP position in New York City in 1931. He shed light on the battles of the bands, on orchestras, and on the fans. Once he admitted that he "unlimbered his own stiff stumps and bounced about for a measure or two" at a Moten dance ("dance gossip by e. w. w.," Kansas City *Call*, September 18, 1931, 10. See Wilkins's obituary, "Earl Wilkins of the *Call* Staff Dies," Kansas City *Call*, January 17, 1941, 1, 4. See also Roy Wilkins with Tom Mathews, *Standing Fast: The Autobiography of Roy Wilkins* (New York: Viking Press, 1982), 111.
9. Kansas City *Call*, January 26, 1931, 7. Ira ("Bus"), Bennie's nephew, started on piano "picking out melodies when I was about five." His uncle lived with him and guided him, advising him to learn songs in more than one key, and they also performed four-handed piano together. Ira studied at the Kansas City Conservatory, played at parties, and worked with dance groups while in high school. He toured with vaudeville acts and returned to Kansas City in 1929, when he bought and learned how to play an accordion. See Sharon A. Pease, "Moten, Now On Discs, Headed for New Fame," *Down Beat* 16 (July 1, 1949), 12.
10. "Bennie Moten Home in September," Kansas City *Call*, July 20, 1928, 7; "Moten Sweeps Into 3rd Place," *Pittsburgh Courier*, November 19, 1932, Part 2, 8; "Bennie Moten Packin 'Em in Down in Philly," *Pittsburgh Courier*, December 3, 1932, Part 2, 1: "Ellington—61,000 votes; Noble Sissle—43,000; Calloway—42,500 votes; and Moten 24,500"; "Bennie Moten's Home-Coming Dance!" advertisement, Kansas City *Call*, September 7, 1928, 7. On Moten, see Marc Rice, *The Bennie Moten Orchestra 1918–1935: A Kansas City Jazz Ensemble and Its African American Audience*. Thanks to Lewis Porter for informing me of Rice's Ph.D. dissertation.
11. "dance gossip by e. w. w.," Kansas City *Call*, March 27, 1931, 9.
12. e.w.w., "dance gossip," Kansas City *Call*, July 4, 1930, 8.
13. U.S. Bureau of the Census, *Fifteenth Census of the United States, 1930, Population*, Table 12 (Bureau of the Census: Washington, DC), 1338.
14. Ibid.
15. "Bennie Moten Sunday Night" in "Dance Gossip," Kansas City *Call*, January 3, 1930, 7.
16. "Memorial Hall, Jan. 7" in "Dance Gossip," ibid.
17. "New York to Claim Bennie Moten, Favorite Kansas City Orchestra," Kansas City *Call*, February 20, 1931, 8.
18. "Bennie Moten's First 1932 Break O'Day at Labor Temple Saturday," Kansas City *Call*, April 29, 1932, 7A.
19. e.w.w., "The Motenites Return," in "dance gossip," Kansas City *Call*, February 26, 1932, 7B.
20. Ibid.
21. Nat Hentoff, "Jimmy Rushing," *Down Beat* 24 (March 6, 1957), 20, 56; Helen McNamara, "The Odyssey of Jimmy Rushing," *Down Beat* 32 (April 8, 1965), 23.
22. Advertisement for Break O' Day Frolic, Kansas City *Call*, April 11, 1930, 9.
23. e.w.w., "Band Contest Tonight," in "dance gossip," Kansas City *Call*, April 11, 1930, 10.
24. "Dance Gossip," Kansas City *Call*, July 25, 1930, 8; "Another Break O'Day Dance, Bennie Moten on Tomorrow Night," Kansas City *Call*, May 29, 1931, 9.

25. "Paseo Hall Now Summer Garden," Kansas City *Call*, July 4, 1930, 8.
26. "Duke Ellington at Paseo Monday Night," Kansas *City Call*, July 5, 1930, 8.
27. "Dance Gossip," ibid.
28. "More Music for Labor Day," Kansas City *Call*, August 29, 1930, 7; "Monster Labor Day Celebration," advertisement, Kansas City *Call*, August 29, 1930, 7. Only five bands appeared: "Large Crowd at Labor Day Dance," Kansas City *Call*, September 5, 1930, 9.
29. "Large Crowd at Labor Day Dance, Kansas City *Call*, September 5, 1930, 9; "Dance Gossip," Kansas City *Call*, September 5, 1930, 7. Webster lived in Oklahoma City: USMC, 1930, Oklahoma City, ED 55, sheet 16 B.
30. e.w.w., "The Musicians' Ball," in "dance gossip," Kansas City *Call*, September 11, 1931, Part 1, page 8.
31. "dance gossip," Kansas City *Call*, May 6, 1932, 7A.
32. "Bennie Moten's Orchestra Opens Vaudeville Act at Downtown Theatre Today," Kansas City *Call*, January 9, 1931, 7.
33. e. w. w., "dance gossip," Kansas City *Call*, March 6, 1931, 7; "Now A Motenite," Kansas City *Call*, May 29, 1931, 9.
34. "Bennie Moten on WDAF, 6:30 Today," Kansas City *Call*, November 14, 1930, 9.
35. "'A Night in Harlem' Is Offering of Bennie Moten Monday, Nov. 17," Kansas City *Call*, November 14, 1930, 9.
36. "Flashlights Only Illumination At Break O' Day Tomorrow Night," Kansas City *Call*, August 28, 1931, 10.
37. "Pajama Break O'Day Tomorrow Night with Bennie Moten's Band," Kansas City *Call*, August 14, 1933, 8.
38. "dance gossip by e. w. w.," Kansas City *Call*, March 27, 1931, 9.
39. E. W. W., "Dance Gossip," Kansas City *Call*, July 10, 1931, 8.
40. Ibid.
41. "Dance Gossip," Kansas City *Call*, January 3, 1930, 7.
42. Kansas City *Call*, April 18, 1930, 6.
43. "Proceeds from Elks Annual Charity Dance Dec. 9 Will Aid 500 Families," Kansas City *Call*, December 5, 1930, 9.
44. Kansas City *Call*, June 26, 1931, 7.
45. "Musicians Union Offers Nine Bands; Floor Show at Paseo Hall Monday," Kansas City *Call*, November 4, 1932, 3B.
46. "Proceeds from Elks Annual Charity Dance Dec. 9 Will Aid 500 Families," Kansas City *Call*, December 5, 1930, 9; "[Moten?] Orchestra Records Hits for Victor," Kansas City *Call*, November 7, 1930, 9; "Something to Give Thanks for Will Be Moten's Dance Thursday," Kansas City *Call*, November 21, 1930, 9.
47. "Tonite Bennie Moten" advertisement, Kansas City *Call*, September 5, 1930, 7; "Bennie Moten in Farewell Dance," Kansas City *Call*, September 5, 1930, 7.
48. "Homecoming Dance" and "Grand Hallowe'en Ball," advertisements, Kansas City *Call*, October 24, 1930, 9.
49. "Bennie Moten Farewell Dance," Kansas City *Call*, January 17, 1930, 5; "dance gossip," Kansas City *Call*, January 20, 1930, 7, reported that Moten was headed South.
50. "Proceeds from Elks Annual Charity Dance Dec. 9 Will Aid 500 Families," Kansas City *Call*, December 5, 1930, 9; "[Moten?] Orchestra Records Hits for Victor," Kansas City *Call*, November 7, 1930, 9; "Something to Give Thanks for Will Be Moten's Dance Thursday," Kansas City *Call*, November 21, 1930, 9.
51. "New York to Claim Bennie Moten," Kansas City *Call*, February 20, 1931, 8.
52. Ibid.
53. "Benny Moten Says Goodbye to Kansas City" and "Moten Plays Farewell," in "dance gossip by e. w. w.," Kansas City *Call*, February 27, 1931, 7; see advertisement for February 25 job at Cotton Club and Pythian Hall, *St. Louis Argus*, February 20, 1931, 7.

54. "dance gossip by e. w. w.," Kansas City *Call,* March 6, 1931, 7.

55. Ibid.

56. Ibid; "dance gossip by e. w. w.," Kansas City *Call,* March 13, 1931, 7. In his February 25, 1977, interview with Phil Schaap, Durham maintained that the Moten bandmembers carried guns "most of the time."

57. "With Bennie," in "dance gossip by e. w. w.," Kansas City *Call,* March 13, 1931, 7.

58. e. w. w., "dance gossip," Kansas City *Call,* March 6, 1931, 7.

59. "With Bennie" in "dance gossip by e. w. w.," Kansas City *Call,* March 27, 1931, 9

60. "With Bennie," in "dance gossip by e. w. w," Kansas City *Call,* March 13, 1931, 7; Basie, *Good Morning Blues,* 127.

61. George D. Tyler, "Harlem Rambles," Baltimore *Afro American,* April 11, 1931, 9; Herschel Parke Williams, "Bennie Moten Makes Hit in New York," Kansas City *Call,* April 24, 1931, 9; "With Bennie," in "dance gossip by e. w. w.," Kansas City *Call,* April 17, 1931, 7; "At the Lafayette Theater," *New York Age,* April 11, 1931, 6.

62. Herschel Parke Williams, "Bennie Moten Makes Hit in New York," Kansas City *Call,* April 24, 1931, 9; "With Bennie," in "dance gossip by e. w. w.," Kansas City *Call,* April 17, 1931, 7; Herschel Parke Williams, "Bennie Moten Makes Hit in New York," Kansas City *Call,* April 24, 1931, 9. The comedienne Jackie Mabley, later "Moms Mabley," was on the bill (Basie, *Good Morning Blues,* 128).

63. Herschel Parke Williams, "Bennie Moten Makes Hit in New York," Kansas City *Call,* April 24, 1931, 9; "Bennie Moten, Western Jazz King, at the Savoy," *New York Age,* October 10, 1931, 6.

64. George D. Tyler, "Harlem Rambles," Baltimore *Afro American,* April 11, 1931, 9.

65. "With Bennie," in "dance gossip by e.w.w.," Kansas City *Call,* April 17, 1931, 7; "Bennie Moten Royal Theatre Headliner," Baltimore *Afro American,* April 18, 1931, 9.

66. "Five King Circus of Jazz Gives Local Dance Fans Thrilling Night," Baltimore *Afro-American,* October 17, 1931, 9.

67. Ibid.; "Battle of Music," advertisement, Baltimore *Afro American,* October 3, 1931, 2; "Famous Bands on Air," Baltimore *Afro American,* November 21, 1931, 9.

68. e.w.w., "dance gossip," Kansas City *Call,* May 15, 1931, 9. In the May 29, 1931, "dance gossip," e. w. w. says it looks like black bands have a "stranglehold on jobs at Kansas City amusement parks," Kansas City *Call,* 9.

69. e. w. w., "dance gossip," Kansas City *Call,* June 13, 1930, 9; Smith, IJS interview, page 34.

70. e. w. w., "dance gossip," Kansas City *Call,* June 13, 1930, 9.

71. "McKinney's Cotton Pickers vs. Bennie Moten. . . ." *Call,* June 26, 1931, 7.

72. "Musicians Ball on Monday. . . ." *Call,* September 4, 1931, 10.

73. "Bennie Not to Break Up Band," *Memphis World,* March 1, 1932, 7.

74. "Bennie Moten at Paseo Hall Tonight," Kansas City *Call,* February 19, 1932, 7B.

75. Ibid.; Webster joined in Chicago, according to the Driggs interview with Barefield, April 25, 1965, Marr Sound Archives, Miller Nichols Library, University of Missouri, Kansas City, Missouri; see also Barefield interview, IJS, Reel 1, page 44.

76. "Hayes Organizes New Band with Men from Moten, Lee," Kansas City *Call,* February 26, 1932, 7B. For Ed Lewis's account of their departure, see "Ed Lewis' Story," as told to Frank Driggs, *The Jazz Review* 2 (October 1959), 23. See also "Kansas City Brass: Ed Lewis' Story as Told to Frank Driggs," *The Jazz Review* 2 (May 1959), 28.

77. "Cotillion Club Dance," *Bluefield Daily Telegraph,* October 20, 1932, 5.

78. On the Prince of Wales's visit and love of jazz, see "Former King Edward Liked 'Swing' Music Played by Lucky Roberts and His Orchestra," *OCBD,* December 17, 1936, 8.

79. "Jazz Pioneer: Eddie Durham," on National Public Radio program *Horizons* broadcast about Eddie Durham, "Good Morning Blues. Thanks to Marsha Durham for providing me with a tape of the show.

80. "Orchestra Returns from Extensive Tour of East," Kansas City *Call*, December 30, 1932, 3B.

81. "New Type of Supper Club to Open Here," Kansas City *Call*, December 30, 1932, 3B; Eastside Musicians Sunset Club advertisement, Kansas City *Call*, November 9, 1934, 13.

82. "New Type of Supper Club to Open Here," Kansas City *Call*, December 30, 1932, 3B; "Deluxe Night Club to Open On April [date unclear]," Kansas City *Call*, April 7, 1933, 6A.

83. Phil Schaap interview with Eddie Durham, February 25, 1977.

84. Nathan W. Pearson Jr., *Goin' to Kansas City* (Urbana: University of Illinois, 1987), 95.

85. Pearson, 99–100.

86. Pearson, 97.

87. Pearson, 95; Eddie Durham, IJS, Reel 3–4, page 42.

88. Eddie Durham, IJS, Reel 3–4, page 43.

89. Ibid.

90. "Memphis Likes Moton [*sic*] and His Kansas City Orchestra," Kansas City *Call*, February 18, 1933, 9.

91. Charles I. Bowen, "On the Air," *OCBD*, October 19, 1933, 3.

92. Eddie Barefield, IJS, Reel 1, page 45.

93. Driggs interview with Barefield, April 25, 1965.

94. Basie, *Good Morning Blues*, 137.

95. "Hear Bennie Moten Loses Orchestra," *Chicago Defender* September 30, 1933, 9; "Count Basie Now Owner of Bennie Moten's Band," Kansas City *Call*, September 15, 1933, 3B.

96. "Musicians to Hold Ball at Labor Temple May 14," Kansas City *Call*, April 27, 1934, 11; "Musicians' Ball May 14," Kansas City *Call*, May 4, 1934, 13; "Musicians Ball Pleases 1,000 at Annual Dance," Kansas City *Call*, May 18, 1934, 11. On Birch, see "Maceo Birch Acquires KC['s] Oldest Store," Kansas City *Call*, August 25, 1925, 3, and Basie, *Good Morning Blues*, 124–125, 134–136, 152–53.

Chapter 10

1. "Willie Lewis Dies Out West," *Chicago Defender*, November 3, 1934, 9.

2. Miles Davis and Quincy Troupe, *Miles: The Autobiography* (New York: Simon and Schuster, 1990), 41–43.

3. Basie, *Good Morning Blues*, 159; "Slaughter's Hall," in "Amusement Reporter," *OCBD*, August 29, 1937, 8.

4. Basie, *Good Morning Blues*, 70.

5. *Jazz Casual—Jimmy Witherspoon/Jimmy Rushing*, Koch Jazz, KOC-CD-8561.

6. Basie, *Good Morning Blues*, 85–87, 89–94, 97–101. He performed in a "domestic skit" in White's show in St. Louis when they performed in 1927. "Gonzell White and Her Big Jamboree..." in "Theatres," *St. Louis Argus*, June 24, 1927, 4.

7. "New $15,000 Wicks Pipe Organ...," Kansas City *Call*, November 2, 1928, 10: "only such instrument in Negro Theatre in Country," except at Regal Theatre; "equipped with a wide variety of instruments and is capable of producing everything from the voice of the single violin to the volume of a full concert orchestra" in orchestra pit. The Eblon Theatre was at 1822 Vine St.

8. Basie, *Good Morning Blues*, 15–17.

9. Ibid., 160.

10. Ibid., 6.

11. Ibid., 8.

12. Marc Rice, p. 290; Walter Page on page 14 of "About My Life in Music," says their pianist, Thomas B. "Turk" Thomas, left them in Dallas on July 4, 1928, and "Basie made his debut with the band that night."

13. Basie, *Good Morning Blues,* 19.
14. Ibid., 18.
15. Ibid.
16. Linda Kuehl interview with Basie, ca. 1971, IJS, page 21 of transcription.
17. Basie, *Good Morning Blues,* 113.
18. Sharon A. Pease, "Moten, Now On Discs, Headed for New Fame," *Down Beat* 16 (July 1, 1949), 12; USMC, 1920, Jackson County, Kaw Township, Kansas City, MO, ED 243, sheet 11B.
19. Basie, *Good Morning Blues,* 113.
20. Rice, 290–292.
21. Basie, *Good Morning Blues,* 114.
22. Ibid., 116.
23. Ibid., 114.
24. Ibid.
25. Ibid., 115.
26. Ibid.
27. Ibid., 112.
28. Ibid., 117–118.
29. Ibid., 118.
30. Ibid., 122; Sharon A. Pease, "Moten, Now On Discs, Headed for New Fame," p. 12.
31. Nat Hentoff, "One More Time: The Travels of Count Basie," *Jazz Review* 4 (January 1961), 6.
32. Ibid., 6–7, for his reputation as a bandleader.
33. Basie, *Good Morning Blues,* 122.
34. Ibid.
35. Ibid., 123.
36. Ibid.; *Bennie Moten's Kansas City Orchestra, 1929–1930,* Classics 578.
37. Basie, *Good Morning Blues,* 127.
38. Ibid.
39. Ibid.
40. Eddie Durham interview, KC-12, Kansas City Jazz Oral History Collection, Western Historical Manuscript Collection, University of Missouri, Kansas City, Missouri, also deposited at IJS, cassette 22a, page 3 of transcription; Phil Schaap interview with Eddie Durham, February 25, 1977.
41. "New Type of Supper Club to Open Here," Kansas City *Call,* December 30, 1932, 3B; "Noted Comedian Comes to Cherry Blossom Night Club," Kansas City *Call,* May 12, 1939, 7B; "Talisman Club to Give Party at Cherry Blossom," Kansas City *Call,* October 20, 1933, 3B; ibid., advertisement for Cherry Blossom.
42. "Cherry Blossom Night Club Reopening Saturday, Feb. 10," Kansas City *Call,* February 9, 1934, 11.
43. "Deluxe Girls Cabaret Fete Cherry Blossom, March 8," Kansas City *Call,* March 2, 1934, 11; ibid., "Fire Eater Added to Cherry Blossom Show"; advertisement for Cabaret Dance at Cherry Blossom, Kansas City *Call,* March 9, 1934, 11; "George E. Lee Now Permanent Cherry Blossom Attraction," Kansas *City Call,* June 22, 1934, 11.
44. "Somewhere to Go!" advertisement, Kansas City *Call,* June 1, 1934, 11. "Guest artists from the city's leading clubs" also appeared, and Maceo Birch was M.C., ibid., "Sunday Matinee Dances."
45. New Centre Theatre advertisement, Kansas *City Call,* October 2, 1934, 11; Dudley an associate of Irvin C. Miller: "Say Miller Plans New Road Show," Baltimore *Afro American,* October 17, 1931, 9.
46. "Eastside Musicians Sunset Club" advertisement, Kansas City *Call,* November 9, 1934, 13.

47. Advertisement for East Side Sunset Musicians' Club, Kansas City *Call*, January 25, 1935, 12.
48. Ibid., Big Sunday Night Stomp advertisement.
49. "Monster Charity Benefit," advertisement, Kansas City *Call*, May 22, 1936, 9.
50. Basie, *Good Morning Blues*, 146–147.
51. On Moten's death, see Frederick J. Spencer, M.D., *Jazz and Death: Medical Profiles of Jazz Greats* (Jackson, MS: University of Mississippi, 2002), 191–194. Using autopsy records, Dr. Spencer maintains that heart trouble and "chronic arterial and cardiac disease" were major factors contributing to the pianist's death.
52. Basie, *Good Morning Blues*, 157.
53. Ibid., 158–159.
54. Ibid., 159.
55. Phil Schaap interview with Eddie Durham, February 25, 1977, IJS; "Two Kansas Citians Join Lunceford's Band," Kansas City *Call*, January 18, 1935, 11, referring to Ben Webster and Forest La Dent.
56. Basie, *Good Morning Blues*, 159.
57. Author's interview with Leonard Chadwick, August 18, 1985; "Rhythmaires Continue to Pack Ritz, *OCBD*, April 11, 1935, 8.
58. Basie, *Good Morning Blues*, 175.
59. Jimmy Stewart, "Jimmy Says," *OCBD*, April 27, 1946, 6.
60. Jimmy Stewart, "Jimmy Says," *OCBD*, January 17, 1948, 11. See also "Homecoming Atmosphere Marks Count Basie Date Here," *OCBD*, November 28, 1948, 7.

Chapter 11
1. "Count Basie Is Big Hit in Chicago," Kansas City *Call*, December 4, 1936, 9.
2. "James Rushing Coming Home," *OCBD*, April 2, 1938, 12, says the band was a "sensation overnight" there.
3. "James Rushing Coming Home with Count Basie's Band for Easter Dance," *OCBD*, April 16, 1938, 12.
4. "Count Basie to Play at Carnegie Hall," *OCBD*, December 17, 1938, 12.
5. Quotes are from "Are You Thrilled by Orchestra Life?" Kansas City *Call*, March 7, 1941, 1.
6. The history given in "Count Basie and Orchestra Featuring James Rushing to Play Easter Dance Here," *OCBD*, April 9, 1938, 12, says he took over from Moten at his death; see also history in "Count Basie at Trianon March 14," *OCBD*, March 5, 1941, 8, and "Are You Thrilled by Orchestra Life?" Kansas City *Call*, March 7, 1941, 1. In the late summer of 1939, they made the trip to California. They performed twice a day at the San Francisco World's Fair in 1939, and Buck Clayton maintained, "that was the real beginning of Basie's Band." See *Buck Clayton's Jazz World*, by Buck Clayton, assisted by Nancy Miller Elliott (New York: Oxford University Press, 1987), 112.
7. *Kansas City Directory, 1933*, lists "Jas Rushing (Mabel) mus r 2317 Brooklyn"; 1934 and 1936 have the same listing.
8. Ethel in the *DCD* for 1924, Addie in *DCD* 1925, and Ethel in 1927; wife is Ruth Heneretta Jackson on Social Security application December 27, 1939.
9. "Count Basie to Aid Career of New Jersey Convict," Kansas City *Call*, March 14, 1941, 15.
10. See Douglas Henry Daniels, *Lester Leaps In* (Boston: Beacon Press, 2003) and "Basie's Key Men to Return," *Pittsburgh Courier*, December 1, 1945, 16.
11. Walter Page married Sarah Boone on October 15, 1925 (Application for Marriage License, Marriage License, and Certificate of Marriage, Clerk of the Court, Oklahoma County). Oran Page married Zenobie Harris on April 3, 1926 in Corsicana, Texas (Marriage License No. 170, Clerk of the Court, Navarro County) and Mary Elizabeth Law-

son, from Salem, Virginia, on August 6, 1949, in Roanoke, Virginia (Certificate of Marriage No. 185, Clerk of the Court, Roanoke County, Virginia). In the 1930s, Page married Myrtle Steers of Montgomery, Alabama, and they had one child; she died in childbirth in 1946 (author's interviews with Oran Page Jr. and George Page Jr.). Eddie Durham married Elsie McClure in Kansas City (Marriage License Application No. 39751, Office of Recorder of Deeds, Jackson County, Missouri, Kansas City, Missouri, December 7, 1929).

12. Count Basie wed Vivian Lee Winn (Marriage License No. A42292, Office of Recorded of Deeds, Jackson County, Missouri, July 21, 1930). The *St. Louis Argus*, February 6, 1931, Section 2, page 3, has a photograph of her: "one of the charming members of social and literary circles in Kansas City," and her husband is said to be James William Basie, "the well known organist and pianist."

13. Nat Hentoff, "Jimmy Rushing," *Down Beat* 24 (March 6, 1957), 20.

14. Dance, *The World of Count Basie*, 344ff.

15. "Count Tops Negro Bands in 'Ballroom' Popularity Poll," Kansas City *Call*, February 14, 1941, 13; "Lionel Hampton, Count Basie, Top New York Musical Scene," *Pittsburgh Courier*, January 12, 1946, 17. According to Billy Rowe, "Basie Stan Kenton and Hawkins Are Runners-Up," *Pittsburgh Courier*, February 15, 1947, 15, in the *Courier* contest, Basie came in second to Lionel Hampton; Kenton was third, and Ellington was not in the top twelve. See Marshal Royal, with Claire P. Gordon, *Marshal Royal: Jazz Survivor* (New York: Continuum, 1996), 86–118.

16. "Basie Ends Tour in Apollo Theater After 3 Months," Kansas City *Call*, April 11, 1941, 12.

17. Ibid.

18. Ibid.

19. "Count Tops Negro Bands in 'Ballroom' Popularity Poll," Kansas City *Call*, February 14, 1941, 13.

20. Ibid.

21. "Count Basie Again Winner Band Popularity Contest," Kansas City *Call*, August 8, 1941, 15; see "Basie in Red to Tune of $28,000," Kansas City *Call*, January 31, 1941, 7.

22. "Good News from Count Basie Reaches Coast," in Harry Levette, "Gossip of the Movie Lots," *OCBD*, October 28, 1941, 8. His fame and accolades also included the bandleader's mother when she died on November 1941, in Red Bank, New Jersey. The celebrities who attended the funeral were numerous, including Benny Goodman and Les Hite; more than three thousand other people paid their respects. "Telegrams from California to Maine were sent in condolence from actors, artists, musicians and song writers." ("Bury Basie's Mother in N.J.," Kansas City *Call*, November 14, 1941, 10.)

23. "Here's That Guy Basie!" Kansas City *Call*, January 3, 1941, 15; James E. McCarthy, "Count Basie in Come Back," *OCBD*, December 19, 1942, 7.

24. "Count Basie: A: 1," *Metronome* 59 (January 1944), 14.

25. "Los Angeles Plantation," *Pittsburgh Courier*, September 8, 1945, 13.

26. "Count Basie Booked Solid for One Year," *Pittsburgh Courier*, September 29, 1945, 17.

27. Ibid.

28. "Basie to Coin Big Money in One-Nighters in Canada," *Pittsburgh Courier*, May 4, 1946, 10.

29. "Basie Moves to Roxy At Near Record Salary," *Pittsburgh Courier*, June 1, 1946, 19.

30. "Count Basie's Ork Invades Mid-West," *Pittsburgh Courier*, July 6, 1946, 17.

31. Jimmy Stewart, "Jimmy Says," *OCBD*, January 17, 1948, 11.

32. "Amazed at Home Town Growth," *OCBD*, November 27, 1948, 1.

33. "Basie Dance Moved to City Auditorium," *OCBD*, September 14, 1940, 8.

34. "James Rushing Coming Home," *OCBD*, April 16, 1938, 12.

35. "Count Basie, Nation's Number One Swing Band," *OCBD*, September 7, 1940, 8.

36. "Basie Launches Sepia Band Policy at Avodon," *Pittsburgh Courier*, December 7, 1946, 18.
37. Ibid.
38. Ibid.
39. "Jitter, Jive and Jump" advertisement, *AN*, September 3, 1938, Section 2, page 7; Charles W. Edgar, "Jitterbugs At Randall's Are Sent by Bands," *AN*, September 17, 1938, Section 2, page 9; "The 'Gators Tore It Down," Baltimore *Afro American*, June 4, 1938, 10; "The Jive Was Solidly Present," Baltimore *Afro American*, September 10, 1938, 10.
40. First used, it seems, in "Count Tops Negro Bands in 'Ballroom' Popularity Poll," Kansas City *Call*, February 14, 1941, 13; see also "Are You Thrilled by Orchestra Life?" Kansas City *Call*, March 7, 1941, 13.
41. "Count Basie to Aid Career of New Jersey Convict," Kansas City *Call*, March 14, 1941, 15; "Basie Forms Own Music Firm," *Pittsburgh Courier*, November 16, 1945, 16; "James Rushing Coming Home with Count Basie's Band," *OCBD*, April 16, 1938, 5.
42. "Philadelphia Theatre-Goers Go for Count Basie's 'Swing,'" *Pittsburgh Courier*, April 24, 1937, 19.
43. "Count Basie to Aid Career of New Jersey Convict," Kansas City *Call*, March 14, 1941, 15; for his conservatism in politics and social issues, see Nat Hentoff, "One More Time: Travels of Count Basie," *The Jazz Review* I (January 1961), 5. Catherine Basie, his spouse, on the other hand, "hurls herself into an astonishingly full round of activities. She is on the boards of nearly a dozen organizations, works for the Urban League and the National Conference of Christians and Jews, and is actively involved in local politics," ibid., 8.
44. "Robeson Sings 'Louis Blues,'" *OCBD*, October 11 1947, 8; "Paul Robeson to Sing with Count Basie," *Metronome* 57 (September 1941), 1; Frank Marshall Davis, "Ratin' the Records," *OCBD*, December 27, 1941, 8.
45. "Billy Rowe's Note Book," *Pittsburgh Courier*, November 27, 1943, 19.
46. Izzy, "Count Basie Forced to Table Beauty Contest," *Pittsburgh Courier*, August 16, 1947, 17.
47. "Basie Forms Own Music Firm," *Pittsburgh Courier*, November 17, 1945, 16.
48. "Basie Hits Jukes on Three Labels," *Pittsburgh Courier*, March 1, 1947, 19; "'Hit Parade of 1943' Showcases Negro Talent," *OCBD*, August 21, 1943, 7; "Basie's 'One O'clock Revue' Opens at Apollo," *Pittsburgh Courier*, September 27, 1947, 17.
49. "Famous Maestro and His Lads To Make Merry," *OCBD*, October 22, 1936, 8.
50. Ibid.
51. "Count Basie and Orchestra Featuring James Rushing," *OCBD*, April 9, 1938, 12.
52. "Count Basie Is Big Hit in Chicago," Kansas City *Call*, December 4, 1936, 9.
53. "Basie Dance Moved to City Auditorium," *OCBD*, September 14, 1940, 8.
54. "Basie Moves to Roxy," *Pittsburgh Courier*, June 1, 1946, 19.
55. "Atlantic City Spot Keeps Count Basie for Summer," *Pittsburgh Courier*, July 26, 1947, 16.
56. "Count Basie a Sensation at America's Most Exclusive Hotel," Kansas City *Call*, July 18, 1941, 14.
57. "Count Basie, Nation's Number One Swing Band," *OCBD*, September 7, 1940, 8; "City Boy with Basie," *OCBD*, September 14, 1940, 8; Daniels, *Lester Leaps In*, 231–242.
58. "Atlantans Pay $4,000 to Hear Count Basie," Kansas City *Call*, August 22, 1941, 14.
59. G.T.S., "Basie Band Provides Stage Thrill," *Metronome* 57 (January 1941), 14.
60. Ulanov, "Count Basie A; 1," *Metronome* 59 (January 1944), 14.
61. "Basie to Coin Big Money," *Pittsburgh Courier*, May 4, 1946, 10.
62. Used as early as 1941: "Count Basie Continues His 'Triumphs,'" Kansas City *Call*, June 17, 1941, 14; "Basie to Begin Tour," Kansas City *Call*, December 12, 1941,15.
63. Jo Jones, IJS interview, page 32.

64. Ibid., 34.
65. Ibid., 50–51.
66. Ibid., 59.
67. Ibid., 51.
68. Ibid., 54.
69. Ibid., 55.
70. Don Gazzaway, "Before Bird—Buster," *Jazz Monthly* (January 1962), 6–7.
71. McDaniels, "Buster Smith," 13.
72. Ibid.
73. Gazzaway, "Before Bird—Buster," 6.
74. "One O'clock Jump" was in first place, Andy Razaf and Fats Waller's "Honeysuckle Rose" came in third; next were "Tuxedo Junction," "Caravan," and "King Porter Stomp." "One O'clock Jump" placed fifth for best stock arrangement of all time: Marvel Cooke, "Negro Musicians Win Many First Places in Poll," *AN*, April 26, 1941, 20. Smith also arranged "Smarty" on *Count Basie, The Original Decca Recordings*, Decca GRD 3–611; see Gunther Schuller, *The Swing Era: The Development of Jazz, 1930–1945* (New York: Oxford University Press, 1989), 245. Marvel Cooke arranged "The Blues I Like to Hear," one of Smith's favorites. "One O'clock Jump" became the band's theme song for a time, and "Blues I Like to Hear" became part of their main repertoire, compositions that were true to the blues tradition, as opposed to the other songs they played that catered more to commercial taste. "The sun's going to shine in my back door one day," Rushing sang on "Blues I Like to Hear," and also "I been chasin' pretty women since I was twelve years old." "Swinging at the Daisy Chain," on *Count Basie, The Original Decca Recordings*, was another Buster Smith arrangement, according to Chris Sheridan.
75. Billy Rowe, "Jimmie Lunceford And Count Basie Orchestra Battle," *Pittsburgh Courier*, May 8, 1937, 18.
76. Durham, IJS, Reel 3, page 18.
77. "Lunceford Band in 'Command' Performance," *Pittsburgh Courier*, March 20, 1937, 18.
78. Eddie Durham, IJS, Reel 3, page 11; see John Hammond's request for him to join Basie to augment the book, IJS, Reel 3, pages 11–12.
79. In his interview with Phil Schaap, February 25, 1977, Durham said someone bet he could write a song during this train ride, which is what he did. He repeated this story in another Schaap interview on November 7, 1988.
80. "The Cash Box TOP 100 Best Selling Tunes on Records," compiled by The Cash Box from leading retail outlets, Eddie Durham Papers.

Chapter 12

1. See Gunther Schuller, *The Swing Era: The Development of Jazz, 1930–1945* (New York: Oxford University Press, 1989) on Pete Johnson and his playing on "Cherry Red" and "Baby, Look at You." Former Blue Devils Hot Lips Page, A. G. Godley, and Abe Bolar performed on "Piney Brown."
2. General Artists Corporation listing, IJS, Oran Page Vertical File.
3. See "Amusement Reporter," *OCBD*, August 29, 1937, 8. On Simpson in Los Angeles and Chicago, see Jimmy Stewart, "Jimmy Says," *OCBD*, January 16, 1943, 10, and July 17, 1948, 10.
4. "Makes Hit," *Pittsburgh Courier*, July 25, 1942, 20; author's interview with George Hudson; "George Hudson, St. Louis 'Ork' Swing Out," *Pittsburgh Courier*, July 24, 1943, 21.
5. Gazzaway, "Conversations with Buster Smith, Part 2," 15.
6. Tim Schuller, "The Buster Smith Story," *Coda* 217 (December 1987), 4.
7. Gazzaway, "Conversations with Buster Smith, Part 2," 14.

8. IJS, Buster Smith Vertical File.
9. Schuller, "The Buster Smith Story," 4.
10. IJS, Buster Smith Vertical File, handwritten and undated note, April 1937.
11. Ibid., February 1938.
12. Jack McDaniels, "Buster Smith," *Down Beat* 23 (July 11, 1956), 13.
13. Connie Hershorn, "Buster Smith Recalls Career as Jazz Musician," *Dallas Morning News*, August 28, 1978, 19A; see Don Gazzaway, "Conversations with Buster Smith, Part 2," 13–14.
14. Schuller, "The Buster Smith Story," 4.
15. Gazzaway, "Conversations with Buster Smith, Part 2," 14.
16. IJS, Buster Smith, page 135; McDaniels, "Buster Smith," 14; Gazzaway, "Conversations with Buster Smith, Part 2," 14.
17. Ken Parish Perkins, "Fame Was a Melody Lost on Buster Smith," *Dallas Morning News*, August 18, 1991, 3C.
18. Social Security applications: December 27, 1939, for Smith, and October 2, 1937, for Page.
19. Gazzaway, "Conversations with Buster Smith, Part 2," 15.
20. Ibid., 14.
21. *McKinney's Cotton Pickers, 1930–1931/Don Redman and His Orchestra, 1939–1940*, Classics 649; Gazzaway, "Conversations with Buster Smith, Part 2," 14.
22. McDaniels, "Buster Smith," 13–14; Peter Watrous, "Henry Smith, 86, Alto Saxophonist," *New York Times*, Obituaries, August 15, 1991; IJS, Buster Smith Vertical File.
23. IJS, Buster Smith Vertical File, handwritten and undated notes; *Hot Lips Page and His Band*, Classics 561.
24. Schuller, *The Swing Era*, 797–798.
25. IJS, Buster Smith Vertical File, handwritten and undated note; *Hot Lips Page and His Band, 1938–1940*, Classics 561.
26. Schuller, "The Buster Smith Story," 5.
27. Ibid.
28. IJS, Buster Smith, pages 97–98.
29. Ibid., page 97.
30. Schuller, "The Buster Smith Story," 5.
31. IJS, Buster Smith, pages 98–99.
32. Ibid., pages 99–101.
33. Gazzaway, "Conversations with Buster Smith, Part 3," 15.
34. Ibid.
35. Schuller, "The Buster Smith Story," 5; see Gazzaway, "Conversations with Buster Smith, Part 2," 15.
36. Gazzaway, "Conversations with Buster Smith, Part 2," 15.
37. Author's interview with Buster Smith.
38. Tim Schuller, "The Buster Smith Story," 5.
39. Gazzaway, "Conversations with Buster Smith, Part 2," 15.
40. Eddie Durham interview, KC-12, page 31, Kansas City Jazz Oral History Collection, Western Historical Manuscript Collection, University of Missouri, Kansas City, Missouri.
41. Leonard G. Feather, "32-Year-Old Trombone Veteran," *Melody Maker*, May 21, 1938 (probably the first article on Durham), IJS, Durham Vertical File; in 1937, Feather reported that Durham passed through London with Lunceford. Chris Sheridan, "Obituaries: Freddie Green and Eddie Durham," *Jazz Journal* I:40 (1948), 8; "Leads Girl Band," *Pittsburgh Courier*, November 28, 1942, 21.
42. Leonard Feather, "31-Year-Old Trombone Veteran," *Melody Maker*, May 21, 1938, IJS Durham Vertical File.

43. Chris Sheridan, *Basie: A Bio-Discography* (Westport, CT: Greenwood, 1986), Appendix 2, page 1092.

44. Sheridan, Appendix 2, page 1094.

45. Record of the Works of Eddie Durham, Eddie Durham Papers.

46. Ibid.; Val Wilmer, "Durham: The First Man to Plug-In," *Melody Maker* 59 (December 13, 1975), 46.

47. Eddie Durham, IJS, Reel 3, pages 36–37.

48. Ibid., page 39.

49. "Teddy Wilson, Eddie Durham Choose Men," *Down Beat* 7 (June 1, 1940), 4; "Eddie Durham Rehearses," *Down Beat* 7 (June 15, 1940), 14.

50. At the time of this article, they had not yet signed with anyone; "Eddie Durham's Band Features A Guitar Like A Clarinet," *Metronome* (June 1940), IJS, Durham Vertical File; IJS, Reel 3, page 54. Durham complained that at this time "the politicians was on me on one hand and the racketeers on the other." IJS, Reel 3, pages 55–56.

51. Sally Placksin, *American Women in Jazz: 1900 to the Present, Their Words, Lives, and Music* (New York: Wideview Books, 1982), 95–96.

52. Ibid., 97.

53. Ibid., 96.

54. Ibid., 96–97.

55. " 'Sweethearts of Rhythm' Loom As Broadway Surprise Package," *Pittsburgh Courier*, May 22, 1943, 20; Billy Rowe, "No Hope Seen On Transportation," *Pittsburgh Courier*, July 18, 1942, 21.

56. Eddie Durham, IJS, Reel 3, page 49.

57. Placksin, 97–98.

58. "Leads Girl Band," *Pittsburgh Courier*, November 28, 1942, 21; "Billy Rowe's Notebook," *Pittsburgh Courier*, December 13, 1941, 20; "Four of the International Sweethearts," *Down Beat* 9 (March 15, 1942), 12; Billy Rowe, "Arranger Eddie Durham Embarks On New Venture," *Pittsburgh Courier*, December 12, 1942, 20.

59. Placksin, 145–148.

60. "All-Girl Orchestra Praised by Arranger," *Pittsburgh Courier*, February 21, 1942, 21.

61. "Swing Battle of the Sexes Is Set," *Pittsburgh Courier*, April 4, 1942, 21.

62. Barry Ulanov, "Women in Jazz: Do They Belong?" *Down Beat* 25 (January 1958), 17, 50.

63. Eddie Durham, IJS, Reel 3, page 58.

64. One of his tenor saxophonists, a spectacular soloist, was Vi Burnside, from Los Angeles. See Placksin, 133–134, 139.

65. Eddie Durham, IJS, Reel 3, page 59. On the band's origins, see "17-Girl Band Which Quit School," *Pittsburgh Courier*, April 19, 1941, 21, and "$30,000 Spent on Sweethearts of Rhythm," *Pittsburgh Courier*, May 31, 1941, 21.

66. "Eddie Durham's All-Girl Band," *Courier*, July 10, 1943, p. 22; "Ella Fitzgerald, Four Keys, Durham's Band at Apollo," *Amsterdam News*, February 27, 1943, 14; "Band Routes," *Courier*, July 10, 1943, 22; "Arranger Eddie Durham Embarks on New Venture," *Courier*, December 12, 1942, 20; "Band Routes," *Courier*, July 10, 1943, 22; "To California," *California Eagle*, April 20, 1944, 13.

67. "Eddie Durham," in "Stage Show Reviews," *Metronome* 60 (June 1944), 32.

68. Eddie Durham, IJS, Reel 3, page 61.

69. Ibid., pages 60–61.

70. Ibid., 59–60; "Ella Fitzgerald, Four Keys," *AN*, February 27, 1943, 14.

71. Placksin, 149.

72. Ibid.

73. Ibid., 149–150.

74. Application for Marriage License, April 23, 1939, Clerk of Porter Circuit Court, Valparaiso, Indiana.

75. "All-Girls Band and Rochester Film at Regal Theatre," *Chicago Defender,* April 14, 1943, 12; see marriage certificate, Durham Papers.
76. "Sweethearts War Proof Orchestra," *Pittsburgh Courier,* June 20, 1942, 21; "Sweethearts in There!" *Down Beat* 9 (July 1, 1942), 19.
77. Placksin, 149–150.
78. Ibid., 150–151.
79. Ibid., 150–151; see "Gingervating, Clamorous, Gorgeous Gals," *OCBD,* January 8, 1944, 6.
80. Freddy Doyle, "Swingtime in H'wood," *California Eagle,* October 23, 1941, 4B.; see also "Hollywood," *AN,* June 7, 1941, Part 2, page 21, which lists band members, including journalist Freddy Doyle, guitarist and singer.
81. Freddy Doyle, "Swingtime in H'Wood," *California Eagle,* January 3, 1942, 2B.
82. Ibid., March 19, 1942, 2B, and February 26, 1942, 3B.
83. Ibid., *California Eagle,* November 6, 1941, 4B.
84. Ibid., *California Eagle,* April 2, 1942, 3B.
85. Ibid., *California Eagle,* May 7, 1942, 2B, and May 14, 1942, 2B.
86. Ibid., *California Eagle,* May 14, 1942, 2B.
87. Ibid., *California Eagle,* July 9, 1942, 2B; on Morris, see Lillian Greene, "Joe Morris' Plantation Club Tops West Coast Night Spots," *Pittsburgh Courier,* August 12, 1944, 13.

Chapter 13
1. Landon Laird, "K.C. Reunion in New York," Kansas City *Call,* January 10, 1941, 13.
2. "Release Kansas City Jazz Album Dedicated to Kay Cee's Musicians Local Number 627," Kansas City *Call,* May 30, 1941, 12.
3. Author's interview with Lorraine Chadwick, widow of Leonard Chadwick.
4. See Oran Page letters of October 12, 1953 and August 18, 1954, Oran Page Vertical File, IJS.
5. Max Jones, "'Hot Lips' Page Dies in New York," *Melody Maker* 70 (November 13, 1954), 1; "Oran Page," *The Record Changer* (December 13, 1954), 9.
6. Jimmy Stewart, "Jimmy Says," *OCBD,* November 13, 1954, 12.
7. Leonard Feather, "6 Trumpet Men Carry Lips to Rest," *Melody Maker* 70 (November 20, 1954), 6.
8. Edward Murrain, "Mourn Trumpet Ace at Funeral," IJS Oran Page Vertical File.
9. Leonard Feather, "6 Trumpet Men Carry Lips to Rest," 8.
10. "Oran Page," *The Record Changer* (December 13, 1954), 9.
11. "Two Huge Memorials For Page Raise Almost $5 G's," *Down Beat* 21 (December 29, 1954), 3.
12. William Ewald, "They Came to Play Goodbye to 'Hot Lips,'" *Oakland Tribune,* November 19, 1954, 22.
13. Author's interview with Oran Page Jr.
14. Dan Morgenstern, "Hot Lips," *Jazz Journal,* 4, IJS.
15. "Reminiscing with Hot Lips Page," *Jazz Hot,* September 1951, 10.
16. Henry Kahn, "That's How Mr. Page Swings—Like a Pendulum," *Melody Maker* 67 (July 28, 1951), 3.
17. "Oran 'Hot Lips' Page, Famed Trumpeter, Dead," Kansas City *Call,* November 19, 1954, 8.
18. Author's interviews with George Page Jr., Oran Page Jr., and Tracy Page Willis.
19. *Oran 'Hot Lips' Page—1942–1953,* Foxy 9006A.
20. "Final Bar," *Down Beat* 25 (February 6, 1958), 10.
21. *Oran 'Hot Lips' Page—1941–1953,* Foxy 9006B.
22. Ibid.
23. "Walter Page, a Great Rhythm Man, Is Dead," *Kansas City Times* (the morning edition of the *Kansas City Star*), December 21, 1957, 4, IJS, Page Vertical File.

24. Ralph J. Gleason, "How Count Basie Found Walter Page," *San Francisco Chronicle*, ca. 1957, IJS Vertical File.
25. Joseph Berger, "Mr. Five by Five Sang His Song…Blues King Jimmy Rushing Dead," *New York Post*, June 9, 1972, IJS, Rushing Vertical File; Douglas Hague, "Jimmy Rushing Tells His Story to Douglas Hague," *Jazz Journal* (September 1957), 2–3.
26. Nat Hentoff, "Jimmy Rushing," *Down Beat* 24 (March 6, 1957), 20.
27. Ibid.
28. "Rushing Swings the Singing Smiths," (periodical not identified), September 9, 1961, IJS, Rushing Vertical File.
29. Helen McNamara, "McNamara's Bandwagon: Those Smith Girls Get the Rush From Rushing," *Toronto Telegraph*, August 18, 1961.
30. John McClellan, "Rushing Real Jazz Singer," (periodical not identified), February 23, 1958, IJS, Rushing Vertical File.
31. Helen McNamara, "Pack My Bags and Make My Getaway: The Odyssey of Jimmy Rushing," *Down Beat* 32 (April 8, 1965), 24.
32. Patrick Scott article in Jimmy Rushing Vertical File, IJS.
33. S. Trail, "Jimmy Rushing—In My Opinion," *Jazz Journal* 17 (January 1964), 14.
34. John McClellan, "Rushing Real Jazz Singer," (periodical not identified), February 23, 1958, IJS, Rushing Vertical file.
35. George Hoefer, "Jimmy Rushing/Dave Brubeck Quartet," in "Caught in the Act," *Down Beat* 17 (March 2, 1961), 44–45.
36. " 'Gotta Feel Blue to Sing the Blues,' " *Toronto Daily Star*, November 18, 1961, IJS, Rushing Vertical File.
37. "Rushing to Write About His Singing," *Philadelphia Afro-American*, August 30, 1947, 18; Rushing Archives (in the possession of the Rushing family); "Jimmy Rushing's Autobiography," *Variety* 241:51 (November 24, 1965).
38. Robert A. Rotner, University Publisher, in undated letter, IJS, Rushing Vertical File.
39. Morris Duff, "Mr. 5 by 5: Target of Bombs," *Toronto Daily Star*, Rushing Vertical File, IJS.
40. Author's interview with William Staton.
41. Ralph Ellison, "Remembering Jimmy," *Shadow and Act* (New York: Signet Books, 1966), 239.
42. Rushing Vertical File, "Rushing Rites Draw 300 Including Basie," (periodical unidentified), June 13, 1972, 16; author's interview with Lynn M. Staton, daughter of William Staton.
43. "Wynonie Harris, Larry Darnell Here April 25," OCBD, April 12, 1952, 7.
44. Durham interview with Phil Schaap, February 25, 1977.
45. Record of the Works of Eddie Durham, Eddie Durham Papers.
46. Stanley Dance, "Kansas City All-Stars," in "Caught in the Act," *Down Beat* 36 (May 15, 1969), 31–32.
47. Ibid., 31.
48. Stanley Dance, "Lawrence Lucie/Eddie Durham," in "Caught in the Act," *Down Beat* 37 (January 22, 1970), 30–31.
49. Val Wilmer, "Eddie Durham," *Coda* 158 (November–December 1977), 7.
50. Harlem Blues & Jazz Band Tour, April 28–July 10, 1983, in Durham Papers.
51. John S. Wilson, "Old Timers Get a New Bandstand," *New York Times*, February 27, 1981, C24; Stephen Holden, "Pop and Jazz Guide," *New York Times*, February 27, 1981, C19.
52. Hospital Show Tour #5 program, Durham Papers.
53. Chip Deffaa, "For Eddie Durham," *New York Post*, August 25, 1986, IJS, Durham Vertical File.
54. Judith Cummings and Laurie Johnson, "Notes on People," *New York Times* April 16, 1980, B4.

55. Invitation to Algerian reception, Durham Papers.
56. "Jazz Legend Eddie Durham Dies," IJS, Durham Vertical File.
57. Letter of Edward Durham Jr. to New Jersey Jazz Society, November 24, 1989, Durham Papers.
58. Jesse H. Walker, "Big Apple Jazz Women Honor Eddie Durham," IJS, Durham Vertical file.
59. Cyril Mumford, "The Note Book," *Dallas Express*, August 12, 1944, 12.
60. "Buster Smith to Play Regal," *Dallas Express*, November 11, 1944, 12.
61. "Buster Smith's Ork. Rocks Greenville" and Cyril Mumford, "The Note Book," *Dallas Express*, November 25, 1944, 13.
62. Jimmy Stewart, "Jimmy Says," OCBD, April 21, 1951, 10.
63. *The Legendary Buster Smith*, Atlantic 1313.
64. "Weekend Happenings: Music and all that Jazz," *Dallas Herald*, stamped September 1, 1979, Jazz Vertical File, Dallas Public Library.
65. Donna Fieldler, "Quartet Pours out Smooth Renditions," *Denton Record Chronicle*, January 16, 1981. Thanks to Adolphus Sneed for providing me with a copy of this article.
66. Ibid.
67. Ken Parish Perkins (staff writer of *Dallas Morning News*), "Fame Was a Melody Lost on Buster Smith," *Dallas Morning News*, August 18, 1991, 3C.
68. Ibid.
69. Author's interviews with Leonard Chadwick and his son, Leonard Jr.
70. *Ray Charles Blues + Jazz*, Rhino R2 71607.
71. "Jazz Tradition, Religious Heritage, and the Transformation of a Blue Devil—Leroy 'Snake' Whyte," *Jazzforschung* 26 (1994), 143–155.
72. Oklahoma Jazz Hall of Fame Induction Banquet program, Tulsa, Oklahoma, June 14, 1995, page 8.
73. Charlie Christian and Zelia Breaux were inducted in 1989.

Page numbers in italics refer to photographs.